Vie de Bohè

A Patch of Romantic Paris

Orlo Williams

Alpha Editions

This edition published in 2024

ISBN : 9789362928108

Design and Setting By
Alpha Editions
www.alphaedis.com
Email - info@alphaedis.com

Contents

I

LA VRAIE BOHÈME

La Bohème, c'est le stage de la vie artistique; c'est la préface de l'Académie, de l'Hôtel-Dieu ou de la Morgue.

MURGER: "Scènes de la Vie de Bohème."

IF there is one reason for which the growth of newspapers during the last century may be looked at askance, it is the journalist's persistency in perpetuating phrases. Phrases and catchwords at the moment of invention are works of a peculiar genius, of which some men have an abnormal share, though it may crop out suddenly in the most unlikely places; but a good catchword, that crystallization of a drop of some elusive current that is momentarily passing through public opinion, that apt naming of some newly formed group of men or ideas, never comes out of an inkpot: it is essentially, as the French finely recognize, a *mot*, a pearl of speech. It darts out in some happy moment of human intercourse, often almost unconsciously, when the words on a man's lips are less than usual rebellious to the expression of his thoughts, or when the exhilaration of some public utterance has charged the air so that the little telling point, hitherto cold and dormant, flashes suddenly into incandescence. Such a phrase, born on the lips of one, can only be nurtured on the lips of many: its success implies continued utterance. It becomes a heaven-sent convenience to save human circumlocution, a new topic for the dullards, a new toy for the *blasés*. In these communicative days, indeed, journalism increases a thousand-fold the possibilities of its radiation, but a good catchword has always made its way without the help of print. There has never existed a human society, at any developed stage of civilization, that has not been perfectly capable of hitting off a new idea or a new group in some telling phrase or name without the intervention of a scribe. At the same time, conversational man, left to himself, is no less quick to forget than to invent. A new phrase properly fades as soon as the novelty of that which inspired it, but once it has appeared upon a single written page it has been given an artificial life of varying but incalculable duration. This artificial existence has been infinitely increased by the newspaper. The journalist, who has little time to think, is naturally loth to let a convenient label go, so that, long after its original parcel of ideas or beings has passed away, he will keep tagging it on to other parcels with a certain show of relevance which effectually conceals the fact that it ought long ago to have been filed for the etymological dictionary.

A phrase which has thus lingered artificially in common use is the word "Bohemian." Nobody can deny that it is a useful label, simply because it is so vague, conveying as it does the sense of some deliberate divergence from the usages of polite society, without being in the least embarrassingly clear as to the degree or direction of that divergence. It is a term, so apparently specific, so really loose, equally capable of carrying blame and admiration, which people will go on applying to men and women, their lives and their clothes, without inquiring whether there is in fact any answering reality. It would be easy enough to confuse its simple users by a few question. They might be asked, for instance, what a Bohemian is, when they would probably reply, in the slipshod phraseology of to-day, that he is an odd person who wears funny clothes and does quaint things. But then, it might be pointed out, a docker from Limehouse is equally odd and quaint from their point of view, though they do not call him a Bohemian; on which they will rather pettishly explain that they mean artists and musicians and so on, people who don't "work." To help them out on this point, in fine, they mean people who potentially rank with the members of learned professions, but who choose to live a less respectable life, in which paying calls, dressing for dinner, and attending to the dictates of social morality are considered of small importance, though the exact degree of social unorthodoxy is left as undefined as the qualifying degree of artistic performance. The same lady will comprehend in the term the middle-aged civil servant who haunts studios of an evening, wears pale tweeds, but is otherwise a pearl of inartistic chivalry, and the scaramouch of a painter, whom she calls "charming" because he is clever, and whose absorption in art has entirely ruined him as a social being. I propose another question. Why are Bohemians so called? The answer seems easy—because they live in Bohemia. And Bohemia? Again the label produces a difficulty. To pursue any geographical inquiries concerning Bohemia in a Socratic spirit would quickly produce exasperation in any catechumen, and I will presume the result without the method. The answers would generally amount to this: that it seems agreed, simply since the word is used, that there is a Bohemia, but its latitude and longitude are indefinable. It is not confined to Chelsea or St. John's Wood, or even, of course, to England; apparently it transcends the ordinary differences of nationality, existing always and everywhere. The possibility of its having existed once and somewhere—I give away freely at this early stage the foundation of this book—never occurs, for labels have a tremendous potency of suggestion. Bohemia is commonly assumed to exist now in the midst of this commercial day. It is generally accepted—with more or less warmth according to individual tastes—as an institution not, perhaps, entirely desirable for itself, but a necessary patch in the motley dress of civilization. It is proclaimed gleefully or admitted under constraint, as the case may be, that clever, artistic men and women, wisely or perversely, choose to gather there, and that certain epithets, such as quaint, amusing, unconventional—the ethical implications of the adjectives differing with their user—are applicable to it. But *la vie de Bohème*, once so vivid a reality, has now no tangible substance: it wanders about, the palest ghost of a legend, formless and indistinct. The young may look forward to it and the old pretend to look back on it, but young and old, in either case, are turning their mind's eye upon a mere abstraction. The word "Bohemian" has become as conventional as "gentleman," with less content for all its greater glamour.

The glamour of Bohemia, too, is projected from a paradox. On the assumption that it exists, those who wish to live in Bohemia idealize it; those who have lived in it boast of it; and those who might have lived in it, but did not, pretend that they did. Yet those who wish to live in it know nothing of it, and those who lived in it, for all their boasting, have left it. It seems to take shape, like a mirage, only in prospect or retrospect. There are witnesses to the distant glint of its magic towers in the rosy mists of sunrise or the golden haze of sunset, but of the light and shade within its streets there are none, for those who might be supposed to be passing through its gates are strangely reticent, and seem mysteriously to lose the sense of their glorious nationality. A man may say with a thrill, "I will be a Bohemian," or with a glow, "I was a Bohemian," but of him who said, "I am a Bohemian," the only proper view would be one of deepest suspicion. He would certainly be a masquerader.

Yet many people, at least in England, do so masquerade—people who affect Chelsea, slouch hats, and ill-cut garments, who haunt Soho restaurants, talk and smoke cigarettes in half a dozen studios, toady sham genius, flutter in emancipatory "movements," and generally do nothing on quite enough a year. Not long ago a distinguished artist, genially inspired by dinner at a club of Bohemian traditions and most respectable membership, gave utterance to the view that, though the velvet coat had disappeared before evening dress, the Bohemian still existed. Upon that a writer in an evening paper made the wise comment:

"There are people, it is true, who indulge in mild unconventionality; they feed in Soho, and talk of cabarets. But these people are seldom artists and never Bohemian. The unconventionality of these people is a mere outward pose, which compels any artist who wishes to preserve his individuality and good name to pay careful attention to the external forms. Bohemianism, such as it was, sprang up in Paris, and that is sufficiently good reason for its failure in England."

The journalist has here risen above the temptation of the label, and his words are just. The gist of the matter lies, perhaps, in his last sentence, but that point must wait its turn. There is no doubt that there exists in London, not to speak of other cities, a large body of people of varying ages, occupations, beliefs, and principles who keep up a masquerade of Bohemianism. As a body they are worthy citizens enough, whose intelligence on some subjects is above the average, but they are masqueraders none the less if they wish to pass as *enfants de Bohème*. A reason for this masquerade may be found partly in the very human love of "dressing up" which is never to be discouraged, partly in the glorification of Bohemia in which writers of novels and reminiscences are prone to indulge. Probably George du Maurier's "Trilby" has been responsible for more misconceptions on this matter than any other single book, on account of its very charm, a charm that needs no further praise at this date. The author himself, who wrote about that which he knew, made no extravagant claims to have drawn Bohemia in the early part of "Trilby," but it is that which in the eyes of most of his readers he is unavoidably represented as doing. So far as Taffy, the Laird, and Little Billie are concerned, they are simply transplanted Britons of the Victorian era, art students with means enough to pursue their studies without pot-boiling and to keep open house for a collection of other joyous young people, of whom Svengali was alone the complete Bohemian, while Trilby herself with perfect propriety mended their socks. Trilby's part in this studio life is a sentimental idyll which nobody would wish to destroy, but it is none the less true, in spite of her creator's plea for her *quia multum amavit* in a delightful page of circumlocution, that he has effectually distilled out of her any essence of Bohemianism which she is dimly represented as possessing. George du Maurier knew Paris when Bohemia was no more, but even he must have known the rougher, wilder, less comfortable side of the Quartier Latin. Yet that he glossed it over is perfectly comprehensible. Even those who lived to write about the Bohemia that once was could not help tinging their memories with the romantic yearning of middle age. In a life where hardship and happiness kaleidoscopically alternate, pain—especially in the shape of material want or the sense of unjust neglect—obscures in the moment of struggle the more brightly coloured glasses of health and joy which more often than not surround it. In retrospect, by a merciful dispensation, the sombre lines almost entirely disappear, only to be recalled by an unnatural effort of memory. What stood out in retrospect, in the special case of *la vie de Bohème*, was the happiness of youth that would never return, its *insouciance*, its untrammelled companionships, the poetry of its first love, its gaiety and irresponsible humour, its courage, its ready makeshifts in adversity. The ex-Bohemian had, what the Bohemian had not, a contrast by which to measure his regrets—the cares of domesticity, the wearisome demands of society upon its members, the responsibilities and cares of an assured position, howsoever humble, the dulling of pleasure's edge, joints stiffening, hair bleaching. The snows of yesteryear were falling upon others now; and that the young rogues might not be too uplifted, he must write his *militavi non sine gloria*, hinting the while that the special glory of Bohemia paled at the precise moment of his exodus. George du Maurier poured over "Trilby" some of this romantic recollection, and other less gifted novelists have done the same for certain *coteries* that have lived in London. To them is due much of the glamour still implied in the phrase "Bohemian," a glamour which is seldom corrected by a reading of George Gissing's "New Grub Street." Yet no conception of Bohemia into which the sombre details of that book will not naturally fit can possibly approach the truth.

This last sentence, I am aware, may be used to challenge my acquaintance with the truth since I assume its existence. To any such challenge the whole of this book is an answer, and its reader will at the end, it is hoped, be in possession of at least as much truth as its author, if not the little more which criticism supplies. In the case of a subject so little complicated an elaborate initial summary of aims and processes and steps of proof will be unnecessary. Those who wish to do so will have little difficulty in following a study, which provided no little entertainment to the student, of the life that was truly to be called Bohemian. I have been so far concerned to hint that I do not deal in any heterogeneous parcels which have come to pass under an old label. The label was applied at a particular time to a particular parcel, and the one and only original parcel is the *vie de Bohème* which in this book I attempt to unwrap.

It might be supposed from the commonness of allusions to Bohemia and Bohemianism that the terms were contemporary, at least, with the intrusion of artists and men of letters into society, and that before the existence of the Bohemia whose capital is Prague the name of some other nation was, in the same way, taken in vain. However, this is not the case. The *græculus esuriens* to whom the Roman poet so scornfully refers had no doubt many Bohemian qualities, but the emphasis of the taunt is laid on his foreign nationality, not upon his mode of existence. Even after the Bohemia of the atlas came into being it knew for many centuries no usurper of its name. Will Shakespeare, Ben Jonson, and the merry company of the "Mermaid" tavern neither called themselves nor were called Bohemians. Samuel Johnson, Goldsmith, and the other less distinguished inhabitants of Grub Street suffered many verbal indignities, but not that. Coleridge and Charles Lamb might be alluded to as Bohemians now, but in their day the term had even yet not been invented. Murger's preface to "Scènes de la Vie de Bohème" proves that so late as 1846 a universal understanding of his title could not be taken for granted, since he begins by carefully distinguishing the geographical Bohemia from the artistic. The modern sense of the term originated, in fact, in Paris at the time of the Romantic movement, being only an extension of the meaning of "gipsy" or "vagabond" long attached to the word *bohémien* in France. Our "Bohemian" was introduced into the English language by Thackeray, who learnt it during his student-period in Paris.

This piece of etymology, nugatory as it may appear, is, in fact, very important. It is the first real delimitation of our inquiry. *La vie de Bohème* is essentially a

French term, and it is therefore fitting that we should examine its implications in that language. Murger in his preface is contradictory, but his very contradiction is pregnant and valuable. At the outset he applies the term *bohémien* to the literary and artistic vagabonds of all ages. "La Bohème dont il s'agit dans ce livre n'est point une race née aujourd'hui, elle a existé de tous temps et partout, et peut revendiquer d'illustres origines." Homer, he says, was the first Bohemian of Greek antiquity, and his tradition was carried on by the medieval minstrels and troubadours; Pierre Gringoire and François Villon, Clément Marot and Mathurin Regnier, Molière and Shakespeare, Rousseau and D'Alembert were the leading citizens of their contemporary Bohemias. This brings Murger to his own day, of which he says: "Aujourd'hui comme autrefois, tout homme qui entre dans les arts, sans autre moyen d'existence que l'art lui-même, sera forcé de passer par les sentiers de la Bohème." If Chelsea were here to make a triumphant interruption, it would have spoken too soon, for he proceeds to give the definition which serves as an epigraph to this chapter, and, without a word of warning, contradicts what he has said before in the sentence: "Nous ajouterons que la Bohème n'existe et n'est possible qu'à Paris." This is a highly serious matter. It leaves old Homer nothing but a Greek poet, and Chelsea—well—little more than Chelsea. However, I cannot imagine Homer objecting, and Chelsea must forgive me, if I accept Murger's statement in the strictest possible way. Further, the Paris implied is the Paris of Murger's own day. That this was so may appear more clearly in the sequel, but for the present it must suffice to say that the Paris of the Romantic period, which gave birth to Bohemia, was unlike the Paris of earlier days in many respects, and no Romantic had any conception of the cosmopolitan Paris of to-day. *La vie de Bohème*, far from being a vague label, was a phrase packed with intimate meaning, meaning which at the time was not at all so fully manifest as under criticism and comparison it may now appear. It depended for its peculiar qualities upon the social and material conditions of Louis Philippe's Paris, which have long since passed away.

We go, therefore, beyond Murger and strike out Villon, Gringoire, and Marot from the roll of Bohemia. At most they were only potentially enrolled and lived, like Socrates, in a state of unconscious grace. Whether or no Bohemia can be said to exist to-day or to have existed in the Middle Ages, at least it can only be by analogy from the very definite and localized *Bohème* which was part of Paris between 1830 and 1848. Though Louis Philippe, the *bourgeois* king, the admirer of the *juste milieu*, was her ruler, the life of Paris never beat with a quicker pulse than in those days; never was she more gay, more witty, more intellectually scintillating, more paradoxical, in fact more absolutely Parisian than when Victor Hugo, Sainte-Beuve, Alfred de Musset, the Princess Belgiojoso, Théophile Gautier, Gérard de Nerval, Nestor Roqueplan, and Baudelaire were among her citizens, when Roger de Beauvoir was dazzling upon a truly brilliant boulevard, when the dandies gracefully lounged and quizzed upon the steps of Tortoni's, when Alexandre Dumas gave his famous fancy-dress ball which drew all Paris, when Marie Dorval shone beside Mademoiselle Mars, when Fanny Elssler and Taglioni danced while Duprez and Grisi and Rubini sang, when Gavarni and Daumier drew their caricatures, when Musard conducted his furious quadrilles, when there were still *salons* in which men and women still knew how to talk, when life was still an artistic achievement in an artistic setting. Memoirs and reminiscences abound of this enchanted city in the time when her intense inner light had not paled before the glare of commercialism and cosmopolitanism, but such sketches and side-views must yield to the all-comprehending picture contained in the works of Balzac, that magnificent magician. Through him the Paris of Louis Philippe shines doubly brilliant, for its world of flesh and blood was not more wonderful than the fictitious world with which he peopled it, a world of high and low, rich and poor, squalor and splendour, vice and virtue, wit and stupidity—miraculous issue from one poor mortal brain. The Princesse de Cadignan, Madame D'Espard, Madame Firmiani, and Mademoiselle des Touches were its higher, Coralie, Esther, Jenny Cadine, Florine, and Madame Schontz its lower, divinities, and their worshippers were de Marsay, the engaging Lucien de Rubempré, the remarkable Rastignac, Maxime de Trailles, La Palférine, and all the corrupted crew of Crevels, Malifats, and Camusots; in it the greasy, dirty Maison Vauquer contrasted with the splendid boudoir of a Delphine de Nucingen, the illuminated poverty of a D'Arthez with the vicious luxury of the Nathans and Finots, the huge *coups* of a Nucingen with the petty usury of a Père Samanon, the simplicity of a Cousin Pons with the malignity of a Cousine Bette. Into this world of feverish movement and poignant contrasts fits *la Bohème*, lighted by its double facets of fact and fiction. As the actual Bohemians from Pétrus Borel and Théophile Gautier to Baudelaire and Murger play their part in the world of fact, so the fictitious Bohemians from Raphael de Valentin and D'Arthez down to Rodolphe, Marcel, and Schaunard play theirs in the world of fiction. They are all part of that pageant which, though it took eighteen years to pass and declined in bravery towards its close, may conveniently be called the pageant of 1830.

To disentangle the Bohemian contingent from its accompaniment of press and bustle is my aim in this book, which was suggested, I may frankly say, by some meditations on a second reading of Murger's "Scènes de la Vie de Bohème," a work of perennial delight that deserves a better acquaintance in England. In spite of the vivid light thrown by Murger on the life which he is describing, his stories are apt to be misleading unless read in the light of certain knowledge—knowledge which he could presume in his contemporaries and which it is the aim of this book, with all humility, to revive. Murger's little volume, after it has produced its first flush of pleasure and amusement, raises many disconcerting questions to a thoughtful reader. The scene it paints, for instance, is remarkably different from the two sides of literary life depicted in Balzac's "Illusions Perdues." Neither the brotherhood of the Rue des Quatre Vents nor the fast set into which Lousteau introduces Lucien are connected by an obvious link with Rodolphe and his friends. Then there is the question whether Rastignac in his days at the squalid Maison Vauquer was in any sense a Bohemian. Or, again, it may be asked how far fiction agrees with fact. Did Murger himself lead the same kind of life as a Schaunard or Marcel, and if he did, was the same to be said of other writers and artists, of Théophile Gautier or Gérard de Nerval? How did Bohemia arise, and how far was it, as Murger asserts, a necessary stage in the artistic life? These are some of the obvious inquiries to which it has been my part to attempt an answer, and I would crave the reader's indulgence if, at the outset, I seem to shrink from plunging at once into *la vie de Bohème*. The external details of a way of life cannot be seen in a true light if the social conditions and, still more, the state of mind of which it was an expression are not first made clear. For that reason a little "fringe of history" makes its appearance and leads to a short consideration of what French writers have called *le mal romantique*. Nevertheless, I have tried to keep the main subject always in view, and not to be led away into discussing aspects of the Romantic period which are not relevant. This is not, I claim with all deference, a concoction of all the old legends and Romantic love affairs. George Sand, for instance, and Alfred de Musset only poke their heads in; Alfred de Vigny and Marie Dorval, Sainte-Beuve and Madame Hugo play no part. Bohemia alone is our concern, a theme which is displayed for what it is worth without any distracting embroideries.

If, then—to return to the train of thought with which I began—Bohemia turns out to be something definite, with a beginning, a development, and an end, some negative criteria, at all events, will be supplied by which to judge the applicability of the label "Bohemian" to any set of conditions existing to-day, and to decide whether the disappearance of certain special implications and unique circumstances does not drain the term of all definite meaning except as applied, in retrospect, to the very persons, manners, and ideas which it originally described. By analogy from that meaning, there is no harm in saying that there have always been, and always will be, Bohemian individuals with a Bohemian state of mind. Richard Steele was a Bohemian; Lamb, perhaps, was a little too staidly settled at the India House, but his friends, George Dyer, George Burnett and, above all, Coleridge, were certainly Bohemian individuals. They were of that ultra-Bohemian type which never grows out of its Bohemianism, men who remain permanently in what should only be a "stage" till they pass the age when, as Nestor Roqueplan said, the "bohémien" risks being confounded with the "filou." Such men as Coleridge and Dyer would be called eccentrics even in the true Bohemia; like poor Gérard de Nerval, they were not entirely sane, and the Bohemian *type* had essentially perfect sanity. It is for this very reason that *la Bohème*, at its proper time, could exist, and why before and after that time it did not exist. Sane young men, no matter what their fads, fancies, and enthusiasms may be, have no need and no possibility of making to-day that particular demonstration which resulted in Bohemia. The social forces drive them in other directions. It has long been admitted in France that Bohemia is dead, and that it has been or ever will be revived in England is a delusion resting upon the unintelligent use of a word. Even young Englishmen, as we now consider youth, are too old, far too old, to live the life of which they flatter themselves they are preserving the tradition. The boy who has submitted to discipline for over a dozen years, learned to honour his neighbour on the cricket and football field and to respect society as embodied in the unwritten laws of school life—what has he in common with the youth in France, a bachelor of letters at eighteen, bursting with his own individuality, passionate in pursuit of his own ideas, revelling in his new liberty, dreaming, as only a Frenchman can dream, of glory and love, who could attach no meaning to such a phrase as "playing the game," wayward, capricious, uproarious, and completely unbalanced? Yet it was such who made the traditions of *la vie de Bohème*. To those who are impelled to break away and lead joyous, untrammelled young lives of privation and artistic striving all sympathy is due, but by masquerading under a tattered banner they do not revive its glory nor increase their own. Paris once had room for Bohemia, but London never. Chelsea and Soho, Highgate and St. John's Wood are to-day no more Bohemian, in the true sense of the word, than Piccadilly or Grosvenor Square. In the lapse of years a few accidental attributes of the real Bohemia have come to be regarded as the essentials of the false. We are fond of labels and catchwords, lightly casting away their implications. So it has come to pass that Bohemia—that dirty, hungry, lazy, noisy vale of youthful laughter and tears, so enchanting in prospect or retrospect, so uncompromising in actuality, which many had to pass through and most would have avoided— is looked on as the pleasant home of more or less artistic natures, that men of stable occupations, regular means, and fastidious temperaments may choose for a dwelling-place, just as they may choose a garden city.

Well, let them masquerade, yet Bohemia is dead, and more honour may be done to its memory by recalling how it walked and lived than by casting lots for its old-fashioned garments. Its virtues and its faults were balanced as equally as its good and bad fortunes, but if it were to be revived, the resurrection should begin with that which was its chief glory, the intense artistic enthusiasm that was its charter. "Nous étions ivres du beau," wrote Théophile Gautier. London, indeed, would be the better for the infusion of a more Dionysiac spirit into her æsthetic appreciations and ideals. But that is not of the times. At the end of his charming book, "Les Enfants Perdus du

Romantisme," M. Henri Lardanchet quotes a speech made by the president of some university society to the effect that the youth of to-day, preoccupied with extremely definite problems, has no longer the poetic enthusiasm of the past generation, whereon he is moved to exclaim:

"Ah! ne vous glorifiez pas de l'avoir chassé, cet enthousiasme! Il était à la fois la rose et la chanson au bord de vos vingt ans désolés; il était l'opulence orgueilleuse de votre âge, il était votre grâce, votre génie, votre fierté, ô jeunesse!—toute votre jeunesse...."

Let us take this for the epitaph of *La Bohème*.

II

A FRINGE OF HISTORY: THE REVOLUTION OF 1830

IN the first chapter of Murger's "Scènes de la Vie de Bohème," Marcel, the painter, requires his *concierge*, in return for a tip of five francs, to tell him every morning the day of the week, the date, the quarter of the moon, the state of the weather, and the form of government under which they are living. A hasty generalization from this episode might conclude that the more noteworthy vicissitudes of society, which we call history, were of singularly small importance to those concerned with Bohemia. The main current of events, it would seem, rolled on, leaving the stagnant backwater undisturbed, where, in the easy garment of "art for art's sake," a few geniuses and many *dilettanti* lolled the day through in unpatriotic apathy. Such a conclusion from Murger's picture of Bohemia is, in fact, inevitable, but it is a wrong one, and the fault lies only with Murger. The French people, at any rate the Parisians, are extremely susceptible to the impressions of passing events, political, artistic, or social. They are more excitable, as we say, than ourselves. We only become agitated in response to orders from Fleet Street, whereas they are apt to ferment spontaneously, their natural liveliness of mind acting as the yeast. It is this quality of interest in passing events, fostered by their fondness for discussion, which renders their criticism so trenchant and their partisanship so ardent. So that we can scarcely believe Bohemia, eclectic as it was, to have been unmoved or, at least, uninfluenced by the objects of contemporary comment or debate. For this reason our picture would be seen in a false light without some reference to history. Moreover, I have been rash enough to impose upon myself the limitation of dates, which are dangerous things in themselves, always requiring justification. I put the classic period of *la vie de Bohème* between 1830 and 1848, the exact period of Louis Philippe's reign. At first sight the reign of this *bourgeois* prince would seem to have little enough connexion with the florescence and decadence of the very antitype of *bourgeoisie*, but this is only a further reason for not neglecting history. The Revolution of 1830 was of the highest importance for France: it was the inevitable explosion of dissatisfaction, both political and artistic, with the powers that ruled. What I wish to make clear is that, whereas before this date Bohemia, if it existed, was but an unconsidered fringe on the ancient student life of the Quartier Latin, after 1830 it not only received a population but became a force. For a few years it was an integral part of the larger Paris, a considerable element in public opinion and, to some extent, in social life, a factor that could not be ignored. Disturbance, however, yielded to peace, and the interests of the public shifted. The living spirit of Bohemia gradually hardened into a dead tradition. By 1848 independence and individual liberty, the watchwords of Bohemia, were replaced in the mind of citizens by thoughts of social reform which culminated in the Republic of 1848. Art, for the time, fell from her place of glory, and Bohemia relapsed for ever into obscurity.

The battle of Waterloo seemed to have undone all the good of the Revolution of 1789. The Bourbons came back to power, with Louis XVIII, a lazy man, on the throne, and his brother, the Comte d'Artois, leading a band of ultra-Royalists behind him. The ultra-Royalists, exasperated by the "hundred days," were breathing fire and slaughter, full of zeal to destroy the liberty and philosophy of the Revolution and to replace it with absolutism and priest-rule. Against them was arrayed the party of "Independents" with Béranger, their poet, and between the two were the "doctrinaires" or moderate Royalists. The "Ultras," whose violence began by damaging their own cause, were put into power by the assassination of the Duc de Berry in 1820, and Villèle was their minister. The succession of Charles X only strengthened the forces of reaction, till in 1828 Villèle was defeated and gave place to a Liberal, Martignac. But Martignac's party were not strong enough to support him long, and in 1829 he was succeeded by Polignac and a Royalist ministry. The Liberals now prepared for stubborn resistance. Societies were formed, with branches throughout the provinces, which were joined by all shades of Liberal opinion, and their hero was Lafayette. The blindness of Charles X precipitated events. Exasperated by the adverse result of the elections of 1830, he suspended the constitution by his famous ordinances on July 26. Paris rose at once, and four days later all was over. Louis of Orleans was in Paris by the 30th, and took the oath as King in August. This is only a bald statement of facts, but they are facts that can be seen by the eye of imagination. By 1830 Paris was a boiling cauldron of passionate enthusiasm. Revolution was aflame once more. Barricades—the mere word is a trumpet-call to Frenchmen—had been erected once more in the streets, and once more blood had flowed in their defence. Paris for years had smouldered with indignation, and now her young men glowed with triumph. The people should come to its own again, and they should be its champions. The eyes of France were on them, and they knew that their comrades in the provinces, intoxicated by the songs of Béranger, enraged by the petty vexations of Royalist officials, were envying them their opportunity and eagerly looking for any chance that would bring them to the city that so nobly stood for liberty.

The Revolution of 1830 was not only political, it was also artistic, and the artistic results were really the more permanent. This artistic revolution is generally known as the Romantic movement, about which so much has been written that I need not refer to it at length. Just as the Liberal spirit smouldered for many years against the Royalist oppression, so the Romantic spirit smouldered against the restraints of the dead classic tradition of the eighteenth century. The process of combustion, beginning as it did with Rousseau, was a slow one, and, as it has been said, Romanticism only potentially existed, as a movement, before 1820. In that year Victor Hugo founded his journal, the *Conservateur Littéraire*, gathering round him a brilliant company of writers. For ten years the movement grew in intensity, fostered by the institution of *cénacles* and the only too successful proselytism of Victor Hugo, who disdained no recruit whom he could by flattery enlist. It is not too much to say that the youth of all France was fired by the revolt against classicism in poetry and drama. Every schoolboy wrote verses and every ardent soul longed to enter the very arena in Paris, where the *perruques* of the Institute were so signally defied. Paris became doubly desirable as the field on which political and artistic liberty were being won. The triumph came in 1830 with the performance of "Hernani." That victory of the Romantic army is now a commonplace, but in 1830 it was magnificently new, and it was, moreover, the public manifestation of *la Bohème*. The effect of this double excitement was overwhelming. It literally tore the more intelligent among the young men of France from the roots of all their attachments and interests. To establish liberty, to revolutionize literature, these were their dreams, in comparison with which all ordinary professional prospects seemed dreary and unworthy. So the year 1830 saw Paris harbouring in her garrets a host of enthusiasts, most of them very young, burning with ideals and flushed with apparently glorious victories. They felt themselves incorporated in one great brotherhood of defiance to established authority, so that those who mocked their poverty and lawlessness in the name "Bohemian" were unconsciously justified, for a corporate name is the sign of a corporate existence. *La Bohème* in 1830 was not a haphazard collection of *dilettanti* and artistic eccentrics; it was a fellowship inspired by similar enthusiasms and bound together by the struggle against similar misfortunes.

Misfortunes, indeed, were not slow to come. Society is wonderfully quick to repair the breaches in its walls made by gallant assaulters, and the heroes who have been foremost in the attack find that their bravely made passage has closed behind them, and that they are left to be broken and starved into submission. So it was after 1830. Louis Philippe was at heart a Royalist who had little understanding of the Revolution. His great achievement was to keep on his throne for eighteen years by encouraging the moneyed middle class, thus laying the foundation of French industrial prosperity. *Enrichissez-vous* was the order of the day, an order ironically unsuitable to the reformers of Bohemia. Those among them whose ideals were political rather than literary became uncompromising Republicans, formed secret societies, carried on a violent Press campaign of articles and caricatures against Louis Philippe and his ministers, and plotted further armed risings in Paris, the most serious of which was the ill-fated insurrection of the Cloître Saint-Merri in 1832. They were to find that they had presumed too far upon their strength. In spite of the Legitimist risings in La Vendée, labour troubles at Lyons, and disaffection in Paris, Louis Philippe's government was powerful enough to meet all emergencies. Press laws were made doubly stringent, secret societies were prohibited, caricatures were exposed to a censorship, and the police was exceedingly vigilant. Above all, the *bourgeoisie* held firm. They were tasting prosperity and power, and had no desire to let political disturbance interfere with their enjoyment. Happy were those who could repent of youthful political excesses and return to comfortable homes and settled careers. Those who had no refuge but Bohemia came to know the chill of disappointment and repression. Their bright dreams faded away into grey reality; they found themselves suspects and outcasts, with the problem of subsistence, instead of being miraculously solved, only rendered more acute. They had no outlet for their energies, and those whom neither the barricades nor the cholera of 1832 carried off saw the fellowship of assault followed by the isolation of retreat. They drifted away in little bands to join the societies of social reformers like Saint Simon, Fourier, or Père Enfantin. Consumption, starvation, and suicide were the ends of many of them, and their traces gradually faded from Bohemia, which became identified purely with the lives of its literary and artistic inhabitants.

The poets and artists of Bohemia survived longer, not only as individuals, but as a united brotherhood, mainly because artistic rebellion cannot be put down, as it does not manifest itself, by force, and also because the campaign in which "Hernani" was the central engagement really culminated in a lasting victory. For some years after 1830 there was plenty for the young band to do in reducing block-houses and chasing the persistent critics of the old school, who conducted a most robust guerilla warfare. Yet hardship and misfortune dogged their footsteps also. The Romantic victory of 1830 was won by an army; its spoils were shared by the few leaders—Victor Hugo, Sainte-Beuve, de Vigny—who, as M. Henri Lardanchet has rather unkindly said,[1] "without a word of farewell or a motion of gratitude abandoned their army to famine." To tell the truth, many of the devoted enthusiasts were young men of mediocre talents at a day when the standard was very high. Verses were a drug in the market, and he was a lucky man who could earn a few francs by filling a column or two in a little fashion paper boasting a few hundred subscribers. Journalism was not yet a commercially flourishing business, expenses were high, subscribers few, and Press laws menacing. The starveling poets and dramatists of Bohemia fell upon lean years, in which the weaker and more utterly destitute were destroyed by their privations, like Elisa Mercœur and Hégésippe Moreau. Nevertheless, the Romantics were not crushed out of existence. The stout hearts of those who held out still beat to a common measure, and maintained artistic fellowship in an ideal as an essential element of *la vie de Bohème*.

Bohemia was glorious for a few years after 1830 as it has never been since because it proclaimed a creed, the creed of Romanticism. It was glorious then because, with Romanticism, Bohemia was a living force. Given this connexion, there was some point in the bravado, the extravagances and conceits of Bohemian life. They were an irregular army, those young men, and they rejoiced in their irregularity. *Épater le bourgeois* was a legitimate war-cry when the *bourgeois* stood for all that was reactionary in art. To scare the grocer with a slouch hat and a medieval oath was not only a youthful ebullition, it was a symbolic act. The sombrero defied artistic convention as typified in the top hat; the medieval oath, in its contrast with the paler expletives of modernity, symbolized the return to life and colour in art after a century of grey abstraction. It was with the decline of Romanticism that Bohemia lost its living spirit. Unlike Republicanism, that gathered unseen strength in failure to blossom for a more worthy generation, Romanticism lost its vitality through its very success. It may be likened to some conflux of waters which to force from its way the inert mass of an obstacle rises to a mighty head: the obstacle is swept away, and the seething waters resolve themselves into a workaday river humbly serving the sea. So the Romantic movement has served literature for many decades now, and it was quietly flowing between the banks before Louis Philippe lost his throne. Success, it might be said, came to it too soon, especially as success in that day meant money. The dangers of Republicanism were staved off for the moment by force; the dangers of Romanticism were for ever discounted by payment. Authorship was made to serve a commercial end, and all was over. In 1836 Emile de Girardin founded *La Presse*, which was sold at a far lower price than any other paper. The inevitable followed. Circulation went up by leaps and bounds, contributors were paid respectable prices, expenses were defrayed by the profits of advertisement, and journalism in France was at once on a commercial footing, for other papers were not slow to follow. Literature, from being purely an art, quickly became a trade. The struggle for a new artistic ideal gave way to the struggle for loaves and fishes, which is contemporary with mankind. A man's artistic creed went for nothing, when all the public asked was that he should make himself conspicuous before they gave him their countenance. Once artistic success became a matter of royalties it was an easy prey to *bourgeois* conditions, which were that art and literature should either be merely entertaining or point a respectable moral. Only a few Romantics were proof against this insidious influence. To those recalcitrants we owe the motto "Art for art's sake."

The effect of this change upon Bohemia is not difficult to imagine. *La vie de Bohème* implies youth, so that its generations change as rapidly as those of a university. The generation of 1830 had either disappeared or become famous—that is, potentially rich—in a few years. The struggle which had convulsed all Paris was a thing of the past, and Romanticism was so far accepted, swallowed, and digested that by 1843 the necessity was felt for reverting to the classical tradition again, for a change, with the so-called *école de bon sens*. There was no longer any trumpet-call to which Bohemia could respond as a brotherhood, as Victor Hugo learned when, on wishing to enlist a fresh army to go into battle for "Les Burgraves," he was told "il n'y a plus de jeunes gens." The swaggering heroes of 1830 were now writers of successful novels and comedies, or safely chained, as critics, to the careers of remunerative journals. Rebellion was impossible, for there was nothing to rebel against. Success depended more upon individual enterprise than common enthusiasm. There was nothing left, therefore, for the new generations of Bohemia but to fall back upon tradition. If there was no more certainty in ideals there was at least something definite in slouch hats and medieval oaths, in defying conventions of dress and accepted table manners. So the symbols of Romanticism became the realities of Bohemia after all that they symbolized was as lifeless as a cancelled bank-note. Further, the population of Bohemia lost that great asset in life, personal pride. Their predecessors of 1830 were arrogant, no doubt, but with the arrogance of an advance-guard in a desperate venture. There was no desperate venture now toward, and advance meant, not progress, but prosperity. The poorer brethren of art who peopled Bohemia were now, inasmuch as they were not prosperous, failures. They had no sense of intellectual achievement to keep up their courage, when such achievement was measured in gold. It was inevitable that their *moral* should be affected; the recklessness, which was formerly that of bravado, became that of despair, and a less reputable atmosphere grew up round Bohemia which has never been dispelled from its tradition.

Nevertheless, dead as the spirit was, the tradition of 1830 remained very strong, being kept alive not only by oral transmission, as all traditions are, but also by the art of the sturdy few who remained faithful to the uncompromising standard of disinterestedness in art which it implied. Gautier, Flaubert, Baudelaire, the de Goncourts, and a few others stood out unflinchingly against commercialism on the one hand and prosy doctrinairism on the other. Their struggle was not wholly effectual, but, so far as Bohemia is concerned, was important. After 1848, when everything had to have a social "purpose" and art for its own sake seemed dead, they sat down, like the Psalmist, by the rivers of Babylon and remembered Zion. From their regrets the legend of *la sainte Bohème* arose idealized and purified, and it was made immortal in pages of prose by Gautier and in de Banville's "Ballade de ses regrets pour l'an 1830." This legend, tinged as it already was with sentiment, spread to the public, by whom it was resentimentalized, a fact of which other authors, Murger included, were not slow to take advantage.

"Ils savaient tirer parti des ressemblances réelles entre la vie de Bohème et la vie de l'étudiant bourgeois au 'Pays latin' pour établir une confusion avantageuse, confusion qui est déjà manifeste dans les 'Scènes de la Vie de Bohème.' Chanter ainsi la Bohème c'était un peu chanter la jeunesse bourgeoise."[2]

If this be true, then Bohemia after 1848, when the public interest was purely absorbed in Socialistic reforms, lapsed once more into being a mere fringe on the student life, and, as such, equally negligible. Its classic days were over, never to return, for the society of Paris grew too large to be again convulsed by a purely artistic conflict. The leaders of the new *Parnasse* made a considerable sensation, but they founded, not a new Bohemia, but only another *cénacle*. History establishes the florescence and decline of the classic *vie de Bohème* beyond much doubt, for it went with the florescence and decline of a common spirit.

III

LE MAL DU SIÈCLE

I HAVE identified the classic period of Bohemia with the time of the Romantic victory. It was not then lighted by dim lanterns hung outside the door of every artistic idiosyncrasy, but reflected flamboyantly a general state of mind. I disclaim once for all the intention of adding another to the many studies of the Romantic movement, but in my aim of explaining the living reality out of which grew the tradition of *la vie de Bohème* I am compelled to dwell upon the turgid mental content of the early nineteenth century. The eccentricities of Bohemia were then but slight exaggerations of a universal spiritual ferment, though, after the good wine was made, a later and decadent Bohemia artificially reproduced the symptoms of a process that was formerly natural and necessary. *Le mal romantique, le mal du siècle*, are common phrases upon the lips of French critics, who to-day affect to treat with contempt what was, after all, a new Renaissance. Without adopting their attitude, it must be admitted that, inestimable as were its results, it was an alarming convulsion. The English took it in a milder and earlier form. Its most extreme manifestation, Byron and the "Satanic" school, was a thing of the past before 1830. But the French were thoroughly and virulently affected, and exhibited all the most violent symptoms.

We may best begin, perhaps, by looking at a particular "subject," to use a medical phrase, in the correspondence of J.-J. Ampère, son of the great scientist. The younger Ampère, after a violent adoration of Madame Récamier, who was old enough to be his mother, settled down into a most respectable and successful man of letters, and he was never in any sense a Bohemian. He was a well-educated and perfectly normal man, so that the ravages of *le mal du siècle* may be well judged when he writes to his friend, Jules Bastide, in 1820:

"My dear Jules, last week the feeling of malediction was upon me, round me, within me. I owe this to Lord Byron; I read through twice at a sitting the English 'Manfred.' Never, never in my life has anything I have read overwhelmed me as that did; it has made me ill. On Sunday I went to see the sunset upon the Place de l'Esplanade; it was as threatening as the fires of hell. I went into the church, where the faithful were peacefully chanting the Hallelujah of the Resurrection. Leaning against a column, I looked at them with disdain and envy."

Two months later Jules Bastide delivered his soul in a similar strain:

"I feel that the slightest emotions might send me mad or kill me. The evening of our parting I opened at random a volume of Madame de Staël and read the dream of Jean Paul. When I came to that terrible line, 'Christ, nous n'avons point de père,' a shudder seized me. An hour later I had a fever; it lasted a fortnight."

Another friend wrote to Ampère in 1824:

"All my ideas turn towards Africa.... Is it solitude that I seek in Africa? Yes, but it is not only that; it is the desert, the palm-tree, the musk-rose, the Arab! A romanesque and *barbaresque* future is what ravishes me."

In 1825 Ampère, then twenty-five years old, wrote to Madame Récamier:

"Return, for my life is no longer tolerable without you; my spirit is wholly employed in trying to *support* the emptiness of my days."

In these delirious passages are contained the most marked symptoms of the time, the satanic gloom that drew its inspiration from Byron, the nervous sensibility imitated from the heroes of Madame de Staël, Châteaubriand, and Sénancour, and the longing for a life of Oriental colour which found a later expression in Victor Hugo's poems. However, it would be unfair to put down this spiritual *bouleversement* to the influence of "René," "Obermann," "Werther's Leiden," or "Manfred." They became, indeed, the breviaries of the afflicted, but the cause of the affliction lay deeper in the reaction of the French nation after the Napoleonic wars. Napoleon's victorious campaigns drained France of its best blood and its best energies, leaving an inheritance of anæmia and neurasthenia to the next generation, without diminishing that feverish desire for glory, that determination to work one's will upon a passive world, which was the spirit of Napoleon's armies. Older and more settled people were content to reap the rewards of peace, but the young men, exalted by the exploits of their fathers, looked in vain for some channel in which to discharge their superfluous electricity. Under the restored Bourbons there was none. The fathers had had free play upon historic battlefields, the sons were cribbed and confined in the narrow bounds of everyday life. Moreover, the revolutionary wars had revealed vast, unexplored pastures to the French mind. New countries, languages, and literatures were brought into its view. The gorgeous East, in particular, seized upon the French imagination. The desert was vast and untrodden, the Arab was dignified and free, and under unclouded skies the primitive nobility of mankind revealed itself in splendour and space.

Here, then, is the root of *le mal du siècle* from which the divers symptoms sprang. Of these, perhaps, the most marked and most general was an exaggerated sensibility, a kind of melancholy madness. Young Henri Dubois, who at any other epoch would have been content to learn his trade behind the counter of Dubois and Dupont, cloth merchants, and to settle down into a peaceful home with Mademoiselle Dupont, now plied the yard measure with disgust and yearned for an existence more worthy of his "complicated state of mind." He was a perfect magazine of pent-up emotions, ready to expire in a delirium of joy or an ecstasy of despair after the manner of René and Werther. He was quite willing to love Mademoiselle Dupont on the condition that she would lend herself to a tempestuous passion, allow her hands to be bathed in tears for hours together by her prostrate cavalier, receive folios of hysterical ravings by the post, and dread the fatal dagger if she had smiled from her desk at a customer. She was urged daily to fly to a brighter destiny upon distant shores, and nightly trembled that the coming morning would find Henri transfixed by his own poniard. It was impossible to be reasonable; only a clod, dead to all beauty, could be so brutal. M. Louis Maigron, who in his book, "Le Romantisme et les Mœurs," gives some very remarkable instances of these aberrations in actual correspondence, says very truly: "Une foule de 'cratères' ont alors superbement fumé au nez des bourgeois." The Romantic ideal supposed a sensibility always stretched to its utmost, *des âmes excessives*, as M. Bourget says,[3] capable of constant renewal, and a consumption of emotional energy which is irreconcilable with the laws of any organism. If a young man failed for a moment to find food for melancholy broodings in the shortcomings of society, he could always fall back for a good groan upon his own insufficiencies of sensibility. Now, of course, the "feelings of malediction" which afflicted the Henri Dubois are of small moment in themselves. Time comfortably settled them down. It was the young men of real sensibility and imagination, the coming poets and artists, in whom the ravages of *le mal du siècle* were more than a passing phase. The boundless yearnings that found expression in such lines as these:

Amour, enthousiasme, étude, poésie!
C'est là qu'en votre extase, océan d'ambroisie
Se noîraient nos âmes de feu!
C'est là que je saurais, fort d'un génie étrange,
Dans la création d'un bonheur sans mélange
Être plus artiste que Dieu[4]—

could not but lead to a profound dissatisfaction with existence, which Maxime du Camp in his reminiscences very happily describes:

"It was not only a fashion [he says], as might be believed; it was a kind of general prostration which made our hearts sad, darkened our thoughts, and caused us to see a deliverance in the glimpse of death. You would have thought that life held in chains souls that had caught sight of something superior to terrestrial existence. We did not aspire to the felicities of paradise: we dreamed of taking possession of the infinite, and we were tortured by a vague pantheism of which the formula was never found.... The artistic and literary generation which preceded me and that to which I belonged had a youth of lamentable sadness, sadness without cause and without object, abstract sadness, inherent in the individual or in the period....

"Nobody was allowed to be without an *âme incomprise*; it was the custom and we conformed to it. We were 'fatal' and 'accursed'; without even having tasted life, we tumbled to the bottom of the abyss of disillusionment. Children of eighteen years, repeating phrases gathered from some novel or other, would say: 'J'ai le cœur usé comme l'escalier d'une fille de joie,' and one of Pétrus Borel's heroes went to the executioner to say to him: 'I should like you to guillotine me!' This did not prevent us from laughing, singing, or committing the honest follies of youth; that was also a way of being desperate; we imagined that we had a satanic laugh, while we really possessed the fair joy of spring."

These exquisite sensibilities, when they were not turned back upon themselves in black despair, roamed far and wide in search of new sensations upon which to exercise themselves. This *exotisme*, as the French have called it, is another of the most marked symptoms of Romanticism. The time was ripe for its satisfaction. The French mind, shut for so long in the formalism of the eighteenth century, now found that there were innumerable new ways to *rêver la rêve de la vie*. The men of learning who followed in Napoleon's wake renewed the interest in archæology by their discoveries; the historical novels of Scott and the history of Michelet revealed the full and generous life of earlier ages; the forged poems of Ossian caused a perfect rage for Celtic mysticism; and the bold lawless life of the East, with its tyrannous Ali Pashas and its Greek patriots, shone out with a new splendour. An unsatisfied longing for another age and another clime animated every young breast. Societies even were formed in provincial towns in which subscriptions were pooled, and the winner of the lucky number drew the money to take a voyage in Italy. The glories of Greece and the grandeurs of Rome, as savouring of the classical, appealed only to a few; other eclectics fed upon German mysticism and the fantastic weirdness of Hoffmann's supernatural tales. A far greater number became Celts in imagination; dressed in the dignity of outlawry and the garb of an Irish bard or a Scotch chieftain, they defied the haughty English. Maxime du Camp, for instance, wrote a poem in his school-days called "Wistibrock l'Irlandais." "When I am depressed," he says in his reminiscences, "I read it again, and there is no vexation that resists it." Anybody who wishes to gain some idea of the *genre frénétique*, as Nodier called it, in its Celtic dress will derive considerable entertainment from Pétrus Borel's "Madame Putiphar." It is full of murders and intrigues and tirades which foam at the mouth. The hero, Patrick FitzWhyte, falls in love with Deborah Cockermouth, daughter of Lord and Lady Cockermouth, the opening dialogue of whom upon the battlements is magnificent. My lord, who is described as "one of those gigantic fungous and spongy zoophytes indigenous to Great Britain," permits himself to address my lady as "Saint-hearted milk soup!" After a good deal of clandestine philandering and interminable translations of imaginary Irish ballads the young couple elope to Paris, where Madame Putiphar (Madame de Pompadour) seduces the heroine, and the hero after a series of dreadful adventures is imprisoned in a loathsome dungeon in the Bastille, the taking of which by the people of Paris is described with quite astonishing force.

The Spirit of Romanticism

Wild adventures, horrors and tragedies in any age were fondly dwelt upon in comparison with the insupportable monotony of contemporary life; but the Middle Ages made a stronger appeal than any. There was a perfect mania for medievalism. Nothing pleased overwrought imaginations more than to picture existence amid all the riot and magnificence of those more spacious days. How they would have rattled a sword and clanked a spur, how defiantly tilted their plume, how breathlessly loved and how destructively fought! Why did they not live in the joyous time when every minute brought an adventure instead of spilling one more drop from the cup of *ennui*, and when a man shaped his own ends according to his passions, throwing a curse to the poor and a madrigal to the fair? Then, all their life was not grey. Splendour of colour with ample grace of form decked out existence like a picture by Veronese. Costly satin vied with magnificent brocade; all was a riot of velvet and purple dyes, fur and old lace; drinking cups, worthy of giants, chiselled by a Cellini, offered wine worthy of the gods; swords were masterpieces of the finest Toledo; jewelled harness caparisoned fleet Arab horses; feasts were Gargantuan, jests more than Rabelaisian; and all this wonderful wealth of glittering colour was thrown into magnificent relief against the solemnity of antique battlements and the sombre shadows of Gothic architecture. This, apart from all innovations of dramatic form, was the secret of the delirious popularity of "Hernani," "Lucrèce Borgia," "Le Roi s'amuse," and the "Tour de Nesle," and of the craze for historical novels, verses in baroque metres, slouch hats *à la Buridan*, velvet pourpoints, daggers, mysterious draperies and massive chests, drinking cups made out of skulls, and illuminated breviaries of which Gautier makes such fun in "Les Jeunes France." To it we owe Balzac's splendid "Contes Drolatiques," Lassailly's "Roueries de Trialph," and Roger de Beauvoir's "L'Écolier de Cluny." Gautier in his early poems was as romanesque as any of his "Jeune France," as those who know his early poems must admit. "Débauche" is a frank orgy, and "Albertus" is a gem of the Gothic, with its supernatural setting, the "fatality" of its hero, the horror of its *dénouement*, the wild fantasy of its witches' chamber, and its amorous wealth of descriptive detail in which old fabrics, old furniture, swords, daggers, and hangings abound. Victor Hugo, above all, was the chosen bard of the Gothic and the romanesque. Besides his dramas, his "Odes et Ballades" were in the mouth of every child who could pay four halfpence for an hour's luxury in the *cabinet de lecture*; and schoolboys would declaim for hours in antiphon such passages as the invocation of "La Bande Noire":

O murs! ô créneaux! ô tourelles!
Remparts! fossés aux ponts mouvants!
Lourds faisceaux de colonnes frêles!
Fiers châteaux! modestes couvents!
Cloîtres poudreux, salles antiques,
Où gémissaient les saints cantiques,
Où riaient les rires joyeux!
Églises où priaient nos mères,
Tours où combattaient nos aïeux!

or the frenzied descriptions of the witches' dance in "La Ronde du Sabbat," or lines from "La Chasse du Burgrave"—which even Hugo called "un peu trop Gothique de forme"—or with a

Çà, qu'on selle,
Ecuyer,
Mon fidèle
Destrier.
Mon cœur ploie
Sous la joie
Quand je broie
L'étrier

proclaimed their attendance at the "Pas d'Armes du Roi Jean."

The star of the Gothic and the medieval was indeed high in the heavens, but it paled before the full sun of Araby and the East. Napoleon had dreamed of a Mohammedan empire, and before his dream could fade Navarino and Missolonghi fired men's minds again. Victor Hugo was also the champion of Oriental rhapsody. Even in 1824 he had seen the possibilities of Oriental colour in French verse, when he wrote "La Fée et la Péri," a poem in which the Peri, who stands for romanticism, says:

J'ai de vastes cités qu'en tous lieux on admire,
Lahore aux champs fleuris, Golconde, Cachemire,
La guerrière Damas, la royale Ispahan,
Bagdad que ses remparts couvrent comme une armure,
Alep dont l'immense murmure
Semble au pâtre lointain le bruit d'un océan.

His collection of poems entitled "Les Orientales" was published in 1829 and took Paris by storm, provoking passionate enthusiasm and equally passionate protest. In the preface he asserts that Orientalism is a general preoccupation. "The colours of the East have come, as if spontaneously, to impress themselves upon all his [the poet's] thoughts and all his musings; his musings and his thoughts have become, in turn, and almost without his willing it, Hebrew, Turkish, Greek, Persian, Arabic, even Spanish, for Spain, too, is the East." There are fine poems in "Les Orientales"—"Les Djinns," for instance, will always be famous—but it is impossible to read the volume through to-day without considerable amusement, so very full-blooded are they. There are lofty apostrophes to Byron and the Greeks, followed by dreadful tales of Turkish cruelty, gruesome ballads like "La Voile," in which four brothers kill their sister, epigraphs like "O horror! horror! horror!" valiant Klephtes, houris, scimitars, and all the catalogue which the poet himself gives in "Novembre":

Sultans et sultanes,
Pyramides, palmiers, galères capitanes,
Et le tigre vorace et le chameau frugal;
Djinns au vol furieux, danses des bayadères,
L'Arabe qui se penche au cou des dromadaires,
Et la fauve girafe au galop inégale.
Alors éléphants blancs chargés de femmes brunes,
Cités aux dômes d'or où les mois sont des lunes,
Imams de Mahomet, mages, prêtres de Bel ...

Then, as if Victor Hugo did not whip the passions enough, Alfred de Musset lent a hand in the hurly-burly with his "Contes d'Espagne et d'Italie," which made the young maniacs frantically demand:

Avez-vous vu dans Barcelone
Une Andalouse au sein bruni?
Pâle comme un beau soir d'automne!
C'est ma maîtresse, ma lionne!
La marquesa d'Amaëgui.

Delacroix, too, was sending the critics into ecstasies of rage with his vivid Eastern scenes and the horrors of his "Massacre of Scio." The ideas of the young men with inflamed sensibilities seethed in turbulent disorder. To be in the movement they had to have at least a poniard and a narghile, a medieval cloak and an Oriental divan. Those with money to spare decorated their rooms like sombre Gothic manors, those with no money enriched their conversations with a wealth of medieval diction. No make-believe was too ridiculous to shut out the actual place and time in which they lived. Balzac's novel "La Peau de Chagrin," which has won a celebrity far beyond its merits, is most unmistakably marked with the frenzies of 1830. His revelling in the supernatural, the massed effects of careful detail in the description of the curiosity shop where the wild-ass skin hangs, the wild riot of the orgy, the terrific excesses in which Valentin ruins his life, the duel and the horrible end, are just as much the *genre frénétique* as anything by Pétrus Borel. The hero, Valentin, is simply a type of his time, and his tirade on taking the supernatural skin is hardly an exaggeration:

"Je veux que la débauche en délire et rugissante nous emporte, dans son char à quatre chevaux, par delà les bornes du monde, pour nous verser sur des plages inconnues! Que les âmes montent dans les cieux ou se plongent dans la boue, je ne sais si alors elles s'élèvent ou s'abaissent, peu m'importe! Donc, je commande à ce pouvoir sinistre de me fondre toutes les joies dans une joie. Oui, j'ai besoin d'embrasser les plaisirs du ciel et de la terre dans une dernière étreinte, pour en mourir. Aussi souhaité-je et des priapées antiques après boire, et des chants à réveiller les morts, et de triples baisers, des baisers sans fin dont la clameur passe sur Paris comme un craquement d'incendie, y réveille les époux et les inspire une ardeur cuisante qui les rajeunissent tous, même les septuagénaires!"

As for the "orgy," it was so much a fashion that Gautier in his "Les Jeune France" scores a delightful hit with the story of a society of young men who combine for a colossal feast, in which various sections follow out in exact detail the descriptions of orgies given by their favourite novelists and the end is a farcical confusion.

Building castles in Spain is a fascinating pastime, but the ingenuities of imagination cannot entirely shut out the individual from his surroundings. From 1820 to 1830 the young man of France was continually running against the sharp corners of the world and receiving the elbow prods of his fellow-men. Exalted by his excited sensibility, he conceived at once a contempt and a hatred for the insensibility of society, which produced in him a feeling of moral superiority and solitude. This abnormal vanity, shown in the deification of "l'homme supérieur" and a proud contemplation of his social outlawry, is a third marked symptom of *le mal du siècle*.[5] It broke out in several different forms. One was a romantic worship of energy and strong will, as typified by the career of Napoleon. Given these qualities, a man could rise from the lowest depths to impose his wishes on the world. However, self-styled supermen have invariably found their theories rebellious to practical application, and Henri Dubois, if he started upon a Napoleonic path, soon discovered that society selects its "homme supérieur" when it wants him, and that uncalled-for aspirants receive the point of its toe. He reserved his superiority, therefore, more usually, for less material manifestations and conflicts. His rare spirit, susceptible to all "the finer shades," stood mournfully but prudently on high, scorning the base, unfeeling throng below it, and calling out through space for kindred spirits to cherish. "My friend, take care of yourself," writes young Ampère to his friend. "Obermann cries to us, 'Keep close together, ye simple men who feel the beauty of natural things.' Let us help one another, all of us who suffer." So Henri Dubois and his friends suffered and helped one another, shedding pints of tears and being just as ridiculous as they could be.

Solitary suffering makes men philosophers or poets. Philosophy requiring some intellectual capacity and mental preparation, Henri Dubois often took the further step from crying in the wilderness to enshrining his laments in metre, being encouraged in this by the certain fact that young men and true poets were indeed striking the Romantic harp to a new and surprising tune.

The poet was the real "homme supérieur" of the time, not only in fancy but in fact. Henri accordingly proceeded another stage towards sublimity by way of the faulty syllogism: "The poet has an exquisite soul; I have an exquisite soul; therefore I am a poet." The Romantics conceived the poet as a God-sent prophet. This was the attitude, above all, of de Vigny; Lamartine and Sainte-Beuve adopted it in their early days, and certain passages of Victor Hugo—for instance:

O poètes sacrés, échevelés, sublimes,
Allez, et répandez vos âmes sur les cimes,
Sur les sommets de neige en butte aux aquilons,
Sur les déserts pieux où l'esprit se recueille,
Sur les bois que l'automne emporte feuille à feuille,
Sur les lacs endormis dans l'ombre des vallons!

—show that he was not averse to it. So every youth who could rhyme "âme" with "flamme" put on the aureole of a "poète échevelé," revelled in the ecstasies of solitary contemplation, and sneered magnificently at all who attended to business as soulless *épiciers*. This was a harmless enough delusion, but it became less harmless when combined with the idea that for the sake of experience the poet should abandon himself entirely to his passions. The great artist, indeed, has his own morality, but Victor Hugo's "Mazeppa" or Lamartine's stanza

Mais nous, pour embraser les âmes,
Il faut brûler, il faut ravir
Au ciel jaloux ses triples flammes:
Pour tout peindre, il faut tout sentir.
Foyers brûlants de la lumière,
Nos cœurs de la nature entière
Doivent concentrer les rayons,
Et l'on accuse notre vie!
Mais ce flambeau qu'on nous envie
S'allume au feu des passions

were dangerous matchboxes in the hands of children. It was a fatality, too, that several poets of some merit died during these years of want or neglect. Gilbert, the satirist, expired in hospital, breathing piteous plaints, and Hégésippe Moreau, the poet of "La Voulzie," was equally unfortunate. Society can hardly be blamed for not supporting all its lyrically inclined members, but it was natural that the "poète échevelé" should smoulder with indignation at such disasters, and cheer the sentiments of de Vigny's drama "Chatterton" till his lungs gave out. It was still more of a fatality that certain other poets attained a momentary celebrity by committing suicide, leaving rhymed farewells to a stony-hearted society and a tedious life. To win fame by a pathetic death in a pauper's hospital, or to bid defiance to the world with a superb gesture of self-destruction, was a far too common ambition. Sainte-Beuve himself observed that "la manie et la gageure de tous les René, de tous les Chatterton de notre temps, c'était d'être grand poète et de mourir." A perfect epidemic of suicide was due to *le mal du siècle*, as M. Louis Maigron shows in his work that I have already cited. Among other strange stories he gives at length the confession of an old man who in his youth was president of a suicide club, formed in a provincial town by a set of romantic schoolboys as late as 1846. Happily the club was short-lived, but it resulted in the self-destruction of one of its most gifted members. In the letter with which he announced his coming death from Lucerne he wrote:

" ...I have no precise reason to have done with life except the insurmountable disgust with which it inspires me. Chance of birth gave me a certain fortune; I am not denied an intelligence perhaps slightly above the common level; it would have been in my power to marry an adorable child: so many conditions of happiness, in the eyes of the vulgar. But my poor soul, alas, cannot content itself with them. Nothing can charm my heart any longer, 'mon cœur lassé de tout, même de l'espérance'; it will be closed, without ever having been opened."

He left his little library to the club, specially reserving for the president "Werther," "René," "Obermann," "Jacques," and the works of Rabbe. They were his breviaries, he said, covered as they were with notes that revealed all his soul.

The pose of pathetic despair was not, however, the only one in which the feeling of moral solitude showed itself. Another very common attitude was that of revolt against society, an aping of Mephistopheles, the fallen angel doomed to everlasting unhappiness, strong only in his disillusionment and his clear vision of the canker in the heart of every bud. The word "satanism" summed up this attitude: its breviaries were "Manfred" and Dumas' violent tragedy, "Antony." It rejoiced in the cult of the horrible, in Hoffmannesque dabblings in the supernatural, in pessimistic poetry like Gautier's "Tête de Mort," and such lines in his early sonnets as:

Mais toute cette joie est comme le lierre
Qui d'une vieille tour, guirlande irregulière,
Embrasse en les cachant les pans démantelés,
Au dehors on ne voit que riante verdure,
Au dedans, que poussière infecte et noire ordure,
Et qu'ossements jaunis aux décombres mêlés.

Its effects, in society, were chiefly obtained by the satanic laugh. Gautier soon grew out of his satanic mood, Dumas was never anything more than a fine romancer, while Victor Hugo, Lamartine, and de Vigny were too lofty poets to indulge in such artificialities; but satanism deserves mention because it was a traditional business with one party in the romantic Bohemia—the party of the *Bousingots*.

Bousingots

The origin of the term *Bousingot* has been a matter of dispute among French writers. Philibert Audebrand in his memoir of Léon Gozlan says it was invented by that brilliant journalist to satirize the young republican enthusiasts of 1832 in the *Figaro*. Charles Asselineau in his "Bibliographie Romantique" says that after some hilarious souls had been arrested for singing too loudly in the streets "Nous avons fait du bousingo"—*bousingo* being the slang for "noise"—it became a popular designation for the more furious Romantics. The matter seems to be settled more or less in Asselineau's manner by a passage in the letter written by Philothée O'Neddy to Asselineau after the publication of the "Bibliographie Romantique" to give a more correct account of the second *cénacle*. He asserts that there never were any self-styled *Bousingots*, but that after the arrest of the hilarious revellers the affair got into the newspapers and the term remained as a *bourgeois* hit at the Romantics. The proper spelling of the word was *bouzingo*, and Gautier exclaimed one day: "These asses of *bourgeois* don't even know how *bouzingo* is spelt! To teach them a little orthography several of us ought to publish a volume of stories which we will bravely call 'Contes du Bouzingo.'" The suggestion was thought a happy one, and the book was even advertised as imminent, but it was never written. Gautier's promise of a contribution was afterwards redeemed in "Le Capitaine Fracasse," but Jules Vabre's famous treatise "Sur l'incommodité des commodes" did not progress beyond the title. In common parlance, however, the name remained *Bousingots*, and its general meaning was quite clear. Just as the Gothic frenzy made the party of *Jeune-France*, who were the Christian-Royalist section of the Romantics, so the political agitation, combined with the feeling of antagonism to society, made the *Bousingots*. The meaning became subsequently enlarged to express all the extravagances of the Romantics, their idealization of the artist and their disorderly ways; but this extension was illegitimate. Literature and poetry were, it is true, the preoccupation of the more prominent *Bousingots*, but their distinctive mark was a profession of ultra-democratic views and manners. The leader of them all was the mysterious Pétrus Borel,[6] whom I have already mentioned as the author of "Madame Putiphar." His other chief work was a volume of poems entitled "Rhapsodies." The young men of 1830 worshipped him as the coming champion before whom the star of Victor Hugo was ingloriously to wane. They were grievously disappointed. After the first crisis of *le mal du siècle* his inspiration faded away, and he died an obscure official in Algeria. Baudelaire, in "L'Art Romantique," says of him:

"Without Pétrus Borel, there would have been a lacuna in Romanticism. In the first phase of our literary revolution the poet's imagination turned especially to the past.... Later on its melancholy took a more decided, more savage, and more earthy tone. A misanthropical republicanism allied itself with the new school, and Pétrus Borel was the most extravagant and paradoxical expression of the spirit of the *Bousingots*.... This spirit, both literary and republican, as opposed to the democratic and bourgeois passion which subsequently oppressed us so cruelly, was moved both by an aristocratic hate, without limit, without restriction, without pity, for kings and the bourgeoisie, and by a general sympathy for all that in art represented excess in colour and form, for all that was at once intense, pessimistic, and Byronic; it was dilettantism of a singular nature, only to be explained by the hateful circumstances in which our bored and turbulent youth was enclosed. If the Restoration had regularly developed in glory, Romanticism would have never separated from the throne; and this new sect, which professed an equal disdain for the moderate party of the political opposition, for the painting of Delaroche or the poetry of Delavigne, and for the king who presided over the development of le *juste-milieu*, would have had no reason for existing."

Charles Asselineau fills up the picture. The *Bousingot*, he says, was as rough and cynical as the *Jeune-France* was dandified and exquisite, and showed genius in discovering at once the *plastique* of his idea. In contrast to the extravagant luxury affected by the medievalists, he adopted the manners of the people in habits and dress, smoking clay pipes and drinking the "petit bleu" of low pot-houses. Instead of raving about cathedrals, he spent his ingenuity in devising bitter satires against the king and his officers or fresh settings in caricature for Louis' famous *tête de poire*. "The fusillade of St.-Merry and the laws of September were the *Bousingot's* Waterloo. From the moment he was forbidden to protest in a visible manner, and was deprived of his insignia, his waistcoat, his stick, and his pipe with a pear-shaped bowl, the *Bousingot* had to retire. He became serious, an economist or a humanitarian philosopher, and showed his revolt against society and power by writing novels 'in which the idea predominated over the form.' The novel with a tendency, that literary monstrosity, is the only legacy left by the *Bousingot* to the literature of the nineteenth century."[7]

In Balzac's wonderful gallery of portraits there is a picture of a *Bousingot*. Raoul Nathan, the author, appears frequently in his Parisian scenes, but his outlines are only elaborated in the little-read "Une Fille d'Eve." There was something great and fantastic in his appearance, as if he had fought with angels or demons. He was strongly built, with a pocked face and a tanned complexion. His long hair was always untidy, but his eyes were Napoleonic and his mouth charming. His clothes always looked old and worn, his cravat was askew, his long, pointed beard untended. The grease from his hair stained his coat-collar, and he never used a nail-brush. His movements were grotesque, his conversation caustic and full of surprises. His talent, great but disorderly, had shown itself in three novels and a book of poetry: he was critic, dramatist, vaudevillist. Jealous ambition led him to embrace politics. Beginning at the extreme of opposition, he went from Saint Simonism to republicanism and through all the stages to ministerialism, being rewarded by a government appointment.

"Nathan offre un image de la jeunesse littéraire d'aujourd'hui, de ses fausses grandeurs et de ses misères réelles; il la représente avec ses beautés incorrectes et ses chutes profondes, sa vie à cascades bouillonnantes, à revers soudains, à triomphes inespérés. C'est bien l'enfant de ce siècle dévoré de jalousie ... qui veut la fortune sans le travail, la gloire sans le talent et le succès sans peine, mais qu'après bien des rébellions, bien des escarmouches, ses vices amènent à émarger le budget sous le bon plaisir du Pouvoir."

Balzac, we all know, was a little too ready to believe in the depravity of human nature, particularly when men of letters were in question. Moreover, he was profoundly antagonistic to the creed of the *Bousingots*. His portrait of Nathan is distinctly ill-natured, but it bears out the profound remark of Baudelaire, that if the Restoration had developed in glory Romanticism would never have separated from it. In another extravagant tirade (in "Béatrix") Balzac complains that the Revolution of 1830 opened the flood-gates of petty ambition, and the result of modern "equality" was that everybody did his utmost to become conspicuous. This complaint was very largely true, but as far as the *Bousingots* are concerned Baudelaire puts the facts in a truer light. The policy of *juste-milieu* inevitably caused revolt among the over-excited young men of the day. The *Bousingots* were part of this revolt, but the best of them had no thought of self-advancement. On the contrary, the testimony of contemporaries goes to show that the saving virtue of the Romantic Bohemia, *Bousingot* and *Jeune-France* alike, was disinterestedness. Baudelaire says in extenuation of Pétrus Borel himself: "He loved letters ferociously, and to-day we are encumbered with pretty, supple writers ready to sell the muse for the potter's field." Asselineau avers that if there was much of the ridiculous in their excesses, there was nothing sordid. "They never talked of money, or business, or position." The artist Jean Gigoux,[8] in regretting the past, says that the *rapin* of his later years, if better dressed, knew less than those of his young days, and was greedy of honours and money, things which the *rapins* of old sincerely despised. Indeed, it is impossible to read much about the Romantics of 1830, high or low, aristocratic or Bohemian, without coming to the conclusion that they were neither jealous nor mercenary. So the *Bousingots*—though some rolled their eyes and knitted their brows "as if they would bully the whole universe," others "fixed their dark glances on the ground in fearful meditation," others, "gloomily leaning against a statue or tree," threw "such terrific meaning into their looks as might be naturally interpreted into the language of the witches in 'Macbeth'"[9]—did these things in all sincerity, with an ambition, not to "get on," but to "do something."

We cannot, then, judge the classic *vie de Bohème* in a true light without taking into account this *mal du siècle* which with its various symptoms infected the greater part, certainly the more intelligent part, of the younger generation. Many outlived the fever and smiled at its remembrance; but at its height it was powerful. It was a healthy fever in so far as it implied devotion to an ideal, *the* ideal of true art, which was then born again. Moreover, the ideal consumed in its fire many pettinesses of the artistic soul, the commercialism of some, the haughty vanity of others. Balzac's Lucien de Rubempré was not a true son of 1830 when he sold his independence to corrupt journalism, and Victor Hugo was not only intriguing when he intoxicated young poets by flattering letters. There was a true fellowship of art such as has not existed since. The poet or artist whose name was in everyone's mouth did not for that reason deny his friendship to one who had never published a line or exhibited a picture. If a man had talent he was greeted as brother by all his fellow-craftsmen, high or low. This common brotherhood inspired by one ideal of art suffused and welded together Bohemia with a radiant heat. Only when the radiance became dim did the mass grow cold and crumble in pieces which retained but the semblance of a spark. Bohemia, to change the metaphor, was not then a block of model dwellings, with nothing in common but steel girders and a stone staircase, but it was a corporation fed by common hopes and warmed at a common hearth. Its more ridiculous defects—its vanities and morbid excitability, its violent defiance of social convention, its passion for the exotic and the vivid, its fits of melancholy and its uproarious rejoicings—were not individual vices, but marks of a generation. Its grandeur and its follies are traceable to a common source. Its greatest fault was not extravagance, for that is a venial folly, but ignorance, which even youth cannot wholly excuse. The seed of dissolution really lurking in Bohemia was what Philibert Audebrand has truly called its *enfantillage de l'esprit*.[10] In the flush of Romanticism the zealots neglected those studies which give firmness to the mind. They rejected history and philosophy; being young, they were not well read and they did not care to become so. Foreign literature was a closed book to them, in spite of their professed admiration for Dante, Goethe, Shakespeare, and Byron; even of their own literature their knowledge was sadly defective. "Tout bien vu," says M. Audebrand with a shake of the head, "ils n'avaient pas d'autre docteur que la Blague." This cap will not fit all the heads, but it has an undeniable texture of truth. When the first ebullition was over, and the Bohemians of 1830 had departed from their joyful college to spread its doctrines in a workaday world, they left nothing but a tradition behind them. Their house had been built upon a light soil, and the time had come to make new and solid foundations. But the tradition did not include such wholesome industry, and Murger's generation, denied the excitement and warmth of building, were content to sit down in the hasty edifice to enjoy only the pastimes of their predecessors, stopping up the ever-widening crevices, that let in a cold blast of public opinion, with the unsatisfactory makeshift of *la blague*.

IV

PARISIAN SOCIETY—LE TOUT PARIS

THE events of the time, the spiritual exaltation of young France, and the *éclat* of the Romantic struggle gave to Bohemia a definite position. This position was accentuated by the smallness of Parisian society. The diversity and complexity of life in a great modern city are such that, even if all other obstacles were swept away, this alone would still make it impossible for Bohemia to rise again. Bohemians must live where rents are low—on the outer circumference, that is, of a city. In the larger capitals of Europe the inner circle, which contains the commerce and luxury, the hurry and bustle, has extended enormously in the last fifty years or so. The increase of middle-class prosperity has thrown far back the alleys and mean houses, to give place to "residential" districts; the easiness of modern travel has brought vast hotels and a constant foreign population; shops and theatres fill immeasurably more space. Bohemia is driven to the extremities of the spider's web, so that, in Plato's phrase, it is no longer one, but many. It would be absurd to imagine a solid cohort formed from Hampstead, Chelsea, and Camden Town, to say nothing of Wimbledon or Hampton Court, for the purpose of forcing some "Hernani" upon the London public (or its newspaper critics). Public opinion can hardly be corrected when the agents of correction are forced to disperse in the last motor omnibus. Moreover, this extension of the inner circle has made its inhabitants less susceptible to sudden assaults. Unconventional demonstrations have upon it no more effect than the poke of a finger upon an india-rubber ball. The interests of Bohemia, even if this circle be not entirely indifferent to them, are only a fraction of its multitudinous preoccupations, which include the fluctuations of the money market, the results of athletic contests in all parts of the globe, the progress of foreign wars, the crimes and railway accidents of the week, the development of aviation, and the safest method of crossing the street. Bohemia can no longer be pointed to and felt by society as part of itself, and when this is the case the name is nothing but a metaphor.

Speaking of the year 1841, Baudelaire in "L'Art Romantique" says:

"Paris was not then what it is to-day, a hurly-burly, a Babel inhabited by fools and futilities, with little delicacy as to how they kill time. At that time *tout Paris* was composed of that choice body of people who were responsible for forming the opinion of the others."

Les Champs Elysées

The glory of Bohemia rests partly on this fact. During Louis Philippe's reign this state of society, comparable in some respects with the ideal polity of the Attic philosophers, was, it is true, being disrupted from within. The balance of power between wealth of gold and fecundity of ideas was gradually changing—a change of which Balzac is the immortal epic poet. Yet, though the power of a Nucingen was increasing, and Paris was about to start on its new prosperity as the pleasure-ground of Europe, this precious *tout Paris* lasted till the reign was over. Paris was small, in extent, in population, in the number of those who formed its opinion. Of its actual compactness as a city I shall speak in a later chapter; suffice it now to say that the boulevards of Montmartre and Montparnasse bounded it on the north and south, that the Champs Elysées was still a wilderness, and that outside the fortifications lay open country. The population about 1835 was only 714,000; railways were hardly beginning, factories only tentatively being erected. The working classes were chiefly engaged in commerce or *petits métiers*, and the heights of Ménilmontant smiled as green and as free from slums as the Champs Elysées were free from luxurious hotels. The passing foreign population, though there was a certain number of English attracted by cheap living, was almost negligible. Brazilians and Argentines, Germans and Americans were hardly to be seen; even French provincials walked delicately instead of forming, as they do now, the chief *clientèle* of the Parisian theatres. *Le tout Paris* was, therefore, a nucleus within a circle of three segments—the middle class, the aristocratic families, and Bohemia.

The middle class, though the most numerous, was only potentially important at the time. Politics and money-making were its only preoccupations. It was divided, of course, into an infinity of grades, all of which may be illustrated from characters in Balzac's "Comédie Humaine." There were the bankers and usurers from the Du Tillets down to the Samanons, the successful merchants like Birotteau, the world of officials so accurately described in "Les Employés," the judges like old Popinot, and all the men of law from a Desroches down to his youngest clerk. Some were as sordid and bourgeois as the Thuilliers, others luxurious debauchees like the Camusots and Matifats, others, like the Rabourdins, fringed upon the *beau monde*. The sons of men enriched and decorated by Napoleon formed perhaps the cream of the middle class, and of these Balzac has given his opinion in describing Baron Hulot's son, who plays so large a part in "Cousine Bette":

"M. Hulot junior was just the type of young man fashioned by the Revolution of 1830, with a mind engrossed by politics, respectful towards his hopes, suppressing them beneath a false gravity, very envious of reputations, uttering phrases instead of incisive *mots*—those diamonds of French conversation—but with plenty of attitude and mistaking haughtiness for dignity. These people are the walking coffins which contain the Frenchman of former times; the Frenchman gets agitated at moments and knocks against his English envelope; but ambition holds him back, and he consents to suffocate inside it. This coffin is always dressed in black cloth."

This sombre portion of the background need, therefore, trouble us no further. It dominated politics and was ignored by *tout Paris*.

The aristocracy of the Faubourg St.-Germain is almost equally negligible. Being legitimists, they sulked after 1830, either living on their country estates or shutting themselves gloomily within the gaunt walls of their *hôtels* in the Faubourg. This retirement, too, was not wholly due to *bouderie*, for many of them, like Balzac's Princesse de Cadignan, suffered heavy financial losses by the Revolution. Their self-denying ordinance caused a great diminution in the general gaiety of Paris for some years. Legitimist drawing-rooms, where a brilliant host of guests had been wont to gather, were hushed and dark while the dowagers gravely discussed the latest news of the Duchesse de Berry. The few official *fêtes* were severely boycotted, and even the entertainments of foreign ambassadors suffered. It was an irksome business for the younger members, particularly the ladies of the aristocracy, who eventually gathered courage to break out into small entertainments, and in 1835 there was the first of a series of legitimist balls, the subscriptions for which went to recompense those whose civil list pensions had been suppressed in 1830. After this the Faubourg St.-Germain became more lively, and certain houses were opened to a wider circle of guests. Eugène Sue, for instance, till he became impossible, was to be found in many legitimist drawing-rooms. Nevertheless, the Faubourg St.-Germain avoided attracting the public eye by any conspicuous festivities, and this had two effects. In the first place, it brought the more joyous festivities of *tout Paris* and the riotous celebrations of Bohemia into greater relief; and, in the second, the men of the aristocracy, like the Duc d'Aulnis, were driven to find distraction and amusement in a gayer world into which their own womankind was debarred from penetrating. It was they who formed a certain section of *tout Paris*; they were the *viveurs*, the *dandies*, the young bloods of the newly founded Jockey Club, the members of the *petit cercle* in the Café de Paris, who joined hands with what may be called *la haute Bohème*.

There was, however, a certain amount of neutral ground between the aristocracy of birth and that of wit to be found in the literary *salons* of the day, which, if not quite so illustrious as they had once been, shone with a considerable amount of brilliance. Among the legitimists these were, of course, not to be found, but the aristocracy of Napoleon was represented by the *salons* of the Duchesse de Duras and the Duchesse d'Abrantès. The latter, widow of Napoleon's marshal Junot, was a particular friend of Balzac, who was the most notable figure to be found at her house. She was always dreadfully in debt, and after being sold up she died in a hospital in 1838. The *salon* of the Princess Belgiojoso in the Rue Montparnasse attracted particular attention because, with an aristocratic hostess, it had all the *entrain* of more purely artistic gatherings. Till troubles in Italy called them back to their estates the Prince and Princess Belgiojoso were among the gayest of the gay. The Prince with his boon companion, Alfred de Musset, ruffled it merrily on the boulevard, while the Princess, who had many of the most brilliant men of the day for her lovers, filled her apartments with poets, artists, writers, and, above all, musicians. One who frequented her drawing-room hung with black velvet, spangled with silver stars, says she had a "fierté glaciale, mais curiosité suraiguë." The splendour of her entertainments was royal, and her concerts were magnificent. To this the *salons* of Madame Ancelot and Madame Récamier were a striking contrast. The former was composed chiefly of serious men of letters and politicians, while at L'Abbaye-aux-Bois Madame Récamier acted as priestess to the adoration of the aging Châteaubriand. The *salons* of the pure Romantics made no pretence of splendour and were entirely free from the atmosphere of officialdom. The chief of them were those of Madame Hugo, of Madame Gay (who was succeeded by her daughter, Delphine de Girardin), and of Charles Nodier, the genial librarian of the Arsenal. In all of these, as in the *salon* of the Princess Belgiojoso, *tout Paris* was to be found in force. The gatherings round Victor Hugo were a little too much flavoured by the fumes of the censer, but those of the Girardins and of Nodier were of the most charming gaiety. Balzac, in a humorous article, drew a malicious sketch of the exaggerated enthusiasms of Nodier's guests when a poem was read before them. "Cathédrale!" "Ogive!" "Pyramide d'Egypte!" were the approved exclamations of ecstatic approbation. Madame Ancelot[11] confesses that she found the conversation very amusing, but very strange. "There was never a serious word," she says, "never anything profound, sensible, or simple; every word was meant to cause laughter, to make an effect. The more a thing was unexpected—that is, the less it was natural—the more prodigious was its success." She, no doubt, was prejudiced, and the fact remains that every guest who wrote in after years of Nodier's *salon*, its merry conversation followed inevitably by dancing, did so with most grateful praise, for Nodier died in 1846, leaving his Romantic friends to write regretful reminiscences. The *salon* of Sophie Gay and her daughter was equally infected by high spirits, but it was less purely literary. Liszt, Thalberg, and Berlioz made music here; Roger de Beauvoir met Lamartine, and the Marquis de Custine sat by Balzac or Alphonse Karr. The de Vignys also had a *salon*, and Théodore de Banville speaks most warmly of their kindly hospitality; but there was a certain aloofness about the creator of "Eloa," and another of his guests found that in his house colouring seemed absent, so that "the regular guests seemed to come and go in the moonlight."[12]

To speak at greater length about the *salons* of the Romantic period would here be beside the mark. Bohemians, no doubt, were often to be found at Victor Hugo's or Nodier's, but on those occasions they were consciously straying outside their own boundaries. Neither the stately house in the Place Royale nor the librarian's dwelling at the Arsenal was within the domains of Bohemia, and no Bohemian of the time would have dreamed of claiming them, as the later "Parnassiens" might have claimed the *salons* of Nina de Kallias and Madame Ricard, for parts of their ordinary existence. The case, however, is different with the relations between *le tout Paris* and Bohemia. *Le tout Paris* was, as I have said, a nucleus, but a nucleus of disparate and constantly shifting particles. This perfectly undefined body had, of course, no definite place of assembly, but so far as it could be identified with any particular locality it may be said to have congregated on the boulevard. The Boulevard des Italiens—*the* boulevard—was the chosen spot for the saunterings of the chosen few, a fact which by itself is a proof of the smallness and privacy of Paris compared with the present day, when this same boulevard is flooded from morning till night by a hurrying stream of indistinguishable humanity. In the days of Louis Philippe nobody, except an ignorant foreigner, ventured to appear on this sacred preserve in the afternoon without some semblance of a title. The title may have been so small as a peculiarly elegant waistcoat, a capacity for drinking, or a happy invention for practical jokes, or it may have been the reputation for a ready wit and a trenchant pen; but whosoever dared to show himself in this select society was sure to have some particular justification for making himself conspicuous, otherwise he was certain to be quizzed out of existence. The newcomer, if he survived a short but swift scrutiny, entered an informal though exclusive club of which every member was known to the others—he was known, that is, to "all Paris." All Paris, in a sense, it truly was, not because the greatest poets and statesmen belonged to it—for they had better things to do than to waste so much time—but because it served as the central intelligence department or, I might almost say, as the brain of Paris. A word uttered there was round the town in two hours; there a poet was made or a play damned—in the twinkling of an eye. One day of its activity furnished all the wit of the next day's newspapers, which is hardly surprising when so many of its members were journalists. *Le tout Paris* was not hide-bound in its requirements; it admitted high birth as one qualification for membership, wealth if accompanied by good manners as another, but a certain way to its heart was by a brilliant handling of the pen. In spite of the exaggeration of the Parisian scenes in "Illusions Perdues," there is no unreality in Balzac's picture of Lucien's sudden rise from impoverished obscurity to fame and money. Lucien, the provincial poet, after his disappointing elopement with Madame de Bargeton, retires discomfited to a garret in the Quartier Latin. The door of rich protectors is shut in his face, no publisher will read his poems or accept his novels. The serpent arrives in the shape of Lousteau, who shows him the devilish power of journalism. By a lucky chance Lucien is asked to write a dramatic criticism for a new paper. He succeeds brilliantly, and he has Paris at his feet. The publisher cringes before his power and publishes all that he had formerly rejected; with money, fine clothes, and a reputation, he can answer stare for stare and return the impertinences of Rastignac and de Marsay; even Madame de Bargeton in the Faubourg St.-Germain cowers from his revengeful epigrams. So long as he remains a power in the Press he is flattered and caressed and plumes himself, a butterfly only just emerged, in the glittering *tout Paris* of his day.

The moral of Lucien de Rubempré, so far as we are immediately concerned, is not ethical, but resolves itself into the truth that there was an open passage between Bohemia and *le tout Paris* which was crossed by not a few. Gautier crossed it, so did Arsène Houssaye, Ourliac, the dramatist, and several others. There were also men who seemed to spend their time between the two, like the elder Dumas, Roger de Beauvoir, and Alfred de Musset, who combined the extravagance of Bohemia with the luxury of the boulevards in different proportions, without ever being entire Bohemians or complete *viveurs*, and who maintained such a continuous communication between the more literary sections of *le tout Paris* and the finer talents of Bohemia that it would be in some cases difficult to say where one left off and the other began. It is therefore impossible to write of the *vie de Bohème* without entering into this larger and more conspicuous life of what may be called *la haute Bohème*. Not only was it the sound-board from which in a lucky moment the struggling whisperer on the left bank might hear his utterances booming forth to a multitude eager for novelty, not only was it an unofficial academy to which every Bohemian might aspire to belong as soon as he had made his mark, but it was also, during the years following 1830, animated by such a spirit of revelry and reckless amusement that the riots of true Bohemia were as pale ghosts before its more notable orgies. There were strong reasons for the merging of the two Bohemias, and the only precise distinction was the possession or want of money. Bohemia proper has no money except what it can make by its art, and as its inhabitants are young that is little enough. *La haute Bohème*, with a less strict limitation of years, makes money and spends it recklessly. Instead of pleading youth as the excuse of its folly, it claims the indulgence due to artistic achievement. However, so far as the generation of 1830 were concerned, this distinction was not absolute, for the Bohemians of 1830 were not invariably so destitute as their successors, so that they were enabled to mix to some extent in the gayer life of the artistic *boulevardiers*.

The most universal word—which I shall adopt—applicable to this *haute Bohème* is the contemporary name for them, *les viveurs*. They were a particular product of the time, and no words of mine can describe them better than a passage from Balzac's "Illusions Perdues." The period of the novel is some years before 1830, but this particular description is far more applicable to the years that followed the second Revolution. I quote it in French, because it is impossible to do it justice in a translation:

"A cette époque florissait une société de jeunes gens, riches et pauvres, tous désœuvrés, appelés *viveurs*, et qui vivaient en effet avec une incroyable insouciance, intrépides mangeurs, buveurs plus intrépides encore. Tous bourreaux d'argent et mêlant les plus rudes plaisanteries à cette existence, non pas folle, mais enragée, ils ne reculaient devant aucune impossibilité, faisaient gloire de leurs méfaits, contenus néanmoins en de certaines bornes: l'esprit le plus original couvrait leurs escapades, il était impossible de ne pas les leur pardonner. Aucun fait n'accuse si hautement l'ilotisme auquel la Restauration avait condamné la jeunesse. Les jeunes gens, qui ne savaient à quoi employer leurs forces, ne les jetaient pas seulement dans le journalisme, dans les conspirations, dans la littérature et dans l'art, ils les dissipaient dans les plus étranges excès, tant il y'avait de sève et de luxuriantes puissances dans la jeune France. Travailleuse, cette belle jeunesse voulait le pouvoir et le plaisir; artiste, elle voulait des trésors; oisive, elle voulait animer ses passions; de toute manière elle voulait une place, et la politique ne lui en faisait nulle part."

A Viveur

Balzac gives his own character, Rastignac, as an instance of the typical *viveur*, but Rastignac had a purpose in his heart, while some of the most prominent among the *viveurs* had none but to amuse themselves. These I name first, for, having no other preoccupations, they set the tone of the whole society. They were chiefly members of the aristocracy who found no place for their energies in a *bourgeois* State which sought no military glory. One of their leaders, the Duc d'Aulnis, who settled down afterwards to serve the State worthily, gives in his memoirs the reason why so many young men of good family gave themselves up to riotous living, as he did under his *nom de plaisir* of Alton-Shee. He and other young legitimists resigned their commissions in 1831 on finding that Louis Philippe, *le roi des barricades*, sided with the insurrectionists, so that, as he says, "the class of idlers was increased by a large number of legitimists who had resigned their commissions and by a contingent of refugees belonging to the Italian, Polish, and Spanish aristocracies. To distract their minds from the thoughts of so many broken careers, so many hopes disappointed, they dashed with an irresistible rush into the pursuit of enjoyment and sought to appease their generous aspirations in an unbridled love of pleasure."

These were the young men who spent all their time in imitating Brummell or the Comte d'Orsay, paying minute attention to every curve of their voluminous frock-coats, the patterns of their waistcoats, and the folding of their cravats; who drove and rode irreproachable horses imported from

England, and founded the French Jockey Club under the auspices of Lord Seymour; who dined copiously at the Café de Paris and adjourned to lounge at the Opéra in the *loge infernale*, where the cream of Parisian dandyism paraded with its *lorgnette* for the edification of the public. In racing and gambling they found their excitement; their consolation was the venal love of a ballet dancer. For no moment of the day did they pursue a worthy ambition, and their only excuse was that, being idle perforce, they attained a certain exquisiteness even in pleasure. Sadly the Duc d'Aulnis sums them up:

"Our generation had the love of liberty, passion, gaiety, an artistic nature, little vanity, the desire to be rather than to appear; then came discouragement, scepticism, the pursuit of amusement, the habit of smoking which fills the intervals, the taste for intoxication, that fugitive poetry of vulgar enjoyments, and every prodigality to satisfy our desires. If one considers what we leave behind us, our baggage is light: the folly of the carnival, the invention of the cancan, the generalization of the cigar, the acclimatization of clubs and races, will be merits of small value in the eyes of posterity.... Of these joyous *enfants du siècle* brought by ruin to face pitiless reality, some escaped from their embarrassments by suicide, others found death or promotion in Africa, others shared their names with rich heiresses; others, persevering at all hazards, swallowing affronts and braving humiliations, lived on the precarious resources of gambling, borrowing, toadying, and parasitism; the most wretched of all fell step by step into the depths of infamy; only a very small number tried to save themselves by hard work."

These men set the pace among the *viveurs*: they were seconded by the more ambitious young men of whom Balzac's Rastignac is the type, who were determined to succeed and uttered in their hearts his famous threat to Paris by the grave of old Goriot, "Maintenant c'est entre nous." These men became *viveurs*, not as a pastime, but as a means. Rastignac, shocked to see that virtuous devotion would not save Père Goriot from a broken heart, and sick of the Maison Vauquer's squalor, determines to play society at its own game and make profit out of its corruption. He becomes the lover of Madame de Nucingen, one of Goriot's ungrateful daughters, and by allowing himself to become a tool in the crafty Baron Nucingen's third liquidation lays the foundation of his own fortunes. Such a man could not live in seclusion—he was forced into the ranks of the *viveurs*, in order to become a conspicuous figure. A smart tilbury and clothes from a first-class tailor were part of his stock-in-trade; he could not afford to run the risk of humiliation before his lady by laying himself open to affront by a more exquisite "dandy" than himself. A Rastignac had to shine to compass his ends, and he shone most brilliantly as a *viveur*, playing at idleness and debauch to cloak his subtle schemes, and drowning the shame of his parasitism in a passionate self-indulgence. Thanks to a strong will he is entirely successful, and out of the wreck of his illusions and his generous impulses builds himself a career as a politician.

Rastignac is one of the most wonderful characters created by Balzac's penetrating pessimism; that he had a special place in his creator's heart is proved, I think, by his frequent appearance on the stage. Those who delight in the fascinating pastime of following Balzac's characters through the whole extent of the "Comédie Humaine" will know that it is impossible to understand Rastignac without reading "La Maison Nucingen," a story which, for pure virtuosity, is second to none of Balzac's masterpieces. They will remember that the scene is set in the year 1836 in a private room at Véry's restaurant, where the impersonal narrator, by overhearing the conversation in the adjoining room, is entertained by the thrilling account of how Rastignac profited by Baron Nucingen's third fraudulent liquidation. The shady financial proceedings of the astute Alsatian—as exciting as a dashing campaign—are related in a marvellous series of *boutades* by Balzac's favourite grotesque, Bixiou, the own brother of Panurge. Now Bixiou and the three friends with whom he is dining are Balzac's examples of the third party among the *viveurs*, that party to which the title *la haute Bohème* is most peculiarly applicable. They were neither aristocratic and wealthy, like a Duc d'Aulnis, nor aristocratic and poor, like a Rastignac, but men of obscure origin and unusual intelligence. They joined the ranks of the *viveurs* neither to banish the *ennui* of enforced idleness, nor out of cold calculation for a diplomatic end— for they were inevitably debarred from attaining any position in the *beau monde*—but simply as a distraction from their pursuit of worldly success as journalists, artists, speculators, and general exploiters of society. They were not single-hearted warriors for an ambition; their aim in life was not purely diversion, it was merely to obtain the maximum of selfish enjoyments, which included a satisfied vanity, a full purse, good food, rare wine, and a pretty mistress. Of them Barbey d'Aurévilly's remark was true: "Qui dit journalistes dit femmes entretenues. Cela veut souper."

They had been pure Bohemians, most of them, in their earlier youth, with higher ideals and more restricted enjoyments; but their gorge, too, had risen at the squalor of their Maison Vauquer, and they had parleyed with the devil. Discovering in themselves some talent for making money, they had exploited it to the exclusion of all others. They traded either in their own art or in that of others. On the boulevard they held their own by their engaging sallies of malicious gossip, by their prodigal extravagance, and, above all, by the fear which their power as journalists, critics, caricaturists, or newspaper proprietors inspired. They were Bohemians at heart, carrying the more pardonable disorders of Bohemia into less exacting circumstances, spending their gifts and their money without a thought, luxurious, venal, insatiable. Their type is to be found to-day in the rich mercantile, especially Jewish, society of all large cities; but in Paris of the thirties and forties they were more powerful and more conspicuous. Though they could never hope to enter the Jockey Club, they were hail-fellow-well-met with the *viveurs* of blue blood; they served the Rastignacs when it was worth their while, and they were so near to the true Bohemia that their example was at once its temptation and its despair. Balzac himself sums up the four friends, Bixiou, Finot, Blondet, and Couture, in a passage which, having myself said so much, I quote in the original:

"C'était quatre des plus hardis cormorans éclos dans l'écume qui couronne les flots incessamment renouvelés de la génération présente; aimables garçons dont l'existence est problématique, à qui l'on connaît ni rentes ni domaines, et qui vivent bien. Ces spirituels *condottieri* de l'industrie moderne, devenue la plus cruelle des guerres, laissent les inquiétudes à leurs créanciers, gardent les plaisirs pour eux, et n'ont de souci que de leur costume. D'ailleurs, braves à fumer, comme Jean Bart, leur agare sur un baril de poudre, peut-être pour ne pas faillir à leur rôle; plus moqueurs que les petits journaux, moqueurs à se moquer d'eux-mêmes, perspicaces et incrédules, fureteurs d'affaires, avides et prodigues, envieux d'autrui, mais contents d'eux-mêmes; profonds politiques par saillies, analysant tout, devinant tout, ils n'avaient pas encore pu se faire jour dans le monde où ils voudraient se produire."

Andoche Finot had risen by his acute perception of the commercial future of journalism. We meet him in his early days in "César Birotteau," abandoning the puffing of actresses and writing of articles to less perspicuous journalists, and devoting himself to what is now grandly called "publicity." It was he who helped the worthy young Anselme Popinot to push the *huile céphalique* which repaired Birotteau's shattered fortunes. In "Illusions Perdues" we find him again, first proprietor of a small paper, then spending his profits and straining his credit in buying a larger one—one of the spiders into whose web poor Lucien fell. By 1836 he is a lord of the Press, a fictitious counterpart of Emile de Girardin, who with Lautour-Mézéray, another *viveur*, made a fortune by selling *La Presse* at half the price of other newspapers. Couture is a very minor character, a financial speculator, who only hung on the fringe of the *viveurs*. Blondet and Bixiou are more important. The former had many counterparts in Paris of the day. He was "a newspaper editor, a man of much intelligence, but slipshod, brilliant, capable, lazy, knowing, but allowing himself to be exploited, equally faithless and good-natured by caprice; one of those men one likes, but does not respect. Sharp as a stage *soubrette*, incapable of refusing his pen to anyone who asked for it or his heart to anyone who would borrow it."

Bixiou is no longer young in 1836. Balzac gives an earlier portrait of him in "Les Employés," when he is a minor official, caricaturist and journalist, poor, ambitious, a real liver of *la vie de Bohème*. But, says Balzac, "he is no longer the

Bixiou of 1825, but that of 1836, the misanthropical buffoon whose fun is known to have the most sparkle and the most acidity, a wretch enraged at having spent so much wit at a pure loss, furious at not having picked up his bit of flotsam in the last revolution, giving everyone a kick like a true Pierrot at the play, having his period and its scandalous stories at his fingers' ends, decorating them with his droll inventions, jumping on everybody's shoulders like a clown, and trying to leave a mark on them like an executioner."

Such, in general, were the *viveurs* who postured in the front of the Parisian stage—equally at home on the steps of Tortoni's or in the Café de Paris, in the Princess Belgiojoso's drawing-room or the luxurious boudoir of a Coralie or Florine, making the talk and spreading the gossip, blowing up the reputations and blasting the characters of the town. To know their habits and eccentricities places those of the true Bohemia in a proper light. In drawing a composite picture of them I have drawn upon fiction, but in another chapter I will justify these generalizations by introducing some of the real heroes of *le tout Paris*.

Fashionables

V

LES VIVEURS

THE most exalted section among the *viveurs*, the members of which were farthest removed from any suspicion of Bohemianism, was formed of young men from noble families. Their names, which do not concern us here, may be found in the list of those who started the *petit cercle* of the Café de Paris. This was an exclusive dining club founded by a set of gay livers who dreaded the political discussions of the one or two regular clubs then existing, but wished to have a place where they could dine together without disturbance by casual strangers. They hired, therefore, some rooms from Alexandre, the proprietor of the restaurant, and continued there till the club broke up in 1848. Little need be said of them as a body, except that they were the arbiters of Parisian elegance. As such, their chief effort was to curb the luxuriance of Parisian taste within the limits of English correctness. Anglomania was all the rage. Every dandy—a word then definitely adopted by the French—had his tilbury or phaeton and his tiny English "tiger," smoked his cigar, suffered from his "spleen," and tried to face life with an insolent air of imperturbability—a crowning proof of good taste when the effort was at all successful. This Anglomania was not entirely confined to the boulevard; it was partly an effect of Romanticism. Lady Morgan[13] laughs at it, giving a most amusing account of a performance of "Rochester" at the Porte St.-Martin. The character that created the greatest sensation, she says, was the Watchman, "who was dressed like an alguazil, with a child's rattle in his hand." Whenever he appeared there was a general murmur of "Ha! C'est le vatchman."—"Regarde donc, ma fille, c'est le vatchman; ton papa t'a souvent parlé des vatchmen."—"Ah, c'est le vatchman."—"Oui, c'est le vatchman." Great play, too, was made with tea. Rochester entertained his merry companions with tea; Mr. Wilkes poisoned his wife in it. This latter incident gave the highest pleasure:

"Dieu, que c'est anglois! Toujours le thé et la jalousie à Londres!"

The Parisian ideas and imitations of English manners were, no doubt, pretty ridiculous, and must have caused considerable amusement to Lord Seymour, one of the few Englishmen who were conspicuous among the aristocratic *viveurs*. He was the illegitimate son of Lady Yarmouth, daughter-in-law of the notorious Lord Hertford. He lived entirely in Paris, where, being extremely rich, he kept a fine house at the corner of the Rue Taitbout and the boulevard. Here he cultivated cigar-smoking and physical exercise with great assiduity. He was a splendid boxer and fencer, and all the finest bruisers and blades, amateur and professional, were to be met in his *salle d'armes*. He took great pride in his strength, which was abnormal, in his skill as a whip and his success on the race-course. French sport owes him a permanent debt for his successful starting of the Jockey Club, but he can hardly have been a very popular member of a society, for he was cold and brutal, a man who took a defeat rancorously and one who had a cynical delight in causing suffering to his hangers-on. His misanthropy was the reason of his gradually dropping out of society after 1842, and it would have been beside the point to mention him here had it not been for the quite undeserved notoriety which he acquired in Paris during the thirties as the bacchanalian lord of misrule at all the carnivals. It was a strange case of mistaken identity which persisted for many years in spite of categorical denials. The more aristocratic of the *viveurs* were not, as I have said, Bohemians; but during the carnival, which was celebrated by all the population with extraordinary licence, some of the more youthful let themselves go and became revellers with the rest. For the last three days of the carnival the streets of Paris, by day and by night, were given up to an orgy. Crowds of masqueraders filled the pavements, the restaurants, and the theatres, where fancy-dress balls were held. The richer masks had carriages drawn by postilions, in which they drove among the crowd, scattering confetti and sweetmeats and even money, indulging in every kind of quaint antic and gallantry, and inciting the vulgar to engage them in a wordy warfare in which volleys of the coarsest expletives were fired on both sides. Riot reached its culmination on the night of Shrove Tuesday, when the revellers, after an orgy of feasting and dancing at the Barrière de la Courtille, on the north-east of Paris, ended by descending the steep hill towards the city in a state of bacchic frenzy. This was the famous *descente de la Courtille*, at which, as at all the other revels, a certain carriage, drawn by six horses and filled by a motley party of young men, was the central object of admiration. No challenger ever worsted the leader of this gang at a bout of blackguarding, no costumes equalled his in originality, no mask so tormented and excited the crowd as he with his harangues, his missiles, and his largesse. This was the man known to all the populace of Paris as "Milord Arsouille," which, as all Paris would have told you, was simply the *nom de guerre* of Lord Seymour. But it was not so. The real "Milord Arsouille" was a certain Charles de la Battut, son of an English chemist and a French *émigrée*. His father, unwilling to compromise his position in England by recognizing him, paid for his adoption by the ruined Breton Count de la Battut. He was educated in Paris, where, even in his youth, he showed a most dissolute character. He delighted to frequent the lowest haunts, and there learnt that mastery of slang and that skill as a boxer which were his pride. The death of his real father gave him a large fortune, which he proceeded to dissipate with the utmost extravagance and bad taste. His house in the Boulevard des Capucines and his personal attire were equally flamboyant. During his short period of glory he was on certain terms of intimacy with the more rowdy among the young bloods of good family, who in after years looked back, like the Duc d'Aulnis, with shame to some of their exploits in his company. His most notable achievement was to introduce the *cancan* into the fashionable fancy-dress ball at the Variétés in 1832, and his perpetual grief was that all his eccentricities were attributed to Lord Seymour, in spite of his utmost efforts to proclaim the difference of identity. In 1835 he died, a shattered *roué*, at Naples.

The only other English name deserving comment in the *petit cercle* of the Café de Paris is that of Major Fraser, whose personality was an enigma. He was one of the most popular characters on the boulevard, and an honoured friend of the most exclusive diners at the Café Anglais or the Café de Paris, yet nothing was known of his personal history. He spoke English perfectly, but was not an Englishman; he never alluded to his parents, and lived as a bachelor in an *entresol* at the corner of the Rue Lafitte. He was never short of money, but the source of his income was a mystery; and when he died no letters were found, but only a file of receipts, including a receipt from an undertaker for his funeral expenses, and a direction that his clothes and furniture were to be sold for the benefit of the poor. In spite of the mystery surrounding him he was a prominent figure among the *viveurs*. His tight blue frock-coat and his grey trousers were models for the most fastidious dandies; his kindness and gentleness to everyone except professional politicians was extreme; he quoted Horace freely and had a complete knowledge of political history with a prodigious memory. Major Fraser's story could be paralleled by the head waiter of many a London club. While he lived he was a favourite; when he died he simply vanished.[14]

There are only two other members of the *petit cercle* whom I wish to mention—Alfred de Musset and Roger de Beauvoir—because they form a link between the exclusiveness of that society and the hurly-burly existence of *la haute Bohème*, to which both more properly belonged. In the early Romantic days Alfred de Musset, with his beautiful, bored face set off by the fair curls that fell over his eyes, was the petted darling of Paris, its perfect dandy wafting the triple essence of *bouquet de Romantisme*. Nevertheless, Alfred de Musset, though his name was on the lips of all dandies and his poetry set a fashion in Bohemia, never took among men the place that seemed to be his due. He might have been a true Bohemian of 1830, but he disavowed his Romantic companions of letters for the greater splendour of fashionable life; while among the exquisites of the boulevard he found it impossible to preserve that impassive demeanour and attention to the niceties of dandyism which were inexorably demanded. His nature was far too passionate to make him for long together a comfortable companion for men, and his personal history, apart from his poetry, is a chapter of relations with women, of whom George Sand is the most notable. The ashes of his career have been raked over with most scrupulous care since his death, but it is no purpose of mine to take part in the scavenging. To have omitted Alfred de Musset's name would have been impossible, but having mentioned him, I can leave him. Though he hymned Musette and drank deeply with Prince Belgiojoso, he had as little place in Bohemia, high or low, as Lamartine or Victor Hugo. Their throne was the study, his the boudoir.

There are no such reservations to be made for Roger de Beauvoir, whom Madame de Girardin called "Alfred de Musset aux cheveux noirs." He was the arch-*viveur*, with one exquisitely shod foot on the boulevard, the other in Bohemia, the gayest of all those who supped, the insatiable quaffer of champagne, the inexhaustible fountain of epigram, the king of *la haute Bohème*, the very incarnation of the *Noctambule* in Charpentier's delightful opera, "Louise." His family was the good Norman family of de Bully, and he took the name of Beauvoir from one of the two estates which were his heritage. Those who were responsible for his early guidance clearly intended that he should make his way in diplomacy—a career in which his good looks, sympathetic voice, and charming manners would have greatly helped his pioneering—for he was sent to be Polignac's secretary when that unfortunate minister occupied the embassy at London. When his chief came back to the stormy days of July, the debonair secretary, judging no doubt that any association with politics was incompatible with gilded ease, abandoned all attempts to play the game of a Rastignac, and pursued his fantasies in airy independence. The Romanticism of the *Jeune-France* party attracted at once the enthusiasm of a young man, just in his majority by 1830, who was naturally a lover of brilliant colouring. He became a fanatical medievalist, who displayed with pride a Gothic cabinet panelled in carved oak, hung with black velvet, and lit by stained-glass windows. The ceiling was covered with coats-of-arms; the chief decorations were a panoply of armour and an old *prie-dieu* on which a missal of 1350 opened its illuminated pages. Even in 1842, when Maxime du Camp first met him, he still dreamt of reviving the age of chivalry, having just created a sensation by waltzing at a ball in full armour, fainting and falling with the clatter of innumerable stove-pipes. Undeterred by this mishap, he proposed to form a company, to be called the "Société des champs clos de France," which was to buy land for a tilting-ground, Arab steeds, and armour for the purpose of holding weekly tourneys. The shares were to be 1000 francs each, but as Maxime du Camp's guardian prohibited the purchase of any by his enthusiastic ward, the project was dropped. Like every true Romantic he wrote a medieval novel, but his novel, "L'Écolier de Cluny," unlike those of the majority, was published and brought him considerable fame. After its publication in 1832, he became in some sort a man of letters, but he never added to his reputation, being far too bent upon the pursuit of pleasure to bear the restrictions of any profession. Having failed as a writer of vaudevilles, he found his true vocation as the leader of a band of revellers and a composer of wicked epigrams in verse. His epigrams, always written *impromptu* upon the pages of a notebook, were a real addition to the gaiety of Paris. Here is one composed when Ancelot—literary husband of a literary wife—was elected to the Academy:

Le ménage Ancelot, par ses vers et sa prose,
Devait à ce fauteuil arriver en tout cas,
Car la femme accouchait toujours de quelque chose,
Quand le mari n'engendrait pas.

His dress was of the highest elegance in a day when men were not confined to a funereal black. His blue frock-coat, tight-waisted with amply curving skirts, broad velvet *revers*, and gilt buttons, fitted as neatly as one of his own epigrams; his blue waistcoats and light grey trousers were treasures, his hat the curliest and shiniest to be seen. In his own apartment he tempered the shadows of his Gothic furniture by wearing a green silk dressing-gown and red cashmere trousers. So long as their fortunes lasted he and his companions bade dull care begone. At midday they left the softest of beds, and, after a serious hour of dressing, met for déjeuner at the Café Anglais, the Maison d'Or, or the Café Hardi. By four they were to be seen in force upon the boulevard, displaying their waistcoats and quizzing the ladies upon the marble steps of Tortoni's. Before dinner they would visit a drawing-room or two, buy a picture or bargain for some *bibelot*—a Toledo blade or a Turkish narghile—with a dealer in curiosities. The evening programme was a set of variations upon the ground bass of dinner, opera, supper. Roger de Beauvoir was one of the company who haunted the famous *loge infernale* at the Opéra, and it is needless to say that their attention was devoted more to the ballet than to the music, for they were all connoisseurs in choreography and had a personal acquaintance with the dancers, which developed in most cases into something more than Platonic affection. The *foyer des artistes* was the enchanted garden of *la haute Bohème*, where they sought their "Cynthia of this minute" as the true Bohemians did at the Chaumière or the Closerie des Lilas.

The science of practical joking was sedulously cultivated by Roger and his friends, who rejoiced to bring off successful "mystifications." One of Roger's best was played upon Duponchel, the director of the Opéra. One day the whole street where Duponchel lived was set all agog by the appearance of a magnificent funeral procession, consisting of a hearse and fifty carriages, with Roger and his friend Cabanon occupying the first carriage as chief mourners; the head of the procession drew up at Duponchel's door, to his great indignation. The joke up to this point was of no especial originality, but Roger gave it a turn of his own. The Romantic fashion dictated that every chapter in a novel should be headed by an epigraph, as extravagant as possible, from the work of some Romantic author. Roger therefore headed a chapter in his novel "Pulchinella," which was just appearing, "Feu Duponchel (Histoire contemporaine)." Even after he was hopelessly in debt he remained a joker. Being saddled with a thin and dirty bailiff, he gave him ten francs a day, washed him, dressed him as a Turk, and gave an evening party in honour of his Pasha, who could only talk in signs. The supreme *mystificateurs*, however, were Romieu and Monnier. Romieu was reputed to be the most amusing man in Paris, and so firmly founded was his reputation that nobody ever took him seriously. When he became prefect of Quimperlé—an easy post which enabled him to take many a holiday upon the boulevard—he was faced with the problem of dealing with a plague of cockchafers in the prefecture. He hit upon the wise and perfectly successful device of offering fifty francs for every bushel of dead cockchafers. The Bretons were grateful enough, but all Paris was in a roar. Here was the crowning farce of which only its lost joker would have been capable, and it supplied the smaller comic papers with copy for several days. Romieu made Monnier's acquaintance in an appropriate way. About eleven o'clock one night the artist heard a knock at his door, which he opened to a stranger, who came in and entered into a polite conversation without a word of introduction. Monnier made no comment, but replied with equal affability. After an hour or so, as the stranger remained, he ransacked his sideboard and entertained his guest with an impromptu supper. Time passed, the small hours struck, and still the stranger made no sign of going. Monnier therefore announced that he was ready for bed and that his sofa was at his guest's disposition. So they parted for the night, and next morning when they met Monnier's first words were "You are Romieu," a compliment returned by "You are Monnier."

Monnier, says Champfleury in his memoir, belonged to Bohemia till the end of his life; but it is clear that this Bohemia was that of the boulevards and cafés. He was no real Romantic, and far too fond of a good time to stay in the Bohemia which Champfleury himself knew so well. As a writer of short stories and dialogues, an actor, and an artist he had a huge success in the thirties, and he followed the pleasures of life with inexhaustible zest. Balzac drew him as Bixiou in "Les Employés." The portrait, according to Champfleury, was very true, but unjust:

"Intrépide chasseur de grisettes, fumeur, amuseur de gens, dîneur et soupeur, se mettant partout au diapason, brillant aussi bien dans les coulisses qu'au bal des grisettes dans l'allée des Veuves, il étonnait autant à table que dans une partie de plaisir; en verve à minuit dans la rue, comme le matin si vous le preniez au saut du lit, mais sombre et triste avec lui-même, comme la plupart des grands comiques. Lancé dans le monde des actrices et des acteurs, des écrivains, des artistes, et de certaines femmes dont la fortune est aléatoire, il vivait bien, allait au spectacle sans payer, jouait à Frascati, gagnait souvent. Enfin cet artiste, vraiment profond, mais par éclairs, se balançait dans la vie comme sur une escarpolette, sans s'inquiéter du moment où la corde casserait."

Innumerable stories are told of his practical jokes. Being an expert ventriloquist, he was wont to enter an omnibus and without moving a muscle utter in a feminine voice: "Je vous aime, monsieur le conducteur," at which there would be tremendous consternation among the petticoats. The dames swept the company with searching glares of outraged decency, the *demoiselles* blushed, and the embarrassed conductor looked in vain for his temptress. One evening he was burdened with a bore in some illuminated public garden. To escape the tedium of conversation he pretended to be greatly interested in some matter which necessitated his walking carefully all round the garden and gazing intently at all the gas-lamps. After half an hour of these mysterious peregrinations the bore, who had been forced to keep silence, asked with impatience what was the matter. "I bet you five francs," said Monnier, "that there are here seventy-nine *becs de gaz* (gas-jets)." The bore accepted the challenge with delight, and another half-hour was spent in silent perambulation and calculation. At length he announced triumphantly that he only counted seventy-eight. "Ah," said Monnier as he made his escape, and pointing to the orchestra, "vous avez oublié le bec de la clarinette."

Monnier, the great artist, the disappointed actor, was at the other end of the scale to Lord Seymour and his friends. They had a position without activity: his activity made his position. No great artist remains long in Bohemia. Some work their way out on foot: he rose from it, one might say, in a balloon, by which, after disporting himself for some years above the mists, he was landed for his later days in the obscurity of a province. Such a man, at home in all society, is restricted by none. As he was not the perfect Bohemian, so he was not the whole-hearted *viveur*, for whose complete picture I must return to Roger de Beauvoir and his set, some of whom are described in Roger's own little book, "Soupeurs de mon Temps." It is a melancholy epitaph of a brilliant company. The sparkling wit of their gatherings has vanished with the bubbles of the champagne they drank, and little is left on record but the capacity of their stomachs. They took an immense pride in their consumption of champagne. Briffaut, a clever journalist and a particular friend of Roger's, was the king of topers. To him was due the invention of "ingurgitation," which consisted in pouring a bottle of champagne into a bell-shaped glass cover, such as was used to protect cheese, and swallowing it at a draught. He once challenged a noted English toper and gave him a glass a bottle; the victory was easily his, for he disposed of a dozen. Among other champions who helped to make Veuve Clicquot's fortune were Armand Malitourne, a singularly gifted man, a journalist, and at one time secretary to the minister Montalivet; Béquet, whose good taste Roger himself extolled; and Bouffé, the director of the Vaudeville. Then there was Emile Cabanon, who lives in

Romantic annals as the author of the extravagant "Roman pour les Cuisinières." Champfleury,[15] on the authority of Camille Rogier, the artist, says that he appeared one day upon the boulevard and won himself forthwith a place by his gifts as a story-teller, becoming a favourite with all from Prince Belgiojoso downwards. He is one of the reputed originals—there are two or three—of Balzac's Comte de la Palférine (in "Un Prince de la Bohème"), who, being struck with the appearance of a lady passing along the street, at once attached himself to her: in vain she tried to get rid of the importunate by saying she was going to visit a friend, for her cavalier came too and mixed with all urbanity in the conversation, rising to take his leave at the same time as the object of his sudden passion. This assiduity so captivated the besieged one's heart that she struck her colours. It is *à propos* of Cabanon that Champfleury refers with some contempt to "les gentilshommes de lettres du boulevard de Gand, qui nageaient comme des poissons dans le fleuve de la dette, se fiaient plus sur leurs relations que sur leur plume, dépensaient de l'esprit comptant en veux-tu en voilà." Alfred Tattet,[16] the rich son of an *agent de change*, who was introduced to the *viveurs* by Félix Arvers, the poet of one sonnet, was another of the crew. Alfred de Musset, Roger de Beauvoir, Romieu, and others made merry at his sumptuous entertainments till he varied the monotony by running over the frontier with a married woman, leaving Arvers to look after his affairs. In 1843 he returned to settle down at Fontainebleau with the wife of a German in Frankfort. Another young man, with the promising name of Chaudesaigues—a corruption of the Latin for "hot water"—came to Paris in 1835 with a fortune of 30,000 francs, which he squandered in a few years, and then struggled on as a journalist till he died of apoplexy.

I should wrong the *viveurs* if I allowed it to be implied that they were all purely pleasure-seekers. Some of them were successful business men besides. Lautour-Mézéray, for instance, who was distinguished by the white camellia in his buttonhole, laid the foundations of his fortune by starting a paper called *Le Voleur*, which was entirely composed of cuttings from other papers. Like Andoche Finot, he went on from small to great, founding *La Mode* and *Le Journal des Enfants*, the first children's paper. He helped to start *La Presse* with Emile de Girardin, who was another of the more solid among the *viveurs*. Doctor Véron, stout and self-important, his face half hidden in a huge cravat, held an important place among them. He began life as a medical practitioner, but made a fortune by exploiting a certain Pâte Regnault and took to political journalism. Between 1831 and 1835 he was an extremely successful director of the Opéra, and in 1838 bought *Le Constitutionnel*, which he sold fourteen years later for two million francs. To him, it is said, is due the invention of the *tournedos*. Certainly, he was a prominent gastronome, and the terror of head waiters, for he was no mere swiller of champagne, but one who insisted on perfect vintages combined with perfect cooking. In the thirties, when

"Robert le Diable" was filling the Opéra and his own pocket, he was a constant diner at the restaurants, but in later years he never dined except at his own house, where Sophie, his cook and majordomo, alone preserved the proper traditions of gastronomy. Mæcenas-like, he made a certain literary set free of his table. Their places were always laid, they helped themselves, and they remained as long as they pleased, whether their host left them or no. Théodore de Banville and many others have celebrated the excellent "cuisine" and its accompaniment of wit, but a reader of Véron's "Souvenirs d'un bourgeois de Paris" will be inclined to suspect that the doctor himself was rather a prosy humbug, who only supplied the appropriate stimulus for the wit of his guests. The chief of these, another celebrated *viveur*, was Nestor Roqueplan, whose toilette was unsurpassed and whose wit inexhaustible. He was a Parisian to the marrow; a day from Paris was to him a day out of Paradise. Like most of his generation, he began as a journalist, but diverged to become a director of theatres. The Panthéon, Nouveautés, Saint-Antoine, Variétés, Opéra, Opéra Comique, and Châtelet passed successively under his sway, and he lost money at them all except at the Variétés, during his management of which he wrote those sparkling "Nouvelles à la main" which are perhaps the freshest examples of purely ephemeral contemporary wit.

The Revolution of 1848 dispersed the *viveurs* for ever. It was not that Paris diminished in gaiety during the Second Empire nor that the *cafés* ceased to be invaded by merry bands of *fêtards*, but simply that Paris became too gay, too large, and too cosmopolitan. The boulevard was no longer to be kept sacred for a chosen few, and a new generation was rising, which found other channels for its energies than ingurgitatory wit-combats. Under the new *régime* there was a court and a more exciting foreign policy. The aristocracy threw off its sulks, the prosperous industrial conquered his diffidence, the pleasure-loving stranger found that all railways led to Paris. The old guard was overwhelmed, or rather would have been overwhelmed if not already well-nigh crumbled away. Men with clear heads and practical aims, who had only devoted their leisure to enjoyment, like Véron, Roqueplan, de Girardin, survived to retire with all the honours of war, forming small *coteries* for the cultivation of wit and good cheer, but shunning, instead of affronting, the public eye. But the rest, the *viveurs* of every hour, where were they? Dead, worn-out, shattered in health, paying the dismal reckoning for the dissipation of their heyday, poor, neglected, forgotten. Misfortune overtook the gay Roger from the moment he married Mademoiselle Doze, the actress. For six years he was pestered with lawsuits for separation, till a divorce was finally procured. He had drunk, as he said, 150,000 francs worth of champagne and written 300 songs. The francs were gone, the songs lost, and nothing was left but the gout.

Jadis j'étais des plus ingambes,
Mais hélas! destins inhumains,
Le papier que j'avais aux mains,
A présent je le porte aux jambes.

He could jest to the last, but in his last days he was a pathetic sight, fat, prematurely old, infirm, confined to a wretched chamber, and denied even the champagne which could charm away his regrets. The dapper figure that had once filled a frock-coat so jauntily was now a shapeless corpulence hidden in the loose folds of a greasy dressing-gown. He died of gout, as Alfred de Musset died of drink. Malitourne, after sinking lower and lower in drunkenness, died mad; apoplexy carried off Chaudesaigues and Charles Froment; Arvers died of spinal paralysis; Béquet ended in a hospital; gout killed Cabanon and Tattet; while Briffaut expired in a mad-house. The mental pronouncement of their funeral orations I leave to any moralist who chooses, bidding him remember that if they failed as individuals to fulfil the highest destinies of mankind they were victims of a strange fever in common with all the generation of 1830.

Of that generation they were a part, perhaps the most conspicuous part at the time. I might almost liken them to the set of "swells" in some public school, privileged themselves yet censorious of others, always in the eye of their small world, influential in their smallest acts, embodying conspicuously the current fashion and expressing the prevailing tone, shining inevitably as a pattern, envied by most, respected, outwardly, by all. In Louis Philippe's time Parisian society was as limited a corporation as a school. Its "swells" attained their position, as all "swells" do, by excelling in a pursuit in which excellence is universally admired. They excelled in tinging their life with a medieval splendour of colouring, they had some prowess in poetry and letters, they performed miracles of wit in the new spirit of busy, ever-bubbling, *bruyant* fun. As the "swells" of Romanticism they justified their position so long as the conditions allowed. Bohemia, in some respects, was like a "house" in the same school, with a smaller corporate life of its own, yet influenced by the powers outside it, the more so because some of its members had risen themselves to the company of "swells." In this not very exalted, but true, simile is my reason for devoting space to the *viveurs*. They were not Bohemians for the most part, but many Bohemians hoped to be *viveurs* as Etonians hope to be in "Pop." On them rested the high lights of the picture, but we can now peer into the background and discern the true Bohemia of 1830.

VI

LA BOHÈME ROMANTIQUE

MIL HUIT CENT TRENTE! *Aurore*
Qui m'éblouis encore,
Promesse du destin,
Riant matin!

Aube où le soleil plonge!
Quelquefois un beau songe
Me rend l'éclat vermeil
De ton réveil.

Jetant ta pourpre rose
En notre ciel morose,
Tu parais, et la nuit
Soudain s'enfuit.
THÉODORE DE BANVILLE

THE Romantic Bohemia has been the theme of so many French writers, from the time when the first reminiscences appeared to the present day, when a Léon Séché and a Philibert Audebrand, following the lead of Charles Asselineau, the pious *chiffonnier* of Romanticism, industriously collect the very last scraps of authentic information, that a foreigner with all a foreigner's limitations may well hesitate to mar the pretty edifice erected to the memory of 1830 by some clumsy addition of his own. Yet I take heart from the consideration that even in France there is, at least to my knowledge, no complete account of this Bohemia. Those who would follow its annals in their original tongue must do so in a multitude of books, published at different times, some of which are rarities only to be found in museums and the largest libraries. Moreover, the French chronicler writes from a point of view which a foreigner cannot adopt, and makes assumptions which a foreigner cannot grant. All the historical and literary associations on which I have touched in a former chapter make it a subject which even to-day excites passionate enthusiasm and equally passionate reprobation across the Channel. The foreigner can approach in a cooler temper, though I postulate in my readers a general sympathy for Gautier's scarlet *pourpoint* and all that it symbolized. In this cooler temper, then, not seeing red, but with a tendency, at least, to see rosy, a foreigner may glance at a life, so essentially limited by its period and its nationality, without challenging unfavourable comparisons.

The Romantic Bohemia was part of Parisian society, a fact of which I have already tried to point out the implications. It might add to the general picture to know how society judged Bohemia. Contemporary record is scarce, not only because Bohemia itself so largely supplied the personal element in the journalism of its time, but also because the conception—indeed, the name—was so new. There is, however, something to be picked up from allusions here and there which is of some service in the definition of boundaries. Nestor Roqueplan, for instance, in his little book, "La Vie Parisienne," defines Bohemia as comprehending "all those in Paris who dine rarely and never go to bed." He distinguishes sloth and debt as the salient faults in the general disorder of its life, and he is not too appreciative of its abilities, though he admits that there is an inner Bohemia, "intelligente et spirituelle," composed of a certain number of young men with the makings of excellent ministers, irreproachable officials, and daring men of business. In conclusion he asserts the great truth that "Bohemia must be young; it must be continually renewed. If the Bohemian were more than thirty, he might be confused with the rogue." This is excellent testimony from a man who, himself no real Bohemian, had extensive relations with Bohemia as one on whom its young playwrights inflicted the reading of their plays. Balzac is the next witness, though it is remarkable that his only specific reference to Bohemia is in the short story, "Un Prince de la Bohème," which tells how the young Comte de la Palfèrine, a penniless son of a general who died after Wagram, satisfied his vanity in the person of his mistress, Madame du Bruel. He was debarred by his position from having a wife worthy of his aristocratic pride, but that at least his mistress might be worthy, Madame du Bruel, an actress married to a writer of *vaudevilles*, worries her husband into the acquisition of riches, political power, and a peerage. At the beginning of this story—one of Balzac's most curious—he gives a general definition of Bohemia:

"Bohemia, which ought to be called the wisdom of the Boulevard des Italiens, is composed of young men all over twenty, and under thirty, years of age, all men of genius in their manner, still little known, but destined to make themselves known and then to be very distinguished; they are already distinguished in the days of the carnival, during which they discharge the plethora of their wit, which is confined during the rest of the year, in more or less comic inventions. In what an age do we live! What absurd authority allows immense forces thus to be dissipated! In Bohemia there are diplomats capable of upsetting the plans of Russia, if they felt themselves supported by the power of France. One meets in it writers, administrators, soldiers, journalists, artists! In a word, all kinds of capacity and intellect are represented in it. It is a microcosm. If the Emperor of Russia were to buy Bohemia for some twenty millions, supposing it willing to quit the asphalt of the boulevards, and were to deport it to Odessa, in a year Odessa would be Paris. There it is, the useless, withering flower of that admirable youth of France which Napoleon and Louis XIV cherished, and which has been neglected for thirty years by that gerontocracy under which all things in France are drooping.... Bohemia has nothing and lives on that which it has. Hope is its religion, self-confidence is its code, charity passes for its budget. All these young men are greater than their misfortunes—below fortune, but above destiny."

The narrator of the story, the witty Nathan, goes on to give some particular *traits* of La Palférine, who would be King of Bohemia, if Bohemia could suffer a king. Some of these are rather vulgar pleasantries which display the bluntness of Balzac's sense of humour rather than La Palférine's wit, as when the Bohemian, angrily accosted by a *bourgeois* in whose face he had thrown the end of his cigar, calmly replied: "You have sustained your adversary's fire; the seconds declare that honour is satisfied." La Palférine was never solvent: once, when he owed his tailor a thousand francs, the latter's head clerk, sent to collect the debt, found the debtor in a wretched sixth-floor attic on the outskirts of Paris, furnished with a miserable bed and a rickety table; to the request for payment the count replied with a gesture worthy of Mirabeau: "Go tell your master of the state in which you have found me!" In affairs of love, though he was impetuous as a besieger, he was proud as a conqueror. After having passed a fortnight of unmixed happiness with a certain Antonia, he found that, as Balzac puts it, she was treating him with a want of frankness. He therefore wrote to her the following letter, which made her famous:

"MADAME,—Your conduct astonishes as much as it afflicts me. Not content with rending my heart by your disdain, you have the indelicacy to keep my tooth-brush, which my means do not allow me to replace, my estates being mortgaged beyond their value.

Farewell, too lovely and too ungrateful friend!

May we meet again in a better world!"

Balzac's account is obviously tinged with literary exaggeration, though the stories of La Palférine were no doubt gleaned among the gossips of the boulevard. He shall be balanced by an adverse witness, one M. Challamel, who, after a severe attack of *le mal romantique* which caused him to run away from his father's shop, settled down to be a staid librarian. In his "Souvenirs d'un Hugolâtre" he says:

"In the wake of the freelances of the pen the *Bohemians* abounded, affecting the profoundest disdain for all that the bourgeois call 'rules of conduct,' posing as successors to François Villon, playing the part of literary art-students, frequenters of *cabarets*, often of disreputable houses, breaking with the usages of polite society, and believing, in fine, that everything is permitted to people of intelligence.... By the side of these sham romantic Byrons there existed some good fellows who fell into the excess of the literary revolution, and who paraded the active immorality of debauch. Sceptics, materialists, loaded with debt, they raised poverty to a system and laughed at their voluntary insolvency. Some shook off early their Diogenes' cloak ... others succumbed prematurely ... all had imitators who ended by forming numerous groups and by founding a school. The spirit of Bohemia became infectious, and engendered the spirit of mockery (*la blague*)."

I conclude this general testimony with some lines from Alfred de Musset's "Dupont et Durand," which is an imaginary conversation between two old school-fellows, one of whom has become a prosperous citizen, the other has failed as a Bohemian. The Bohemian says:

J'ai flâné dans les rues,
J'ai marché devant moi, bayant aux grues;
Mal nourri, peu vêtu, couchant dans un grenier,
Dont je déménageais dès qu'il fallait payer;
De taudis en taudis colportant ma misère,
Ruminant de Fourier le rêve humanitaire,
Empruntant çà et là le plus que je pouvais,
Dépensant un écu sitôt que je l'avais,
Délayant de grands mots en phrases insipides,
Sans chemise et sans bas, et les poches si vides,
Qu'il n'est que mon esprit au monde d'aussi creux,
Tel je vécus, râpé, sycophante, envieux.

With the aid of these lights we may descry some general features of the Romantic Bohemian. He must be young; on this both Roqueplan and Balzac are agreed, placing his proper age between twenty and thirty. The Bohemians of 1830 were, as a matter of fact, nearer to the earlier than the later limit. Most of them were born at the end of the first decade of the nineteenth century, so that 1830 found them in, or not long past, their twentieth year, a happy state of things which Arsène Houssaye celebrated in his poem "Vingt Ans." We Englishmen can hardly understand the magic of this joyous phrase, *vingt ans*; through French prose and poetry it sounds again and again like a tinkling silver bell calling those who have lived and loved in youth to hark back for a moment in passionate regret, in an ecstasy of remembrance. To think of Bohemia without that silver tinkle in one's ears is to do it a grave injustice, for Bohemia throbbed with it then as with a tocsin, as with a summoning bell to a joyous refectory in some transcendant Abbaye de Thélème. It may be well for us that at twenty we are still hobbledehoys whom serious persons are only too glad to get rid of for half the year in universities as peacefully unmoved by our turmoil as their Gothic buildings by the storms of winter; but these frenzied medievalists had no Gothic university to be engulfed in save their own dear Paris, at a time when the university of their own dear Paris was trying its hardest to withstand the new ideas with which they were aflame. If juvenile excesses and absurdities can be tolerated with easy smiles at Oxford and Cambridge, how much more can those of the Romantic Bohemia be excused when its denizens were Frenchmen, hardly more than schoolboys, yet already victorious as champions of a revolution, with their livelihood to gain, with no kind parents to pay their bills and no kind Dean to regulate their mischief! As the college porter says, "Young gentlemen will be young gentlemen," a proverb which condones the excesses of tender, as it reprobates those of riper, years. Bohemia, in Roqueplan's words, must be continually renewed, for the old Bohemian is nothing but a legitimate object for ardent social reformers. So the Bohemians of 1830, some of whom made their names, while others remained obscure, were all youthful nobodies in the eyes of the world, perching in their attics like a colony of singing birds upon the topmost branches.

This youth of theirs, once it is properly grasped, explains a good many of their qualities, amiable and otherwise. Poverty, for instance, was a tradition of Bohemia. "They dine rarely," "the Bohemian has nothing and lives on what he has," "they raised their poverty into a system and laughed at their voluntary insolvency": so say Roqueplan, Balzac, and Challamel. Most young men in this world are poor, in the sense they have nothing of their own. So long as they follow the careers laid down for them, or earn the prescribed salaries in the prescribed professions, they are not without means indeed, but if they take a contradictory line of their own which is not lucrative, especially if they dare to set up as poets, it is considered better for them to knock their heads against the hard corners of life without much extraneous assistance. On the whole this is a wise point of view, and one can hardly follow some of the less talented Romantics in making it an indictment against society that superior soup-kitchens are not provided for the sustenance of all who choose to embrace the arts. There were, of course, degrees of poverty in Bohemia, just as there were degrees of economic adaptability. Some were really, others only comparatively, destitute: some girded their loins daily in search of pence, others waited for pence to drop from heaven. Still, in spite of all degrees and differences, poverty was very real. The market for art and letters was still extremely restricted, processes were costly, the science of distribution still in its infancy; a few celebrities took all the cream of the demand, leaving only the thinnest trickle to satisfy the rest.

The Bohemians knew, or very soon found out, their prospects. Those who were not scared back to their homes made up their minds that at best a moderate income might be theirs in the future, while the present entailed considerable privations to be endured cheerfully for the glory of art. Poverty being their economic condition, it is not to be supposed that the young men who *did* happen to be rich in their own right migrated to Bohemia for the mere pleasure of its society. It is easy enough to find food for laughter in unavoidable discomforts and delight in the makeshifts by which misery is cheated, but, when neither discomfort nor makeshifts are necessary, the point of view inevitably changes, and irritation takes the place of laughter. It is quite contrary to human nature that a man with money to spare for regular meals, decent clothes, and a comfortable room should enjoy hunger, rags, and a bare garret. Between adversity cheerfully borne and a masquerade of scanty means there is a gulf which no imagination is able to span. A rich man, I admit, may stint himself in order to spend all his means on a hobby or a philanthropic object, but in the Bohemian there was no trace of this voluntary asceticism, which would have been entirely contrary to the Romantic creed. A rich Bohemian was a paradox, for the moment a Bohemian had any money he spent it in forgetting the sorrows of Bohemia, a moral pointed by Murger's amusing chapter "Les Flots du Pactole," where Rodolphe, having received a gift of £20, promptly agrees with Marcel to live a regular life. He will work, he says, seriously, sheltered from the material worries of life. "I renounce Bohemia, I shall dress like the rest, I shall have a black coat and appear in drawing-rooms." Unfortunately the preliminaries are so costly that the sum is exhausted in a fortnight, the *coup de grâce* being given to it when the new servant pays without authorization the arrears of rent. "Where shall we dine to-night?" says Rodolphe, once more a Bohemian. "We shall know to-morrow," replies Marcel. Rodolphe and Marcel, and their predecessors just as much, would have regarded a Bohemian with an income as a madman or a monstrosity. With all the will in the world such a man would have found it impossible to live in such a society without being on its economic level. Its joys and pleasures would not have been his, its amusements would have seemed paltry. To have shown his money would have made him shunned by the proud and courted by the sycophants, in any case a stranger. He could only have been a Bohemian at the price of dissipating all his capital, and that he could more easily do among the *viveurs* upon the boulevard.

Bohemia, then, was poor, which had the one excellent result of banishing from it all mercenary spirit. When there was so little money to be had in any case and there were so many other more glorious things to think about, there was no point in financial preoccupations. If one had a few coins one spent them in common with those who had none; if one's pockets were empty one went without and accepted the hospitality of others. Money-grubbing was left to the virtuous *bourgeois* beloved of a *bourgeois* king, to unscrupulous Nucingens and adventurous de Girardins. And Bohemia never went to bed, because it was young and poor, not from viciousness or an artistic pleasure in the sunrise. They were incorrigible talkers, those young men—perhaps this was one of their graver faults—they not only talked, but they shouted for hours together, mixing declamations of Victor Hugo with extravagant tirades in the Romantic fashion. It was not in them to disperse quietly after "Hernani" or "Antony" had lashed them into fury. They had a plethora of matter to discharge from their souls, but they had no comfortable little Chelsea studio in which to perform this function. A cold attic, a straw mattress, a fuelless stove, a dearth of chairs, which was all the majority could boast of, was a poor setting for impassioned conversation compared with the warmth of even a humble *cabaret*. The good M. Challamel, of course, is justified in his strictures. Their morals were lax, they were extravagant, they did not pay their bills. This was partly due to what a humorous undergraduate once called the "generosity of youth," and partly to the example of the "swells" upon the boulevard. The Bohemian naturally yearned to enjoy himself, with his acute capacity for enjoyment, as he saw his more fortunate fellow-men enjoying themselves. They were luxurious at all times; it was impossible for him to restrain occasionally the impulse to luxury, indulging in a superb orgy at the Rocher de Caucale or the Trois Frères Provençaux, ordering clothes which he *meant* to pay for, and forgetting all the while the just claims of a landlord. His vices, at any rate, were inseparable from the conditions of his existence, and if he was disreputable, it was more outwardly than within.

The talents of Bohemia were as diverse as the physiognomies of its citizens. Genius, it might be said with truth, was not more common there than in other walks of life. Real genius is a law and a life to itself; it is no more Bohemian than it is aristocratic, democratic, liberal or conservative. Social labels imply classes to bear them, and classes imply a common factor of intelligence. Genius, being an uncommon factor, is always severely individual. Moreover, so far as Bohemia is concerned, genius, being one kind of wealth, unsuited its possessor for Bohemian citizenship as much as a comfortable income. The trivialities and futilities of some, the extravagant idleness of others, would have estranged genius or forced it to pretend an acquiescence in much that was repugnant to its nature. With the possible exception of Gautier, the Bohemia of 1830 could really claim none of the greatest names of Romanticism. Victor Hugo, Sainte-Beuve, and the other divinities of its worship were, apart from all further possibilities, too old. Balzac was a far too busy man to pay it more than momentary visits; Berlioz, before he went to Rome, was too occupied in writing music which irritated Cherubini; Delacroix, the acknowledged king of Romantic painters, is revealed in his letters as the austerest of hard workers, scarcely leaving his studio but for a walk when the shadows began to fall. Yet, if Bohemia was denied genius, it was not denied a very high average of ability, which was enhanced by its burning and disinterested enthusiasm for art. Like all other societies, it had its fools, its knaves, its dunces, and its awkward squad. The Romantic revolution had attracted many scatterbrained fanatics to Paris, with as little artistic aptitude as good sense in their heads. Out of those who survived the first disappointments were fashioned failures like Alfred de Musset's unfortunate in the verses quoted previously, "râpé, sycophante, envieux." Probably, too, an impartial observer, listening to the nocturnal conversations of a Bohemian group, would often have found the ecstatic admiration of the listeners disproportionate to the turgid periods of the speaker, for to every real artist in Bohemia there was a wind-bag or two. Nevertheless there was a good deal of truth in Balzac's eulogy. Bohemia numbered within its gates a good proportion of the best among the younger generation. They were indeed an "immense force," which might have been better utilized. Every kind of talent was represented there abundantly, because the field of letters seemed to be the only battlefield then left open to willing and eager soldiers. This very fact gave the Romantic Bohemia its imperishable distinction, for after 1848, when young blood again found other outlets, what had been a little world was left no more than a decadent province.

The republic of Bohemia in general had all the follies and virtues, the amiability and brutality of youth. It was generous, noisy, more often hungry than drunk, often on the verge of despair, and always fantastically clothed. It sprang up in Paris as rapidly as the iron shanties of a Canadian township round a proposed extension of the railway. The settlers, self-assured, fervid, rise on a tide of increasing prosperity till some supreme moment when their venture, its markets humming, its saloons crowded, its new town hall nearly built, seems the very embodiment of all their hopes. But if the railway, after all, take another route, the glory gradually dwindles, the workers throw down the tools, and the host of speculators melts away, till only that population is left which the soil will actually support, and what was for a day a city resumes the existence of an ordinary village. Bohemia's history is of a less commercial texture, but of a like pattern, as I have already said. Its rise was swift, it had a brilliant apogee, its decline was gradual. In a posthumous poem by Philothée O'Neddy, whose place in the chronicles of Bohemia will be duly recorded, it is said:

Il est depuis longtemps avéré que nous sommes,
Dans le siècle, six milles jeunes hommes
Qui du démon de l'Art nous croyant tourmentés,
Dépensons notre vie en excentricités;
Qui, du fatal Byron copiant des allures,
De solennels manteaux drapons nos encolures.

These six thousand copies of the "Fatal Byron," if they ever existed, have, for the most part, died without leaving their names to posterity. The historian can deal only with a few individuals, who embodied the salient qualities of Bohemia.

VII

THE SECOND "CÉNACLE"

"PEOPLE always forget," said Théophile Gautier in his old age, "that we were the first Schaunards and Collines, a quarter of a century before Murger. Only," he added with a smile, "we had talent and did not write invertebrate verses like those of that feeble appendage to Alfred de Musset." This saying, reported by his son-in-law, was made on a festive occasion, so that it is unnecessary to regard with concern the discrepancy between this view of Murger and the one which Gautier has expressed in print. That kindest-hearted of writers would never wittingly have hurt the reputation or memory of the humblest among his fellows, and I only quote the passage because, when the malice is discounted as largely as the "quarter of a century," it remains a true reference to the origins of Bohemia by one who was, so to speak, one of its pilgrim fathers. The first Schaunards and Collines, Rodolphes and Marcels, the unknown poets and artists who first raised the standard of common enthusiasm against a common enemy, the *bourgeois*, were the young and lusty friends of a young and lusty Gautier. They were members of a *cénacle*, albeit a less beatific *cénacle* than the brotherhood drawn in Balzac's "Illusions Perdues." In the *cénacle* of the Rue des Quatre Vents he evolved by sheer imagination a compensating mirage of virtue to be contrasted with all the real depravity of society which his eye so unerringly saw, just as Eugénie Grandet shines out impossibly beside her miserly father, and Madame Firmiani in the corrupt circle of his *femmes du monde*. Nevertheless there is a certain sublimity in the *cénacle* to which attention cannot be denied. It was Balzac's picture of an ideal Bohemia in which alone such a nature as his could have found a home. It is of little moment that he dates the action of "Illusions Perdues" a few years before 1830, for the *cénacle* itself is a timeless creation, only limited by the fact that one of its members died in the insurrection of 1832. The young men who composed the *cénacle* bore upon their brow the "seal of special genius." Daniel d'Arthez, upon whom since the death of their leader, the great mystic, Louis Lambert, the mantle had fallen, was a monarchist of noble family, destined to become the greatest writer of the future; Horace Bianchon, the flower of doctors, a materialist of perfect charity and profound science; Léon Giraud, a humanitarian philosopher; Joseph Bridau, a great painter with "the line of Rome and the colour of Venice"; Fulgence Ridal, a sceptic, a cynic, and the wittiest playwright of his time; Meyraux, a scientist; and Michel Chrestien, a red republican who was killed in the Cloître Saint-Merri. They were not ascetics by profession: d'Arthez, for instance, was the last lover of the Diane, the Princesse de Cadignan, in the days of his later glory; Bridau's art was affected by his love affairs; Chrestien was "plein d'illusions et d'amour." They were like the "saints" of the early Christian Church, each going his own way, but true helpers one of another, true champions and honest critics. They were without vanity or envy, having a profound esteem for one another, with a consciousness of their own worth. "Their great external misery and the splendour of their intellectual wealth produced a singular contrast. In their society nobody thought of the realities of life except as subjects for friendly pleasantries.... The sufferings of poverty, when they made themselves felt, were so gaily borne, accepted with such ardour by all, that they did nothing to alter the particular serenity which marks the faces of young men free from grave faults, who have not lost part of themselves in any of those low traffickings which are forced upon men by poverty ill supported, by the desire to get on without any choice of means, and by the facile complacency with which men of letters welcome or pardon betrayals.... These young men were sure of themselves: the enemy of one became the enemy of all, and they would have abandoned their most urgent interests to obey the sacred solidarity of their hearts. All incapable of a mean action, they could oppose a formidable 'no' to every accusation, and defend one another with security. Equally high-minded and equally matched in matters of sensibility, they could think and speak all their mind in the domain of science and intelligence; thence came the innocence of their intercourse, the gaiety of their talk. Sure of mutual understanding, their minds digressed at their ease; and they stood on no ceremony among themselves, confided in each other their sorrows and their joys, pondered and suffered with open hearts." I need speak no further of this imaginary *cénacle*, for "Illusions Perdues" is widely known. It is one of those wonderful fantasies that one feels were lovingly cherished by Balzac, at once his darling dreams and his disappointments. He had a passionate desire to express the beautiful, and he was denied that gift. The lights dance before his eyes, and his very language becomes confused and turgid when he deserts reality. It may safely be said that in the real *Bohème* there was no such goodly company of industrious, gifted, morally austere, intellectually gay, unselfish young men, and that there never will be in any society till the coming of the Coquecigrues.

The Bohemia of artistic tradition began in what Théophile Gautier named the "second *cénacle*." The first *cénacle*, as all the world knows, was that of Victor Hugo, Sainte-Beuve, and the brothers Deschamps, who met regularly at the *cabaret* of Mère Saguet on Montparnasse in the days when Hugo was still hatching the plot of the literary revolution. To trace to them the origins of Bohemia would be an error, for they never had any part or lot in Bohemianism. They were young, it is true, and depended upon their art for a living, but the fact that they were nothing but a small *coterie* of earnest poets, more akin to the band of d'Arthez than the friends of Rodolphe, depends upon two things, their time and their outlook. The first *cénacle* came into existence about 1822, when the throne of the Bourbons seemed solid and royalism went hand in hand with classicism. No standard of insurrection, civic or literary, had yet been raised; the victory was yet to come, and it would have been madness, before the campaign was fully planned or the army gathered, for the chiefs to have aped the style of victors. The merciless ridicule of Paris would have killed them in a week, without support as they were. Defiance of the *bourgeois*, an absolute essential of the true Bohemian creed, was, therefore, not appropriate to the first *cénacle*, who lived openly the life of ordinary, decent citizens, while secretly preparing the proclamations, the standards, and the weapons by which the cataclysmic victory of 1830 was to be won. In such a tense moment Bohemia could not be born. Their outlook, in the second place, was too lofty to comprehend the lower planes in which Bohemia made itself conspicuous. To strike a more human note in poetry was their chief aim: they were concerned with art rather than with life itself; and though Hugo, in the privacy of his room, doffed with relief that *bourgeois* symbol, the high linen collar, he was like a general in his tent drawing up that transcendental plan of operations, the preface to "Cromwell," which was to inspire his troops in their pioneering and shooting, in their whole bodily attack on the classic tradition. As the classic tradition was embodied not only in literature, in contemporary journalism, in professional lectures, but in the social life of all staid citizens as well, the Romantic troops, passionate and fundamental as their literary enthusiasm was, were forced to make social life the field of their assault, all the more because, being poor, young, and unknown, they were unable to inflict such palpable wounds with pen or brush as they could by making a violent protest in every detail of the ordinary way of living. By outraging the accepted standards of decency in dress, in speech, and in demeanour, they made their presence daily felt, and where their presence was felt their ideals were made ostensible. Their tactics, after the event, may be blamed, the effect they produced was, no doubt, smaller than they imagined, but the fact remains that la *vie de Bohème* began neither as a retreat for higher souls nor as a means for reckless self-indulgence, but as a definite method of drawing attention to a new and important artistic creed. For the greater exponents of this creed, a Hugo or a Delacroix, such a material protest would have been out of place; it would have detracted even from the effect produced by their great works of art. Only the rank and file, to whom supreme personal achievement was impossible, collected and commonly inspired, as I have already pointed out, under special historical and social conditions, were justified in adopting the measures that were best suited to their purpose. Their purpose was as temporary as their conditions; their device, *épater le bourgeois*, has now become a hollow phrase, but it meant then the rousing of every shopkeeper, every *garçon de café*, as well as the cultured reader of current literature, to the sense that art was alive again. This was the aim of the second *cénacle*, the first Bohemians. They were successful, and they were necessary.

The second *cénacle* was not a formal organization, so that no definite date can be fixed for its institution. Its members probably came together in the same haphazard way as the small bands of friends at a public school or university, crystallizing so imperceptibly that the moment of incorporation baffles memory, and often so firmly that death alone is their solvent. Théophile Gautier, in his fragmentary "Histoire du Romantisme," has given the fullest details of the *cénacle's* existence, yet neither he nor his biographer, Maxime du Camp, make it clear whether it was formed prior or posterior to the famous first night of "Hernani" in February of 1830. Gautier, no doubt, had forgotten, but it seems fairly safe to assume that if preliminary acquaintance was already made between some of its members before that time, the stormy nights of February strengthened the bond and made the association compact. The story of "Hernani," with the red waistcoat, *vieil as de pique*, and other trimmings, has so often been told, even in English, that it may seem unnecessary to traverse such well-trodden ground; but a historian has no business to take anything for granted, so that "Hernani" can be no more justly omitted here than Waterloo from any work upon Napoleon. It was part of Victor Hugo's agreement with the Théâtre Français that a number of seats should be at his disposal each night, and that the holders of the tickets should be admitted some time before the ordinary public. These were the trenches into which his army of young men were thrown. Minor officers were entrusted with the task of bringing the men to the rendezvous, Jules Vabre, an architect, being responsible for a hundred and fifty men, and Célestin Nanteuil for almost as large a number. Gérard de Nerval, whose translation of Goethe's "Faust," published in 1828 (when he was only nineteen), had brought him considerable fame in Romantic circles, had known Gautier, who was two years his junior, at the Collège Charlemagne. This amiable essayist, whom Gautier likened more than once to a swallow, flitting always in and out among his friends, was not forgetful of his young friend in the days of recruiting. Gautier was at that time studying painting in the studio of Rioult, whither Gérard de Nerval made one day a swallow-like dart and produced six tickets marked with the single but thrilling word *Hierro*, the Spanish for "iron." According to Maxime du Camp he gave these to Gautier with the words:

"Tu réponds de tes hommes?"

To him replied Gautier: "Par le crâne dans lequel Byron buvait à l'Abbaye de Newstead, j'en réponds. N'est-ce pas, vous autres?"

"Mort aux perruques!" resounded in answer through the studio, and Gérard flitted away content.

Gautier, who was a little better provided with worldly goods than some of the Romantic army, then set about devising a costume that should strike death into the heart of the *perruques*. With extreme care he cut out a pattern of a medieval *pourpoint*—a buttonless waistcoat coming right up to the collarbone, and fastening with laces behind like the uniform of Saint-Simon's disciples, which symbolized mutual assistance, because no Saint-Simonian could truss his own points. His Gascon tailor's professional objections were overruled, even though the material chosen was a gorgeous silk coloured a Chinese vermilion, and the garment was made as desired: to it were added a pair of light greenish-grey trousers with a broad stripe of black down each seam, a black coat with ample *revers* of velvet, and a flowing cravat. It was indeed a devastating sight, and one that deservedly became famous. In this fervent spirit was the battle waged over "Hernani"; for thirty consecutive performances the trenches were manfully filled and a fusillade of cheers poured forth at every touch of romantic colour, every bold *enjambement*, every defiance of classic circumlocution, and, above all, every sign of disapprobation on the part of those they rudely styled "wigs" and "bald pates." The battlefield was often a pandemonium, but the result was victory. The Théâtre Français, the very home of Molière, was successfully carried by the Romantic assault. Gautier had magnificently won his spurs, and shortly afterwards he was introduced by Gérard de Nerval and Pétrus Borel to the great hero himself, an ordeal which caused him so much trepidation that he sat for over an hour on the stairs with his two sponsors before he could pluck up courage to proceed. His fears, however, soon vanished after a cordial reception, and as his parents were then living next door to Hugo in the splendid old Place Royale, he soon became the most constant page and attendant of the poet, for whom he preserved a lifelong devotion.

These were the days of the second *cénacle*, for "Hernani" was the Hegira of *la vie de Bohème*. During the long waits in the empty theatre, the passionate mornings of preparation, the fiery reunions after the curtain had fallen, a set of the most ardent Hugo-worshippers had found their affinities. They did not indeed live together—some were dutifully under the parental roof, some had hardly a roof to their heads, one at least was supporting a mother and sister by daily work in a government office—but they formed the habit of meeting and spending many hours of the day and night together and the meeting-place was either the studio of a young sculptor, Jehan du Seigneur, or the sanded parlour of the *Petit Moulin Rouge*, in the *rond-point* of the Arc de Triomphe. Their names were Pétrus Borel, Joseph Bouchardy, Philothée O'Neddy, Alphonse Brot, Augustus Mackeat, Jules Vabre, Napoléon Thom, Jehan du Seigneur, Léon Clopet, Célestin Nanteuil, Théophile Gautier, and Gérard de Nerval. It is almost needless to say that some of the names are Gothic transformations in the Romantic fashion. Pétrus Borel was, of course, christened Pierre, as du Seigneur was christened Jean by his parents; while

Philothée O'Neddy and Augustus Mackeat conceal the persons of Théophile Dondey and Auguste Maquet. But names in -us or Celtic patronymics were all the rage, and even Gautier was called Albertus after his poem of that name published in 1832. A curious feature about the group was that, though it existed to champion the cause of Romantic poetry, the only pure man of letters was Gérard de Nerval. Of the rest, Borel, formerly an architect, was learning to draw in Déveria's studio, Thom and Nanteuil were artists, Gautier and Bouchardy studying art, du Seigneur a sculptor, Clopet and Vabre architects; O'Neddy and Brot, indeed, were professed poets, but in no less an embryonic stage than some of the others who afterwards found in the pen their most successful tool. "This mixture of art in poetry," says Gautier, "was and has remained one of the characteristic signs of the new school, and makes it clear why the first adepts were recruited rather among the artists than among the men of letters. A multitude of objects, images, and comparisons which were thought to be irreducible to the written word were introduced into the language and have stayed there."[17]

Pétrus Borel

The one whom Gautier called the *individualité pivotale* of the group, though Philothée O'Neddy in after years denied that he had more influence than Gautier, Gérard, or Bouchardy, was Pétrus Borel, Le Lycanthrope as he subsequently named himself. His full name was Pierre Borel d'Hauterive, and he was born in Lyons in 1809. His father, captured by the revolutionaries in 1792 and then liberated, fled to Switzerland, whence he returned to Paris, a ruined man, to earn what he could by keeping a shop. At the age of fifteen Pierre was apprenticed to an architect, and in 1829 he set up on his own account without much success. He and Jules Vabre became associated, and so poor were they that they used to use the cellars of the houses on which they were engaged as their dwelling-place. Gautier recalled visiting them once in the cellar of a house in the Rue Fontaine-du-Roi, where they were preparing their frugal meal of potatoes baked in the ashes. "Ah," said Vabre with pride, "but we have salt on Sundays." Borel's ideas were too Gothically fantastic for his *bourgeois* clients, and, after a violent dispute over his fourth commission, he ordered the half-finished building to be demolished, and gave up for ever an ungrateful profession,[18] betaking himself for a season to the study of painting, and writing the while those poems animated by a haughty bitterness which were published under the title of "Rhapsodies." They are dedicated and addressed to the members of the second *cénacle*, among whom he enjoyed an enormous reputation. He was for them the poet of the future, before whom Hugo would crumble to dust. Alas! for youthful predictions; thirty years later Gautier, the most loyal of Romantics, was forced to exclaim: "Dire que j'ai cru à Pétrus!"[19] He exercised over the group, in fact, a kind of unconscious hypnotism. His slightly superior age, his strange, rough, paradoxical eloquence, and, above all, his picturesque appearance imposed on them all. Their ideal was to have an *allure fatale*, a sombre complexion and haughty, Byronic mien. Borel realized it. He looked like a Castilian nobleman out of a Velasquez picture, says Gautier, with his "young and serious face, of perfect regularity, an olive skin gilded with light shades of amber, lit up by great, shining eyes, sad as those of Abencerrages thinking of Granada," his bright red lip which shone under his moustache, "one spark of life in that mask of Oriental immobility," and his fine, full, silky beard perfumed and tended like that of a sultan, at a time when to wear a beard in Paris was an outrage to public decency. He was clothed in black, wearing a high Robespierre waistcoat and draping a long black cloak around him with an air of studied mystery. How could the younger men, whose beards refused to grow, not believe in such a perfect symbol, so magnificently scornful, so profoundly fatal? He was the most republican, too, of them all, the typical *Bousingot* of the *bourgeois* Press, though fanatical republicanism was not, as Philothée O'Neddy afterwards protested in a letter to Charles Asselineau, their representative opinion. Gérard had no political opinions at all, Gautier was obstinately *Jeune-France*, and the others only dreamt of a social Utopia in which æstheticism should replace religion, or of some humanitarian millennium after the manner of Saint-Simon and Fourier. Borel, however, held society in complete disgust, as he showed when he left the gathering at Jehan du Seigneur's, and proceeded one summer to live with some followers on the slopes of Montmartre, all naked as savages, till the landlord drove them out at the price of his porter's lodge, which they burnt down in revenge.

None of the others were quite so remarkably individual as Pétrus Borel, whose character may be described as Jules Claretie describes his book of extravagant stories, "Champavert": "doubt, negation, bitterness, anger, something at the same time furious and comic." Vabre, his partner in architecture, had fair hair and moustaches, without any extravagance in his bearing, but his face twinkled all over with malice and his conversation was madly Rabelaisian. He projected a famous book that was never written, "Sur l'Incommodité des Commodes." An intense love for Shakespeare was his chief Romantic asset. According to Gautier he gave up his later life to studying our language in England that he might make the perfect translation, a task which was never completed. Joseph Bouchardy, who afterwards became a very successful writer of melodrama, was then learning engraving. He, too, was dark, so dark that with the soft, sparse beard that just fringed his face he looked an Indian, and was nicknamed the Maharajah of Lahore. He was less poetry-mad than the rest, but eternally occupied with dramatic scenarios in which all the secret passages, trap-doors, and sliding panels of a novel by Mrs. Radcliffe were brought into play. Jehan du Seigneur, who made medallions of all his friends, was a gentle, modest youth with a very pink-and-white complexion which was his everlasting despair. To atone for this unavoidable defection from Romantic ideals, he wore a black velvet *pourpoint*, a black jacket with broad velvet *revers*, and a voluminous necktie, so that not a speck of white linen was shown, a "suprème élégance romantique," as Gautier remarks. Augustus Mackeat was chiefly conspicuous for the happy transformation of his name, though he returned to the orthodox Maquet when he became a successful playwright. His disguise, however, was nothing to the tremendous anagram which turned Théophile Dondey into Philothée O'Neddy. He, says Gautier, was dark as a mulatto with fair, curly hair. Though he was helping to support a mother and sister by working in a government office, this Philistine occupation did not prevent him from being one of the most frenzied of the gang, a "paroxyst" *ruisselant d'inouïsme*. In 1833 he published a collection of ultra-romantic poems called "Feu et Flamme," which reek with passion, despair, scorn, suicide, and contempt for Christianity. Yet he lived till 1872, and though he published nothing more, he left a collection of posthumous poems all of which breathe an extreme melancholy. In the letter written to Asselineau ten years before his death he admitted that in the days of the *cénacle* he had "une bonne grosse somme d'extravagance et de mauvais goût," but protested warmly against the application to them of the epithet "ridiculous." "Risible" they might have been, but only the *bourgeois* were "ridiculous." Célestin Nanteuil was big, fair, gentle, and so perfectly medieval that Gautier caricatured him as Elie Wildman-stadius, the hero of one of his *Jeune-France* stories, who lived in a Gothic manor on medieval fare, read nothing but medieval illuminated manuscripts, and was killed when the Gothic cathedral, his sole external joy, was struck by lightning. Gautier describes him personally as having the appearance of "one of those long angels bearing censers or playing sambucs that live in the gables of cathedrals, who has come down into the city in the midst of the busy burgesses, keeping his nimbus all the while at the back of his head like a hat, but without the least suspicion that it is not natural to wear one's aureole in the street." He was a furious Hernanist in 1830 (he was then only seventeen), and called "the Captain," for leading the army to the fray. In 1843, when he was asked to bring three hundred young men to support "Les Burgraves" in the same manner, he sadly said: "Tell the master there are no more young men." He might, says Maxime du Camp, have been a great painter, but he was compelled to live by illustrating. Whenever he had made a little money in this way he returned to his colours and his easel till it was exhausted. He ended in the obscurity of Dijon, becoming the director of its school of art.

Célestin Nanteuil

Maxime du Camp compares Nanteuil's fate to that of Gautier, who was forced by circumstances to waste so much of his talent in mere journalism; but in 1830 Gautier, a young man of nineteen, who made long hair serve instead of a beard, was still free as air. In that year he brought out a little volume of poems, and a year or two later produced the fantastic "Albertus," which he followed with "Les Jeune-France." His art studies had soon ceased because he discovered that he suffered from short sight, and we may regard him in the days of the *cénacle* as a poet pure and simple. One figure remains to be filled in, the most pathetic of all the Romantic band, Gérard de Nerval. He was born in 1808, the son of a Doctor Labrunie—the family name of de Nerval was only assumed by him when he began to write. His youth was spent in the pleasant country of the Valois, and he received a very careful education from his father, who taught him not only Latin and Greek, but German, Italian, and the rudiments of Arabic and Persian. Even in his early days he was an eager reader of mystics and utopists, which gave that first fantastical turn to his brain which ended later in complete madness. His development was normal at first. At the Collège Charlemagne he was the snapper-up of every prize, and produced some quite worthless poetry in praise of Napoleon that won high approval from his professors. He followed this by a satire on the Academy, which appeared in 1826, and in 1828 he produced an ode to Béranger of a style to which his Romantic friends could only have applied the new epithet *poncif.* The translation of "Faust," which earned a very high compliment from the great Goethe himself, turned him into his appropriate path and gave him a serious literary reputation which he never lost. He translated other fragments of German poetry, and wrote for the *Mercure de France*, of which Pierre Lacroix, the "Bibliophile Jacob," was then the editor. His adoption of a literary career was a grave disappointment to his father, who had hoped to make a good official of him, and it is probable that parental coldness first caused him to find a congenial asylum in the new Bohemia, of which he was never a typical inhabitant. When he came of age he inherited his mother's dowry, which made the actual earning of money immaterial to him. His success with "Faust" had brought him into touch with Hugo, so that after the days of "Hernani" he held in the *cénacle* the most distinguished, if not the most influential, position as a lieutenant of their demi-god, with notable achievements in the field of letters already to his credit.

Gérard threw in his lot with the *cénacle*, but, though he even wrote some revolutionary poems in 1830, for which he was imprisoned in Sainte Pélagie, he was never quite at ease with Borel and the *Bousingot* faction. The flamboyant side of Romanticism and its noisy gatherings had little appeal for him. He was an eccentric and a solitary by nature, as his writings, with their strong reminiscence of Heine, show. In the time of the *cénacle* he was, according to Gautier, a gentle and modest young man, who blushed like a girl, with a pink-and-white complexion and soft, grey eyes. Under his fine, light golden hair his forehead, beautifully shaped, shone like polished ivory. He was usually dressed in a black frock-coat with enormous pockets, in which, like Murger's Colline, he buried a whole library of books picked up on the *quais*, five or six notebooks, and a large collection of scraps of paper on which he wrote down the ideas that occurred to him on his long walks. He was the perfect peripatetic: as he once said, he would have liked to walk through life unrolling an endless roll of paper on which he could jot his reflections. He lived at this time with Camille Rogier, the artist, in the Rue des Beaux Arts, but his friends could never be sure where to find him. For him no hour was sacred to rest. He wandered about Paris at all times of the day and night, dropping in on a friend for an hour or two, ready to ride a hobby-horse with him in any direction, then darting off again, his thoughts in the clouds, nobody knew whither, and returning in the small hours, only to flit from his bed at the dawn. Of all the gay companions of Bohemia he was the best loved, for his childlike simplicity and his gentle manners won all hearts. He went through life to his terrible death with complete unworldliness, almost like a ghost, unconscious of the material side of existence, directing his feet only by the light of his spirit. Gautier, writing after his death, protested vehemently that his was no ordinary tragedy of neglected genius; he had money enough, but money was nothing to him, so he spent it without a thought; his work was always accepted by editors, and his plays, though not successful, were all produced. But success was the last of his preoccupations. He was a wanderer living in a world of his own fantasies. As he will appear again in these pages, we may bid him farewell for the moment, with the conviction that it would be pleasant to be transported for a season back to that turbulent *vie de Bohème* if only to find the kindly Gérard's arm passed through one's own and to hear his gentle murmur: "Tu as une fantaisie; je la promènerai avec toi."

I ought, perhaps, to apologize for allowing the persons of the *cénacle* to take up so much space before coming to their life, yet I imagine, on the whole, that I have said too little rather than too much. To go back to a past of which one has no experience is a matter of such extreme difficulty that a historian must often despair at the impossibility of reproducing the whole congeries of scattered detail from which alone his own mental picture could have taken shape. The first Bohemia, that of the second *cénacle*, was less a common life than a common recreation. It was an incomplete *vie de Bohème* in so far as its members were united, not by a desire to share all the joys and difficulties of life, but by a particular artistic enthusiasm. There is no record that any of them worked or dwelt together, that they took part in joint expeditions of amusement, or that the mutual acquaintance of those female divinities for whom they plied so "fatally" their emotional bellows is to be presumed—and these are marked characteristics of Murger's *vie de Bohème*. When they ate together it was at the obscure *cabaret* kept by the Neapolitan Graziano for the needs of his compatriots who worked in Paris. Here, in a plain whitewashed room with a sanded floor, a dresser covered with violently coloured faience and plain wooden benches, they were initiated by their host—a man of senatorial presence, with an immense but perfectly correct nose and big black beard, who seemed to dream all the while of his beloved Italy—into the delights of *spaghetti*, *stufato*, *tagliarini*, and *gnocchi*. They were delicious meals, seasoned with good spirits, and—to use the delightful French phrase—"bedewed" with sound wine of Argenteuil or Suresnes christened magnificently with the names of the most exclusive vineyards in Médoc or Burgundy. Still, they were felt at times to be a trifle wanting in Romantic glamour. It was all very well, the grumblers remarked, to be enjoying incomparable macaroni, but when all was said and done there was little that an impartial observer could descry in these banquets to differentiate them from the prosaic meals of a Joseph Prudhomme. Something was wanting, some tincture of the Newstead spirit, some infernal joy in the food, some shudder in the drinking. The macaroni remained obstinately matter-of-fact, but a brilliant idea was mooted that would give a charnel flavour to the wine. Graziano's glasses were only glasses of quite modern exiguousness; the true brotherhood should drink out of a skull. A skull was accordingly procured by Gérard from his father, the doctor, and ingeniously mounted by Gautier, who screwed to its side an old brass handle from a chest of drawers. In truth it was a noble bowl, and the pious company drank from it with bravado, each concealing with more or less ill-success his natural repugnance. Familiarity, however, bred contempt, till one uncompromising youth surprised his companions by noisily commanding the waiter to fill with sea-water.

"Why sea-water?" exclaimed a simple soul.

"Why sea-water! Because the master in 'Hans d'Islande' says 'he drank the water of the sea from the skulls of the dead.' It is my desire to do the same."

Yes, the *Petit Moulin Rouge*, for all its good cheer and its death's-head mounted with a drawer-handle, was too workaday for these eclectics. They reached their true glory only in the gatherings which took place in Jehan du Seigneur's studio. It was a room over a little fruiterer's shop that the *cénacle* sanctified as their conventicle. "In a little chamber," wrote an older Gautier, "which had not seats enough for all its occupants, gathered the young men, really young and different in that respect from the *young* men of to-day, who are all more or less quinquagenarians. The hammock in which the master of the dwelling took his siesta, the narrow couchlet in which the dawn often surprised him at the last page of a book of verses, eked out the insufficiency of conveniences for conversation. One really talked better standing up, and the gestures of the orator or declaimer only gained a more ample scope. Still, it was extremely unwise to make too free with your arms for fear of knocking your knuckles against the sloping ceiling." It was a poor man's room, but not without ornament, for it contained sketches by the two Dévérias, a head after Titian or Giorgione by Boulanger, two earthenware vases full of flowers on the chimneypiece, the inevitable death's-head instead of a clock, a looking-glass, and a small shelf of books. On either side of the glass and in the embrasures of the windows were hung the portrait medallions which Jehan made of his friends. They had no money to get them cast in bronze, so the world has lost in them a valuable appendix to the well-known busts of his contemporaries executed by the more distinguished Romantic sculptor, David d'Angers. Here they would all gather of an evening: Gérard if he happened to be passing in his amiable wanderings, Bouchardy the Maharajah, Gautier—not yet the burly critic of *La Presse*, but a thin youth of nineteen—Nanteuil with his Gothic nimbus, Vabre bursting with some new joke, Borel swinging off his long cloak with a scowl, O'Neddy shedding Dondey in the street, Mackeat and the rest, each bursting with eloquence or roaring the "Chasse du Burgrave" at the top of his voice. When Maxime du Camp once asked Gautier what they talked about, he answered: "About everything, but I haven't the least idea what they said, because everybody talked at once." However, a very good idea of a typical evening in the *cénacle* is given in Philothée O'Neddy's "Feu et Flamme," the first poem in which, called "Pandæmonium," is a gorgeous description of their cave of harmony. It is freely decorated with "local colour," which on a Romantic's lips meant the borrowing of all he could carry away from the medieval stage-property room, but it was drawn from life with all seriousness and sincerity. The poem opens by depicting them all seated round the punch-bowl—punch, it must be stated, was the only really respectable drink for a thorough-paced Romantic. He mixed it in a large bowl and set light to the fumes, as the students are supposed to do in the first act of the "Contes d'Hoffmann," and derived enormous satisfaction from sitting in an obscurity only lit by this bluish flame. Thus to recall the witches' cauldron and the fires of the Inferno had an unfailing success as a stimulant to eloquence. The scene, then, opens thus powerfully:

Au centre de la salle, autour d'une urne en fer,
Digne émule en largeur des coupes d'enfer,
Dans laquelle un beau punch, aux prismatiques flammes,
Semble un lac sulfureux qui fait houler ses lames,
Vingt jeunes hommes, tous artistes dans le cœur,
La pipe ou le cigare aux lèvres, l'œil moqueur,
Le temporal orné du bonnet de Phrygie,
En barbe Jeune-France, en costume d'orgie,
Sont pachalesquement jetés sur un amas
De coussins dont maint siècle a troué le damas,
Et le sombre atelier n'a point d'éclairage
Que la gerbe du punch, spiritueux mirage.

Smoking, it would be well to add, was considered part of the whole duty of a Romantic man. The cigar, being Byronic, was affected by the "fatally" inclined; the pipe came, not from England, but from Germany; it was Faust-like, Hoffmannesque; it was also Flemish, of course, and the Flemish painters, like Steen and Teniers, were in high repute. A pipe signified a more jolly potatory spirit than a cigar, but it was always possible for the irreconcilable satanics to regard the breathing out of smoke from either as symbolically demoniac. The cigarette was not despised, but its popularity was due also to its picturesque associations. Spain was the home of the cigarette, the *papelito* as Borel and his friends fondly called it. When they rolled their fragrant Maryland lovingly in the *papel* they assumed a Spanish *allure*, Granada rose before their eyes, and invisible guitars played "Avez-vous vu dans Barcelone?" However, cigarettes would have been out of place in the prismatic flames of the punch-bowl. Their Spanish nonchalance suited better the light of day: evening shadows were consecrated to gloom and frenzy, Northern spirits. Hence it is not surprising to hear that all the company had

De haine virulente et de pitié morose
Contre la bourgeoisie et le Code et la prose;

Des cœurs ne dépensant leur exultation
Que pour deux vérités, l'art et la passion!

The conversation is compared with some aptitude to a Spanish town devastated by an earthquake, which confounds in one ruin palaces and huts, churches and houses of ill-fame. So in their talk the ideal and the grotesque, poetry and cynical jesting are confounded pell-mell. Silence is made while a passage from Victor Hugo is declaimed, after which four discourses are pronounced. Three are by Borel, Clopet, and Bouchardy respectively, concealed in the names of Reblo, Noel, and Don José, and the second discourse is delivered by the swarthy O'Neddy himself, who,

Faisant osciller son regard de maudit
Sur le conventicule,

pours out a passionate complaint that poets have too long been under the yoke of governments and codes of law. The evening closes with a violent tumult. The punch has done its work, and the *cénacle* is a-screaming with the ecstasy of energumens.

Ce fut un long chaos de jurons, de boutades,
De hurrahs, de tollés et de rhodomontades.

They danced and sang like the demon crew in the master's "Ronde du Sabbat,"

Et jusques au matin les damnés Jeune-Frances
Nagèrent dans un flux d'indicibles démences.

It is to be hoped that the worthy fruiterer was sleeping quietly in another part of Paris, and only the potatoes were kept awake and sleep banished from the pears.

If at this point our reader feels inclined to throw up his hands and exclaim "How disgusting!" he will be well advised to put down the book. One cannot approach Bohemia without a certain sympathy for youthful excesses, howsoever opposed they may be to one's personal predilections. If the *cénacle* indulged in occasional orgies—which, even allowing a good deal for "local colour" in O'Neddy's "Pandæmonium," they certainly did—they had a great many compensating virtues, such as complete disinterestedness and a consuming love of art, which were not conspicuous in Paris at the time. Maxime du Camp in his memoir on Gautier sets the extreme limit to which reasonable criticism of them can go when, after remarking on the promise given by a violent youth for a fruitful middle age, he says:

"From that should we conclude that the young men who composed the *cénacle* were all destined to become great men? Certainly not; there were among them dreamers with illusions about themselves, sterile dupes of the comedy that they played, failures in whose case the brilliant future which they promised themselves fell naturally into obscurity. To more than one of them the saying of Rivarol could have been applied: 'It is a terrible advantage never to have done anything, but it should not be abused.' In short, only one of them has made a name that will not perish: Théophile Gautier. Gérard de Nerval, by whom he had been distanced at the beginning of his life, never passed a very moderate level, did not push his way in the crowd, and came early to grief. On the other hand, most of them were celebrated in the group, I might say in the *coterie*, to which they belonged, but their reputation never went beyond the circle in which they lived."

Maxime du Camp takes a very superior point of view which is less than just. The members of the *cénacle*, it may be admitted, overrated one another's talents and were ready, in some instances, to take posturing for performance; but Bohemia is not to be blamed because all her children were not great men any more than Eton because all her *alumni* are not scholars. As a matter of fact, in this first Bohemia of the *cénacle* there were very few of whom it could be said that their lives were ruined. Gérard died a violent death, but he was afflicted with mental disease. Apart from his eccentricity he was a scholar and a gentleman whose attainments equalled those of Gautier himself, though he could not bring himself to exploit them. Pétrus Borel was the one real failure, the *poseur* who inevitably came to grief. His Bohemian career reached its apogee at his masked ball in 1832—a caricature of Dumas' own famous ball—held at his lodgings in the Rue d'Enfer, an appropriate address. He left Paris shortly afterwards, and, after earning for some years a precarious livelihood and publishing "Madame Putiphar," he became an inspector of Mostaganem, in Algeria, in which country he died wretchedly. The rest, though they did not quite achieve their proud dreams, continued, most of them, in the paths of art with rectitude and some success, Bouchardy and Maquet as dramatists, du Seigneur as a sculptor, Nanteuil as an artist. O'Neddy, once the *cénacle* dissolved, as it did towards 1833, found poetry a resource in solitude, and poor Vabre, if he made no figure in the world, at least set himself the highest of ideals in devoting his life to the study of Shakespeare.

The first Bohemia, for what that is worth, was singularly respectable in its results. Even had they been far worse, sufficient praise to stifle carping would be found in the indelibly beautiful memory which it left on the minds of its members. In 1857 Bouchardy wrote of it to Gautier in these words:

"It was a holy and beautiful comradeship, my dear Théo, in which each was the loving brother, the devoted friend, the fellow-traveller who makes his friend forget the length and the fatigue of the road. It was a more beautiful comradeship than one can say, in which all wished the success of all without insensate exaggeration and without collective vanity, in which each of us offered to lend his shoulder to the foot of him who wished to climb and to reach his goal.... It was a happy time, dear Théophile, of which we ought to be proud, for when one has traversed this life so often saddened by so much bitterness, we ought to be proud of having found in it some hours of joy, we ought to boast of having been happy!"

Even Maxime du Camp admits that the effect of the *cénacle* on Gautier was incalculable: its disinterested friendship and its enthusiasm made his individuality. All his life he remained "the mystic companion of Victor Hugo's first disciples." Weighed down in after years by the irksome tasks of journalism, the slave who remembered his years of freedom with regret, he responded to Bouchardy with tender melancholy from beside the rivers of Babylon:

"No doubt such joy could not last. To be young and intelligent, to love one another, to understand and commune in every realm of art—a more beautiful manner of life could not be conceived, and from the eyes of all those who followed it its dazzling splendour has never been obliterated."

At another time he wrote to Sainte-Beuve: "Nous étions ivres du beau, nous avons eu la sublime folie de l'art."

These words, issuing from a soul ever animated during its days on earth by a Bohemian spirit, cast a protecting spell round the memory of the first Bohemian brotherhood through which no Philistine anathemas can break.

VIII

LA BOHÈME GALANTE

O le beau temps passé! Nous avions la science,
La science de vivre avec insouciance;
La gaieté rayonnait en nos esprits moqueurs,
Et l'Amour écrivait des livres dans nos cœurs!
ARSÈNE HOUSSAYE

THE *cénacle* broke up towards 1833 and its members scattered. All Bohemian *coteries* must be short-lived, but this one was specially doomed to a quick dissolution. It was, I will not say too romantic, but too romantically ritualistic, too much concerned with the vestments and incense and celebrations incident to the profession of "Hugolâtry." It is not hard to imagine how the too mystic significance given to its gatherings, its feasts, and even its individual actions became to some of the brethren, now that Romanticism was firmly established, either unreal or merely tiresome: divergences of taste and opinion began to creep in till, in the end, this attempted Bohemia became a deserted shrine. But the Bohemian spirit could not thus be quenched; indeed, it was only then fully kindled. The deacons and acolytes, whom the mere symbolism had mainly attracted, were gone; paid off the Swiss Guard whom the return of peace called back to civil life. Those who remained, the most advanced of the initiated, saw that the time had come for the casting away of symbols and the cessation of noisy worship. Bohemia had originated in a literary creed, but in its consummation it was to pass beyond the letter and take hold of human life. This consummation came with extraordinary rapidity; there were no feeble tentatives, no half-successes. A new community arose in Paris, almost out of the ashes of the *cénacle*, vastly different though it was from the obscure group in Jehan du Seigneur's humble studio. It was animated by all that was best in Romanticism—its disregard for academic convention, its colour, its joyousness, its warmth of feeling, and its sympathy with all human passions; but, unlike the *cénacle*, it did not trammel itself with Romantic convention, it set creation above imitation, and—greatest of all differences—it was no society meeting at intervals for spiritual and corporeal refreshment, but a genuine life in common lived just for the sake of living by a set of high-spirited, joyous young men, most of them true artists, neither maniacs, nor ne'er-do-wells, nor idlers. The *cénacle* was dead, but *la vie de Bohème* was born, and its golden age came first. The brotherhood of the Impasse du Doyenné was, in A. Delvau's words, "une Bohème dorée, avec laquelle celle de Schaunard n'a que des rapports très éloignés."[20] Delvau, who was of Murger's generation, knew well how quickly the glory departed.

Yet at least Murger's Bohemians had this connexion with what Gérard de Nerval named *la Bohème galante* that they could look back to it as the Romans to the reign of Saturn. It was constituted informally, even fortuitously; it existed without self-advertisement, but it remained, in the phrase of another French writer, "la patrie de toutes les Bohèmes littéraires."

In 1832 another Bohemian of the golden age had come to Paris, a brave and merry soul called Arsène Houssaye, who had only breathed this terrestrial atmosphere for seventeen years. It was not to champion a cause that he came, but he was called thither by the poet within him to take his part in infusing a new vitality into life and letters. Like Gautier, he was a natural *enfant de Bohème*, yet did not at first find the brotherhood which he was to hymn in prose and verse; it was still only a potentiality. For a few months he lived in an odd little Bohemia of his own with a friend called Van dell Hell in a *hôtel garni*. They wrote songs for a living, wore the red hats by which the more violent students of the Quartier Latin proclaimed their republicanism, and consoled themselves for the rebuffs of editors with the smiles of a certain "Nini yeux noirs." Houssaye in those amusing volumes which he called "Les Confessions" bears witness to the deplorable state of the literary market at the time. Novels and plays could not be sold, poetry was not wanted as a gift, and the newspapers regarded mere men of letters as too frivolous for employment. Poverty among the struggling writers was acute, but nobody cared a fig about money when all cared so much about art—a merciful dispensation of Providence. Yet, if commercialism did not affect art, the same can hardly be said of politics. Far too many of the young poets and artists, who would have scorned to drive a mercenary bargain at the expense of their art, exulted in defiling their artistic convictions with the reddest and most insensate republicanism, not seeing that if art does not need to regard gold pieces, neither does it need to trouble itself whether a king's head or a cap of liberty is their stamp. Arsène Houssaye, careless wretch, nearly missed the glory of Bohemia entirely by mixing himself up in the insurrection of the Cloître Saint-Merri. He was arrested, but a friendly commissary of police saved him from trial and imprisonment by sending him home to his wealthy, loyal, and scandalized family. The ungrateful lad, instead of settling down to some solid profession, simply bided his time till the disturbance was over, and returned to Paris, only so far profiting by his warning that he left politics henceforth to look after themselves. Houssaye's father, worthy man, felt that money would be thrown away on such a ruffian, so Arsène was left to his own resources, which, if they were meagre in early days, kept him alive for another sixty-three years.

Bohemia was not to be baulked a second time. The elements were present, and all that remained to do was for somebody to give them a slight push, such as Lucretius gave to his atoms. The push occurred at the Salon of 1833, if Houssaye is to be believed—a condition not inevitably fulfilled. There, one fine day, he met Théophile Gautier and Nestor Roqueplan, the former of whom was certainly a stranger to him. A genial conversation on the merits of the pictures ensued, in which Arsène Houssaye made, as he was destined to do, a very good impression upon his senior. Gautier was not a man to leave hazard any further part after such a promising beginning, and he accordingly proffered an invitation to *déjeuner* next day in the words: "Je te surinvite à venir déjeuner invraisemblablement demain chez les auteurs de mes jours." Houssaye turned up next day at No. 8 Place Royale, where the irrepressible Théo introduced his father as "le respectable bonhomme qui me donna l'être." The other guest at this *déjeuner* was Gérard de Nerval, whom with true instinct Gautier had brought to test and to embrace the newly found brother. The wit and gaiety, the range and the emphasis of their postprandial conversation can be imagined. At last Théo blurted out frankly: "Tu sais que je ne te connais pas: dis-moi huit vers de toi, je le dirai qui tu es." It was not a test which the future author of "Vingt Ans" feared. Gautier found himself able to give an enthusiastic account of the new brother; the two truest Bohemians in Paris were at once bosom friends, and the most wayward of geniuses was a friend of both.

So far the credit had been with Gautier, but Bohemia was still without a dwelling-place, and in this matter Gérard de Nerval deserved pious mention in the Bohemian bidding prayer, for it was owing to him that *la Bohème galante* found a home suitable to the golden age, a unique setting which posterity could remember but never reproduce. It was a rare opportunity, and it might almost be supposed that fortune, approving of Théo's first amiable push, advanced willingly another step, making peripatetic Gérard her tool. In the course of his wanderings he had become acquainted with one of the most singular regions in all Paris, no sign of which remains to-day. Hardly a visitor to Paris omits a look into the Louvre, but very few know that as they walk from the statue of Gambetta to the entrance of the galleries they are crossing the site that Bohemia in its florescence made memorable. On that spot there stood in 1833 part of an older Paris, which in intention had long been cleared away, but in fact remained another twenty years. Those who have read Balzac's "Cousine Bette" have made its acquaintance, though I should wager that the majority of them have taken it for granted with other of Balzac's topographical details. Let me recall to them the sinister quarter where Cousine Bette, at the opening of the story, cherishes the young sculptor Steinbock and makes the acquaintance of the infamous Monsieur and Madame Marneffe. With his practised touch for tragic effect Balzac describes it thus:

"The existence of the block of houses which runs alongside of the old Louvre is one of those protests which the French people like to make against good sense, so that Europe may be reassured as to the grain of intelligence accorded them and may fear them no more.... Anybody who comes towards the Rue de la Musée from the wicket leading to the Pont du Carrousel ... may notice some half-score of houses with ruined façades, which the discouraged owners never repair, and which are the residue of an ancient quarter in course of demolition ever since Napoleon resolved to complete the Louvre. The Rue and Impasse de Doyenné are the only streets within this sombre, deserted block, the inhabitants of which are probably phantoms, for one never sees a soul there.... These houses, buried already by the raising of the Place [du Carrousel], are enveloped in the eternal shadow projected by the high galleries of the Louvre, which are blackened on this side by the north wind. The darkness, the silence, the chilly air, the cavernous depth of the ground combine to make these houses kinds of crypts, living tombs. When one passes in a cabriolet along this dead half-quarter, and one's look penetrates the little alley de Doyenné, a chill strikes one's soul, and one wonders who can live there and what must happen there in the evening when that alley changes into a den of cut-throats, and the vices of Paris, wrapped in the mantle of night, flourish at their height."

This can hardly be called an engaging description, and even Bohemians, it might be supposed, would shrink from such a dreadful slum. But Balzac was writing in 1847, more than ten years after Bohemia had left it, and he was making a protest against the continued existence of this quarter, which had probably deteriorated since the days when he sent there himself to offer Gautier work on the *Chronique de Paris*. However, whether Balzac was right in making the Rue du Doyenné an inferno or was only touching it up with livid tones appropriate to Cousine Bette and the Marneffes, it was certainly a more smiling spot in 1833. True, it was tumbling down, and lay below the level of the Place du Carrousel, in the midst of mournful débris, between the Louvre and the Tuileries, which Napoleon had meant to join after sweeping it away; the houses, as Gautier says,[21] were old and dark, repairs to them were forbidden, and they had the air of regretting the days when respectable canons and advocates were their inhabitants. Yet it was not a den of thieves by any means. Gérard[22] records that many *attachés* and Government officials lived in the quarter, and that by the Place du Carrousel there was a collection of temporary wooden shops let out to curiosity dealers and print-sellers. It was enlivened, too, by the presence of a little Dutch beer-house served by a Flemish maid of considerable attractions. The view from the upper windows included, naturally, the heaps of stones, the rubbish, with the nettles and the dock-leaves by which Nature tries to cover such deformities at once; but it also included a good many trees, and the ruins of a delightful old priory, with one arch, two or three pillars, and the end of a colonnade still standing. This was the Priory of Doyenné, the dome of which, according to Gérard, fell one day in the seventeenth century upon eleven luckless canons who were celebrating the office. Its ruins stood out gracefully against the trees, and of a summer morning or evening, when, amid the peaceful silence of this forgotten corner, the bright rays of the Parisian sun lit up the lichen on its stones and a fresh breeze from the neighbouring Seine gently swayed the branches of its framing trees, it must have been well to be a-leaning out of a window.

However, Gérard de Nerval did more than find a quiet, romantic corner hidden away in the busy heart of Paris with a ruined priory to give distinction to its prospect; he also found an appropriate dwelling. In one of the old houses of the Impasse du Doyenné there was a set of rooms remarkable for its *salon*. It was a huge room, decorated in the old-fashioned Pompadour style with grooved panellings, pier-glasses, and a fantastically moulded ceiling. This decoration had for a long time been the despair of its owner and had driven away all prospective tenants, the taste for curiosities being at that time undeveloped. In vain had the landlord parcelled it out with party walls; it was still mouldering on his hands when Gérard came thither on one of his swallow-flights. He at once persuaded the good-natured Camille Rogier to transfer his household gods from the Rue des Beaux-Arts, the party walls were knocked down, and Bohemia entered on its ideal home. Gérard had still some of his patrimony left, and chose to expend it upon his one hobby, the collection of pictures and furniture. It was a golden time for the collector. Society had as yet not learned to appreciate old works of art, dealers were not too well informed, and the depredations of the Bande Noire, that, under the Restoration, had sacked so many ancient ecclesiastical foundations, had brought a large quantity of precious old furniture, tapestries, and fabrics into the curiosity shops of Paris. Gérard had acquired a wonderful canopied Renaissance bed ornamented with salamanders, a Médicis console, a sideboard decorated with nymphs and satyrs, three of each, and oval paintings on its doors, a tapestry delineating the four seasons, some medieval chairs and Gothic stools, a Ribeira—a death of Saint Joseph—and two superb panels by Fragonard, "L'Escarpolette" and "Colin Maillard," which last he had bought for fifty francs the pair. It was a magnificent studio, worthy of *la Bohème galante*. There was no question of bare attics on a sixth story, their tiny windows looking on a dreary sea of roofs, of rickety chairs and peeling wall-paper. In spite of its bare floors, its faded colours, its chipped corners, and the incongruous presence of plain easels among its ancient splendours, its riches were princely. Bohemian disorder might reign among paints and palette-knives, ends of paper inscribed with scraps of verse might dot its unswept floor, the *débris* of eating and drinking might litter the seats on which fastidious cavaliers once delicately sat, but no realities of a careless existence could spoil its romantic atmosphere. Without its merry clan of inhabitants, no doubt, it would have seemed odd and ghostly; yet if they brought back to it the necessary colour of youth, it tinged, in turn, their life with a patina of old gold that never faded from their reminiscences.

A Festivity in the Impasse du Doyenné

Camille Rogier was the real lessee, and Gérard his sub-tenant. Gautier had a couple of rooms in the Rue du Doyenné, which cut the Impasse crosswise. These at first were the only permanent inhabitants of the new colony, but the great *salon* where Rogier and Gautier worked soon became a meeting-place for a number of friends. Work was stopped at five o'clock, when Arsène Houssaye was certain to appear, Roger de Beauvoir, then in his most brilliant day, half Bohemian, half *viveur*, and Edmond Ourliac, the future dramatist. One evening Houssaye, Roger de Beauvoir, and Ourliac stayed talking till dawn; Roger departed then to his more sumptuous apartments, Ourliac to his parents' house in the Rue Saint Roch, but Arsène Houssaye stayed, on Rogier's invitation, to complete the inner conclave of Bohemia. His camp-bed was sent for next day, and he became Rogier's second tenant, paying him indeed no money, but spending, in revenge, chance gifts from home on luxurious feasts at the Frères Provençaux.

Such a society in such a setting could not long remain unknown. With its circle of guests widening it grew in importance, for in this golden age Bohemia could be important without losing its quality. Gavarni, the inimitable portrayer of Parisian types, Nanteuil, Châtillon, Marilhat, even Delacroix, were among the artists who found the gaiety of the Impasse du Doyenné to their taste; Pétrus Borel looked haggardly in occasionally; the great Dumas would rush in and out like a storm; the Roqueplans, Camille and Nestor, showed there in moments spared from their more elegant wanderings; and the effervescent Roger de Beauvoir as gaily composed there his witty rhymes as at a supper in the Café de Paris. It was no hole-and-corner Bohemia at which the superior person could affect to turn up his nose; it was a truly artistic centre in Paris and, at the same time, a *coterie* admission to which was jealously enough guarded to exclude the half-baked dilettante who is the ruin of most artistic sets and the very negation of Bohemia. For a reason which will be obvious in the sequel, ladies with leanings to artistic society—another impossibility in Bohemia—were equally debarred from appearing. It was a more or less closely knit society of young and gifted men, lovers of the beautiful, despisers of convention without *gasconnade*, neither rich nor desperately poor, avid of pleasure, and fashioning their conduct easily upon the standards of the day, yet crowning all their hours, even the most wanton, with a graceful and light-hearted idealism that shields these pagan heroes of a golden age from any but an æsthetic judgment, a judgment which, in the case of their own countrymen, they confronted with serene self-confidence.

In all, the group was fairly large: its membership radiated dimly as far as the "dandies" on the boulevard and into the obscurer depths of the Quartier Latin. But radiation was from a central nucleus—the original Bohemian brethren whose home was in the Impasse du Doyenné: Camille Rogier, Gérard de Nerval, Théophile Gautier, Arsène Houssaye, and Edmond Ourliac. The rest were visitors, but they alone were the true dwellers in *la Bohème galante*. Of their brotherhood and its life Gautier, Gérard, and Houssaye have all given glimpses, which compose a picture apt for pleasing and, occasionally, envious contemplation. Arsène Houssaye in his "Confessions" is the fullest source of reminiscence, and his words are delightfully illustrated by the poem, originally entitled "Vingt Ans," but in his complete works "La Bohème de Doyenné." The poem, addressed to Gautier, begins:

Théo, te souviens-tu de ces vertes saisons
Qui s'effeuillaient si vite en ces vieilles maisons
Dont le front s'abritait sous une aile du Louvre?
Levons avec Rogier le voile qui les couvre,
Reprenons dans nos cœurs les trésors enfouis,
Plongeons dans le passé nos regards éblouis.

Chimères aux cils noirs, Espérances fanées,
Amis toujours chantants, Amantes profanées,
Songes venus du ciel, flottantes Visions,
Sortez de vos tombeaux, jeunes Illusions!
Et nous rebâtirons ce château périssable
Que les destins changeants ont jeté sur le sable:

Replaçons le sofa sous les tableaux flamands;
Dispersons à nos pieds gazettes et romans;
Ornons le vieux bahut de vieilles porcelaines,
Et faisons refleurir roses et marjolaines;
Qu'un rideau de damas ombrage encore ces lits
Où nos jeunes amours se sont ensevelis.

Gautier, Gérard, and Houssaye have already been introduced, but a word must be said of the other two. Camille Rogier, who was as old as Gérard, was in Houssaye's opinion the most charming man in the world. Already an artist of some repute, he alone of the brotherhood was earning a living by his art— even more than a living, for was he not rich enough to buy riding-boots and wear coats of pink velvet? It was his departure for Constantinople in 1836, where he remained eight years painting the Eastern scenes which won him his chief fame, that caused the disruption of this Bohemian colony. Besides his mastery of the brush he was a very agreeable singer of *chansons* and ballads. Ourliac did not live in the Impasse du Doyenné, but with his parents in the Rue Saint Roch, and filled a small post in the office of the "Enfants Trouvés" which brought him £48 a year. But he never failed to call on his way to work in the morning, to recount a merry story, and on his way home he stayed with them many an hour. He, who in Houssaye's lines,

gai convive, arrivait en chantant
Ces chansons de Bagdad que Beauvoir aimait tant,

was the merriest of all the band, its Molière, says Houssaye elsewhere, ever sparkling with wit, an inexhaustible *raconteur* of inimitable dramatic power. He was a poet, too, a great student of German philosophy, and was at the time working upon "Suzanne," the first work which made his name heard in the world of literature.

It was a jolly life in the Impasse, though money was plentiful but rarely, and fortune had still to be wooed. They rose early in the morning, even after a bacchic evening, and when Théo joined them all four would set to their work, while the Pompadour *salon* was hardly yet awake in the morning sun, each singing the air which the new day found lingering in his head. Théo always painted or drew before he began to write, but his serious task was the composition of "Mademoiselle de Maupin," that masterpiece which was completed, sold for a beggarly £60, and published in the joyous days of Doyenné. Rogier was illustrating Hoffmann's "Tales" and Houssaye writing "La Pécheresse."

"L'un écrivait au coin du feu, l'autre rimait dans un hamac; Théo, tout en caressant les chats, calligraphiait d'admirables chapitres, couché sur le ventre;

Gérard, toujours insaisissable, allait et venait avec la vague inquiétude des chercheurs qui ne trouvent pas."[23]

Gérard, his part in the foundation of *la Bohème galante* performed, felt under no compulsion to confine himself to the nest. His companions, indeed, saw little of his amiable countenance, for he wandered ceaselessly, often only returning when the night sky grew pale, to leave before it was fairly blue. He had a task, nevertheless, and that task was connected with his great romance. It is a story as pathetic as Charles Lamb's second love affair, and the woman who won his heart was also an actress. In the days of the *cénacle* Gérard had fallen desperately in love with Jenny Colon, of the Opéra Comique, an actress of not more than ordinary talent. It was a passion that went to the very roots of his being, an infatuation enriched by all his romantic mysticism. She was the goddess who ruled his dreams by night and day, and it was for her in anticipation that Gérard purchased his wonderful Renaissance bed with its salamanders and carved pillars. No room that Gérard ever possessed was large enough to hold this bed, which was always lodged with his friends, first in the Impasse, and then in other parts of Paris. They respected his frenzy, for the bed never had an occupant, and they kept it sacred till its deluded owner was obliged by straitened circumstances to part with it. Gérard's bed was the epitome of his life—a search for a phantom that his brain itself had fashioned. His Jenny Colon was a phantom, but the real Jenny, though her vulgar heart was unmoved by a shy poet's awkward homage, was not unwilling to accept his services. Commenting himself, in "La Bohème Galante," on Arsène Houssaye's stanza:

"D'où vous vient, ô Gérard! cet air académique?
Est-ce que les beaux yeux de l'Opéra Comique
S'allumeraient ailleurs? La reine de Saba,
Qui du roi Salomon entre vos bras tomba,
Ne serait-elle plus qu'une vaine chimère?"[24]
Et Gérard répondait: "Que la femme amère!"

wrote:

"La reine de Saba, c'était bien elle, en effet, qui me préoccupait alors—et doublement. Le fantôme éclatant de la fille des Hémiarites tourmentait mes nuits sous les hautes colonnes de ce grand lit sculpté, acheté en Touraine, et qui n'était pas encore garni de sa brocatelle rouge à ramages. Les salamandres de François Iᵉʳ me versaient leur flamme du haut des corniches, où se jouaient des amours imprudents.... Qu'elle était belle! non pas plus belle cependant qu'une autre reine du matin dont l'image tourmentait mes journées. Cette dernière réalisait vivante mon rêve idéal et divin."

The question was to secure her *début* at the Opéra, and for that purpose Gérard undertook to write a libretto in verse for a "Reine de Saba" for which Meyerbeer, then at the height of his popularity, was to compose the music. This was the task upon which he was ostensibly engaged when he joined for an hour or two the other workers in the Impasse du Doyenné. For some reason or other the project never came to maturity, perhaps because Gérard could not work to order, perhaps because Jenny Colon married another. All that is left of the "Reine de Saba" is a fragment published later in Gérard's "Nuits de Rhamadan," and the whimsical reminiscence, from which I have quoted, in "La Bohème Galante." In the latter he goes on to explain the "academic air" which he assumed one festive evening when the Bohemians were amusing themselves with a costume ball. He alone was abstracted because he had an appointment with Meyerbeer at seven the next morning. But he could not escape an adventure. A fair mask who sat weeping in a corner of the room appealed to him to take her home. Her cavalier had deserted her for another and dismissed her rudely. Gérard took her out on the ground of the old riding-school hard by, where under the lime-trees they talked till the moon gave way to the dawn. The ball was almost over, and other masks found their way to this retreat. It was proposed to adjourn to an early breakfast in the Bois de Boulogne. No sooner said than done. The revellers set off joyously, Gérard's *belle désolée* opposing only a feeble resistance. But Gérard had his appointment, and wished to work on his scenario. In vain Camille Rogier rallied him on his desertion of the lady. Gérard was firm, and Rogier with a laugh offered her his disengaged arm. He departed, bidding Gérard farewell with mocking bow. And he had entertained her all the evening; poor Gérard! such was his fate. As he remarked: "J'avais quitté la proie pour l'ombre ... comme toujours!"

Gérard's adventure is in the nature of digression. So, indeed, was his whole life; but the others were not more discursive than befitted Bohemians. They slept in their beds and took their meals regularly. Luncheon, after the morning's work, was a frugal meal except for Gautier, who had developed from a weedy youth into a giant with a Gargantuan appetite. They did not entirely fail to earn a penny, but when literary labour was so poorly paid Gautier, who was doing art criticism in a small paper for nothing, was glad enough to see his mother arrive in the morning with two raw cutlets and a bottle of bouillon for his *déjeuner*. Nevertheless, when the afternoon was over and the visitors gone—Roger de Beauvoir to dress for an evening at the Opéra, Borel to rage at society in some poor garret—Rogier, Gautier, and Houssaye, now and then capturing Gérard, set out to roam in the busy city whose festive lamps were glittering on the boulevards and twinkling along the Seine. They dined—they were not too poor for that—in the Palais Royal more often than not, and wandered for the rest of the night where their fancy took them. Now the theatre would entice them with some romantic play by

Hugo or Dumas, after which a supper with much punch would be indispensable; now they would invade the *Chaumière* or some other place of dancing. At that time everybody danced deliriously,[25] the quadrille being in great vogue since it lent itself readily to choreographic invention on the part of the individual. Ourliac and Houssaye, for instance, attracted great attention by dancing a quadrille which represented Napoleon at all the critical periods of his life—the siege of Toulon, the Pyramids, Waterloo, and St. Helena. Another evening, Gautier having gone to visit his parents and Gérard absent, Houssaye might return quietly to the white and gold *salon* with Rogier, who would talk with him or sing him songs while the cats purred on their knees; or, yet again, they might carouse in the Flemish *cabaret* hard by, served by the young *tavernière*

Qui tout en souriant nous versait de la bière.
Quelle gorge orgueilleuse et quel œil attrayant!
Que Préault a sculpté de mots en la voyant.

Cette fille aux yeux bleus follement réjouie,
Les blonds cheveux épars, la bouche épanouie,
Jetant à tout venant son cœur et sa vertu,
Et faisant de l'amour un joyeux impromptu,
Fut de notre jeunesse une image fidèle;
Ami, longtemps encor nous reparlerons d'elle.

So sang of her Houssaye, whose souvenirs of Bohemia at the magic age of *vingt ans* are deeply tinged with amorous memories. In fact, *la Bohème galante*, as its name implies, was not a monastery, and its life was not shared, but illuminated by a number of divinities whose aureoles had been over more than one windmill. The chief of these was "la Cydalise,"

Respirant un lilas qui jouait dans sa main
Et pressentant déjà le triste lendemain.

She was treasure-trove of Camille Rogier's, a beautiful woman, and titular mistress of the Bohemian encampment. They were all jealous of Rogier's good fortune, for, since he was twenty-five, they considered him a patriarch, and Théo could not understand how Cydalise could put up with such an old man. She lived quite happily in the Impasse, making the afternoon tea, sitting as a model, and inflaming all their hearts. Théo's passion was of a frantic heat. He besieged Cydalise with long and violent apostrophes, swearing to kill the senile tyrant who kept her in his power, threats for which Rogier, ever smiling, did not care a button. Poor Cydalise, she was a butterfly whose day was short. To Rogier's great grief consumption seized her. For some weeks he enlivened her sick-bed by singing her songs and drawing pictures for her amusement; but the day came when her ears no longer heard and her lovely eyes were closed. Gérard, Gautier, Roger de Beauvoir, and Ourliac went to her funeral, and Bohemia lost its official mistress. Yet there were others. Gérard draws a picture of Gautier, on a Gothic stool, reading his verses while Cydalise or Lorry or Victorine swung herself carelessly in the hammock of Sarah *la blonde*, and Arsène Houssaye at the end of "Vingt Ans" recalls them in the lines:

Judith oublie Arthur, Franz, Rogier et le reste,
En donnant à son cœur la solitude agreste;
Rosine à Chantilly caresse un jeune enfant
Plus joli qu'un Amour et plus joueur qu'un faon.
. . . . . .
Ninon au Jockey Club vend chacun de ses jours;
Charlotte danse encore—et dansera toujours.
Alice?—il faut la plaindre et prier Dieu pour elle,
Elle est dans les chiffons, la pauvre Chanterelle;
Armande?—Un prince russe épris de sa beauté
Travaille à lui refaire une virginité.
Olympe?—un mauvais livre ouvert à chaque page—
Ce matin je l'ai vue en galant équipage....

The loves of Doyenné were true *enfants de Bohème*, neither great passions nor elective affinities, but pastimes leaving regrets for inspiration; not devouring flames, but pleasantly crackling experimental fires, drawn chiefly from those great hearths, the stage and the *corps de ballet*. How much fantasy went to their burning is illustrated in a story told by Houssaye of Gérard, who, on one occasion, to the despair of his friends, became obsessed with a mad desire to set out that instant for Cythera and revive the gods of Greece. Prompt measures were necessary, and Houssaye devoted himself to the rescue by professing to enter into the scheme with joy, only remarking that it would be well to have lunch first. This seemed to Gérard a reasonable preliminary, so they adjourned to the Café d'Orsay, where over the first bottle Gérard developed his scheme with growing eloquence. But the first stage on the way to Cythera lasted for several bottles, and at the commencement of the next Gérard met a provisional goddess in the shape of an attractive *grisette*. Houssaye, convinced that his companionship was now no longer necessary, abandoned the voyage, and left Gérard to continue it up several flights of stairs. The end of this ascent marked his farthest point; after a halt of two days he descended and turned his footsteps back to Bohemia. The loves of Bohemia which gambol so trippingly in the tongue of France are ill at ease in our austerer medium, for our Northern spirit has ever refused to admit, as the French do with engaging candour, that man, particularly the artist-man, is naturally polygamous. Lorry, Victorine, Armande, and the rest were the only appropriate feminine attachments of Bohemia, even of the golden age, the pagan loves of pagan heroes, who were greedy of their caresses without hungering for their souls, grew jealous at their eyes' wayward glances, but took no umbrage at the inward abstraction of their minds, and were content with the homage of their play-hours without seeking to rival the ideals of their artistic contemplations. But the mark of the golden age was that they played for love and not for money: they would dance the heels off their slippers in the barren land of Doyenné when all the millions of a dull prince would have moved their agile toes only to the most significant of kicks. It was a mad little world, but good because Mammon had not corrupted its natural spontaneity. True, it was deficient in some virtues, but some virtues are frankly middle-aged, to be put on with a less tricksy cut of the clothes. Bohemia was young; it loved and feasted and, being poor, made debts. There is not much to be said for getting into debt, in spite of Panurge's ingenious discourse, except that it is an unavoidable corollary of certain conjunctions of temperament and circumstance. It is difficult, anyhow, not to pardon Gérard for dissipating his capital and running up bills on account of his delightful inspiration of receiving a pressing creditor, a furniture dealer, with the recitation of a touching poem, "Meublez-vous les uns les autres," which affected the dun to tears.

"We had no money, but we lived *en grands seigneurs*," wrote Arsène Houssaye, looking back. Indeed they did, if it be princely to have pretty actresses to perform impromptu comedies and dancers of the Opéra for one's partners in a quadrille. I suspect that these occasions were not so frequent as the exuberant narrator would have us suppose. Gérard more frankly says they spent much valuable time making eyes at the landlord's wife, who lived on the ground floor, which argues an occasional dearth of desirable objects for idle glances. Nevertheless, dances and comedies they did have, and towards the end of its epoch *la Bohème galante* had one supreme festival. It was a combined dramatic entertainment and fancy-dress ball, which took place in November 1835. The idea, says Gautier, was Gérard's own, who thus made amends for his frequent absences by being responsible for the crowning glory of the first Bohemia. His suggestion rested on the artistic ground that it was a pity to inhabit a room and never to receive there a company worthy of it: a *bal costumé* alone could produce a gathering that would not clash with the decorations. That was all very well, but the general finances were in a melancholy condition, and a reception, even in Bohemia, required capital. Gérard brushed the objection lightly aside. People who are without the necessaries of life, he pointed out, must have the superfluities, or they would have nothing at all, which would be too little, even for poets. As for refreshments, they would do better than give their guests cups of weak tea or rum punch; they would feast the eye instead by having the room specially decorated with mural paintings by their friends, the artists. Only princes and farmers-general could indulge in such magnificence, and the fame of the Impasse would be undying.

The idea was not entirely new, for Dumas at his great ball in 1832 had done very much the same. For him all the leading artists of the day, including Delacroix, had painted the walls of the ballroom, as he narrates in a spirited passage of his "Memoirs." But Dumas had not dared to make art take the place of bodily refreshment, for he declares that his guests consumed the bag of several days' shooting and some thousand bottles of wine. *La Bohème galante*, though younger and less known artists were at its command, placed art upon her proper pedestal. Ladders were quickly erected, panels and piers were parcelled out, and the work began. It is a scene on which to dwell in envious imagination. They were perched on ladders, the merry band, smoking cigarettes, singing Musset's songs or declaiming Victor Hugo, with roses behind their ears—a counsel of Gérard's, who, contenting himself with a general survey of operations, recommended a return to the classic festal usage of garlanding the head with flowers. Camille Rogier, smiling through his beard, was painting Oriental or fantastically Hoffmannesque scenes; the burly Gautier executed a picnic in the style of Watteau, a tantalizing subject for thirsty dancers; Nanteuil, with his long golden hair, limned a Naiad; and Adolphe Leleux produced topers crowned with ivy in the manner of Velasquez. Other friends were pressed into service, Wattier, Châtillon, and Rousseau; Chassériau contributed a bathing Diana, Lorentz some revellers in Turkish costume, and Corot on two narrow panels placed two exquisite Italian landscapes. Any comrade might lend a hand, and it was on this occasion that Gautier first made the acquaintance of Marilhat, the Oriental painter, whom a friend brought in and who drew on a vacant space some palm-trees over a minaret in white chalk. It is to this acquaintance that we owe Théo's recollections of this remarkable day. If that room, decorated thus because a few *louis d'or* for refreshments were not forthcoming, were now existing, only a millionaire could buy, and only a great gallery worthily house, it. Yet regrets are misplaced, for it served its day, and it is well that the *salon* of Doyenné, with its furniture and its painted panels, in which the happy, money-scorning Bohemians danced at their culminating festival, should vanish before mercenary dealings could soil its freshness.

The *fête* was gorgeous. True, the landlord's wife had refused their invitation—a severe blow. But the hosts with some consideration, knowing that their revels would make sleep impossible in the quarter, invited all their bachelor neighbours on the condition that they brought with them *femmes du monde* protected, if they pleased, by masks and dominoes. The wonderful evening began with the pantomime of "Le Diable Boiteux," in which many actresses from the boulevard took part. Then there were two little farces in which Ourliac covered himself with glory as the *buffo*. The first was "Le Courrier de Naples," and the second, written by Ourliac himself, "La Jeunesse du Temps et le Temps de la Jeunesse," was introduced by a prologue by Gautier, read from behind the curtain. Ourliac was buried in bouquets, and the noisy orchestra brought in from a *guingette* struck up. The ruined quarter woke to life again, as in some ghost story; the desert streets resounded with songs and laughter; Turks and *débardeurs* affronted the frown of the staid old Louvre, and only the landlords and *concierges*, tossing sleeplessly, consigned Bohemians to everlasting flames. The dance, sustained only by good spirits, never flagged, till in the final galop every mask with his partner rushed pell-mell from the room, leaped wildly down the rickety stairs, dashed up the Impasse, and came to rest under the moonlit ruins of the old priory, where a little *cabaret* had opened, and only the late dawn of winter drove Bohemia to its bed, to dream of the Pompadour salon, of Ourliac's satirical buffoonery, and of Roger de Beauvoir's magnificent Venetian costume of apple-green velvet with silver embroidery, and his inexhaustible wit, for once born of no champagne.

It is melancholy to go back to a deserted ballroom, and we may spare ourselves the pain. That joyous evening, little as it may have seemed to do so, marked the passing of the golden age. Bohemia's sun henceforth descended the skies. The next year saw marked changes. The landlord of the old house in the Impasse du Doyenné saw with relief—Gérard says he gave them notice to quit—the departure of his turbulent tenants. If Rogier had not gone to Constantinople it is possible that, even if the band had been compelled to change its quarters, some reconstruction of *la Bohème galante* might have been possible. With him, the stable, the earner of money, absent, there was no hope. The heroes of Bohemia had to leave their enchanted garden for the ordinarily circumscribed dwelling of impecunious mortals, and, like the heroes of Valhalla when Freia is snatched from them, a certain wanness came over the complexion of their lives. Joy and beauty and work and love were left, but the magic bloom had just faded. With smaller resources and in a colder light the resettlement of Bohemia was a work of compromise, not spontaneous achievement. Rogier was gone; Ourliac, who produced "Suzanne" with success, married before long, grew serious, and ended his days in the fullest odour of piety; Roger de Beauvoir found the boulevard more to his taste than any less brilliant Bohemia. Gautier, Gérard, and Houssaye were left, a trio of markedly divergent tastes. They made one attempt at a common life in the Rue Saint-Germain-des-Prés, which seems to have lasted a year or two. The details of it given by Gautier[26] and Houssaye[27] differ considerably. According to Gautier they did their own cooking: Arsène Houssaye was perfect in the *panade*, Gautier prepared the macaroni, no doubt remembering Graziano, while Gérard "went, with perfect self-possession, to buy galantines, sausages, or fresh pork cutlets with gherkins at the neighbouring cook-shop." Houssaye, on the other hand, says that they had a rascally valet and a cook called Margot, and that they broke up because they were at variance on the degree of luxury to be maintained, Gérard, whom anything satisfied, departing to a bare *hôtel garni*, Gautier to a sumptuous apartment in the Rue de Navarin, and Houssaye sharing rooms in the Rue du Bac, on the left bank, with Jules Sandeau. I do not trouble to reconcile these two accounts, for the memories of Bohemia are invariably picturesque. The fact remains that the old days could not come back. The first Bohemians were growing older, and the world was beginning to claim its once youthful defiers as servitors. Though Gérard's bed remained with Gautier as a memory of freer days, he knew too well that the gates of the prison were closing upon him. For a year or so he might pretend to mock destiny by producing another book of verses and a novel, or by making a voyage in Belgium accompanied by Gérard: but he was a doomed man. About 1838 he became the dramatic critic of *La Presse*, entering the mill in which he was to grind for over thirty years. Well might he say in 1867, in an autobiographical notice: "Là finit ma vie heureuse, indépendante et prime-sautière." Houssaye kept up the pretence a little longer. Life in the Rue du Bac was gay; there were suppers with Jules Janin and Sandeau at which Gautier and Ourliac sometimes appeared; there was dancing; there were the bright eyes of a certain Ninon, who inspired some pretty stanzas. But these were the last echoes of *la première Bohème*, as he had to admit. When they died away he completed the chapter of his youth, as Gautier had done, by travelling.

Gérard de Nerval

Gérard alone escaped the inevitable superannuation of Bohemia, because he was too ethereal to become amenable to the ordinary dynamic laws of society. An attempt was made to catch him in the machinery by making him Gautier's assistant as dramatic critic of *La Presse*. The sprite within him would not submit to the drudgery, and in a little while he gave it up. He preferred, as ever, to wander at his will and at his own hours, or to sit reading at the dead of night by the light of a brass chandelier balanced on his head. It is not part of this book's plan to give complete biographies of those who appear in its pages, but an exception shall be made in the case of Gérard de Nerval. Between 1837 and 1839 he stayed in Paris, writing a comic opera, "Piquillo," with Dumas, in which Jenny Colon appeared, several plays, with a certain number of articles and reviews. His way of life was always eccentric, but he had his first definite attack of madness in 1839 or 1840, and was placed in the famous establishment of Doctor Blanche. He came out in 1841 and resumed a career of wider vagabondage than ever, now with money, now without, but caring little in any case and ready to go to the ends of the earth with a whim and without a coin. In 1841 he joined Camille Rogier in Constantinople, and wandered subsequently in other parts of the East—an experience which gave rise to some of his best descriptive work. He returned to Paris again, where his spirit dwelt in the clouds and his body anywhere, though he often allowed it to rest with one of his many friends, with whom he would leave a shirt to be washed against his next coming. He continued to write not very successful plays between 1846 and 1850, when he again went completely mad and retired to Dr. Blanche's house. His second stay here was longer, but as he soon became perfectly reasonable his friends were allowed to take him out for the day occasionally. Once more apparently cured he came out, but though he made one or two voyages his faculties remained permanently clouded. Of this he himself was perfectly conscious, but he bore his afflictions with perfect cheerfulness. His money was all gone, and the flashes of sanity too rare for him to earn much; he was homeless, but not friendless, for he never appealed to his friends in vain. He came for crumbs like a bird in winter, but like a bird he would not stay. He would have been an appropriate guest at some strange *Nachtasil* such as Maxim Gorki describes so powerfully. Who knows, too, in what haunts he was not a familiar? His comrades of older days could do no more than greet him and tend him when they saw him, and his equanimity was too great to drive them to forcible detention. As Paul de Saint-Victor wrote after his death:

"In vain his friends tried to follow him with their hearts and eyes; he was lost to sight for weeks, months, years. Then, one fine day, one found him by chance in a foreign city, a provincial town, or more often still in the country, thinking aloud, dreaming with open eyes, his attention fixed on the fall of a leaf, the flight of an insect or a bird, the form of a cloud, the dart of a ray, on all those vague and ravishing beauties that pass in the air. Never man saw a gentler madness, a tenderer folly, a more inoffensive and more friendly eccentricity. If he woke from his slumber, it was to recognize his friends, to love them and serve them, to double the warmth of his devotion and welcome as if he wished to make up to them for his long absences by an extra amount of tenderness."

It was with a profound shock, therefore, that Paris heard, one morning in 1857, that Gérard had been found in the small hours, hanged to an iron railing by a woman's apron-string, in one of the lowest and most ill-famed streets in Paris, the Rue de la Vieille-Lanterne. The mystery of his death has never been cleared up. The inquest brought little light, save that the inmates of a filthy little drink-shop probably knew more than they would tell. What Gérard was doing in that foul haunt will never be known. It is possible that he may have been murdered, but, as he had no money and was the gentlest of men, it is more probable that with some dreadful cloud upon his brain he destroyed himself. Yet his very gentleness had made such an end unexpected, for he seemed to be under the protection of the children's guardian angel. Some sudden impulse brought him a death alien to the character of his whole life. "Il est mort," said Paul de Saint-Victor, "de la nostalgie du monde invisible. Paix à cette âme en peine de l'idéal!"

From Gérard's death, which Gustave Doré made more hideous in a ghoulish picture, it is a long cry back to the Impasse du Doyenné and the Pompadour *salon* of which he was the discoverer. Yet I will end this chapter, as it was begun, with this once festive haunt. Not long did it outlive its Bohemian colony. The landlord, explosively wrathful at the sight of the wall paintings, at once covered the mess, as he no doubt called it, with a coating of distemper. The treasures might, even then, have been saved in part, had anyone but Gérard de Nerval bought from the demolishers Corot's panels, the pictures by Wattier, Chassériau, and Châtillon, and Rogier's portraits of Cydalise and Théophile Gautier. His hand was one to baulk destiny only for a little. This moonstruck captain of a rickety craft let his cargo fall needlessly into the seas while he contemplated the stars and allowed the waves to swing the rudder. So passed *la Bohème galante*, leaving only a gilded legend.

IX

SCHAUNARD AND COMPANY

La Bohème carottière et geignarde d'Henry Murger ...
LEPELLETIER: "Verlaine"

TO follow the heroes into exile would be depressing as well as unprofitable. It is better to stand respectfully aside from the *Götterdämmerung* and wait till Bohemia emerges again from the mists, when a lapse of years has wrought some patent changes, for it is easier to contemplate a result than to trace a process. By leaping forward some ten years from the dispersal of the brotherhood that sanctified by its presence the Impasse du Doyenné it is possible to steal a march on Time and anticipate with a rapid glance his changing hand. Yet to catch this later view it is necessary for the nonce to abandon the world of flesh and blood and to turn from the acts and reminiscences of actual mortals to the imaginary scenes and fictitious characters of a book of stories. The tide of life was too strong upon Théophile Gautier and Arsène Houssaye for them to pause and stamp out firmly the features of those precious days in *la Bohème galante*; they only caught fugitive impressions in retrospect. Henry Murger, less prodigal because less endowed, crystallized as it passed a moment of Bohemia, the Bohemia of common mortality, in "Scènes de la Vie de Bohème." As a confectioner encloses a fresh grape in a transparent coat of candied sugar, so he, even while he tasted, sour and sweet, the fruit of his days, caught stray berries in a light film of art and presented them as dessert to the readers of the *Corsaire*, a small but amusing journal. Sharp and savoury as they were, Time would have destroyed them, as he destroyed the ambrosial lusciousness of the Doyenné feasts, but for that light film. Nobody remembers reminiscences, but a well-told story preserves even the most trivial events.

Murger's "Scènes de la Vie de Bohème" is a book which has now lived for nearly seventy years and does not seem likely as yet to pass into the lumber-room. At the same time, it is to be wished that more people in England knew it, if only because the presupposition of such knowledge would make this chapter easier to write. It is not, of course, difficult to criticize the "Scènes de la Vie de Bohème"; many of Murger's countrymen, indeed, have done so. Its ethics, its humour, and its style have been attacked. M. Boucher, an estimable civil servant interested in literature, in his "Souvenirs d'un Parisien" calls it an effort to depict the life of low-class students, accuses Murger of insipidity and repetition, and denies any wit to his "étudiants demi-escrocs, demi-canailles." M. Pelloquet, who was good enough to pronounce a discourse over Murger's grave, said: "It is an unhealthy book, in which vice grimaces, youth paints its cheeks like a superannuated coquette, and a fictitious *insouciance* conceals, not a laziness that is sometimes poetic, but the cowardly indolence of men without courage and without talent." He was also rash enough to predict that it would not live. Jules Janin, the critic, in a wiser appreciation, asserted that with a little more art and a little more poetry Murger might have created more pardonable heroes and no less charming heroines. Gautier's dictum about the invertebrate verses of "that feeble appendage to Alfred de Musset" has already been quoted, and the opinion of Verlaine's biographer appears at the head of this chapter. Murger's gravest fault, however, in the eyes of French people is that he wrote bad French. To them the mishandling of that difficult, elusive, and withal limited tongue is a crime of which we can hardly comprehend the enormity. It is perfectly true that Murger was culpable in this respect; he was deficient in scholarship and in rhythmic sense, so that his poems are weak and his prose, even where he tried to give it an air of respectability, betrays its imperfections no less manifestly than M. Jourdain betrayed his birth. We in England, fastidious as our critics are in the matter of language, have not our ears tuned to this painful degree of precision. So long as a style effectively harmonizes with its environment we are content to let it stand: the Gothic grandeur of English can suffer without disfigurement the intrusion of the quaint. To sympathies so trained Murger's style in "Scènes de la Vie de Bohème" should make a particular appeal, since in that book, for the most part, he makes no attempt to ape the academician, but writes in the extravagant jargon of the very Bohemians he is describing—a language full of comic inversions, extravagances, and lapses from grammar, which are an essential part of the book's gaiety and charm. Though his matter is unmistakably Parisian, his humour is, in some respects, remarkably English, delighting in broad and bustling effects rather than subtle strokes and sudden flashes. As for the life and the characters that he depicts, criticism of them will be implicit in the remainder of this chapter; of the book as a whole no more need be said than that it has survived when all the rest of Murger's work has been forgotten. It is not a book to be placed unwarily in the hands of the young and tender; parts of it are exaggerated, parts may be wished away, but, when all has been said, it remains, not the picture of *la vie de Bohème* at its best and brightest, but the classic expression of the Bohemian spirit—a frank confession, not the pseudo-pathetic souvenir of a prosperous greybeard. Its pages are among those rare ones in the world's library that have caught and held for a moment the intangible freshness, the poetry, and the gaiety of youth. For this alone it deserves never to grow old.

Murger's Bohemia is described in a series of scenes taken from the life of four young men, a quartet as fascinating to read of as Dumas' Musketeers, though possibly less comfortable companions. They were Rodolphe, the sentimental poet; Marcel, the painter; Colline, the peripatetic philosopher and bookworm; and Schaunard, painter and musician, incomparable rogue whose masterpiece was a symphony "Sur l'influence du bleu dans la musique"—a sly hit at debased Romanticism. Chance brought them together. Schaunard, unable to pay his arrears of rent, was forced to leave his lodging with his furniture in pawn. A day's peregrination in search of a loan brought him three francs in cash, which he spent in dinner, together with the less tangible benefit of Colline's and Rodolphe's acquaintance. He swore brotherhood with Colline over a dish of stewed rabbit in a little eating-house, and the pair collected Rodolphe in the Café Momus, where, at Colline's expense, they passed the rest of a not too abstemious evening. Meanwhile Marcel, the painter, who had taken Schaunard's room unfurnished in advance, though having no furniture of his own but a second-hand scenic interior from the stock of a bankrupt theatre, had been persuaded to take the lodging furnished with Schaunard's furniture, and had duly moved in. Late in the evening, when a sharp shower of rain was falling, Schaunard, in bacchic absence of mind, offered asylum to his two new comrades. Hastily buying the elements of a supper, they gaily invaded the apartment of Marcel. Explanations were difficult, but were accomplished during supper, and next day Marcel and Schaunard agreed to live together. A dinner and a magnificent supper inaugurated the foundation of the new clan, which was united, so long as their Bohemian days continued, by an unbroken bond of friendship. It is these young men whom Murger's readers follow through their straits and shifts, their love affairs, their extravagances, their boisterous jokes, and their naïve pleasures—the poet, the artist, the savant, and the musician, characters drawn from Murger himself and his living friends, whose coats were ragged and whose pockets almost always empty, who were the bane of respectable *concierges* and proprietors of *cafés*, who bore short commons with cheerful bravado and succumbed to innocent gluttony in times of unexpected prosperity, who were really funny even if they were sometimes vulgar, whose expedients for catching the elusive *pièce de cent sous* were as amazing as their puns, who made life, even in a garret, a sentimental poem and a rollicking ballad, and who had the sense to become prosaic before the sentiment grew threadbare or the ballad grew stale. It is a great temptation to follow some of their adventures in greater detail from the day when Marcel went out to dine in the sugar-merchant's coat while Schaunard painted the latter's portrait in his own colour-stained dressing-gown, to the day when Rodolphe by composing a didactic poem at fifteen sous a dozen lines for a celebrated dentist, Marcel by painting the portraits of eighteen grenadiers at six francs a head, and Schaunard by playing the same scale all day and every day for a month to revenge a rich Englishman on an actress's parrot, earned enough to give their mistresses new dresses and take them for a holiday in the fields of Fontenay-aux-Roses. Yet the impulse to discursive commentary must be checked, for plucking flowers is a distraction from comparative botany.

Murger, after all, tells his own story infinitely better than any translator could do, and the purpose which is proper to the present book is to inquire what kind of a Bohemia appears in Murger's light-hearted pages.

So far as Bohemia was concerned, the generation of 1830 had entirely passed away by 1846, when Murger's sketches actually appeared, and the young men of whom Bohemia was composed were formed under less violent influences. The last flashes of Napoleon's glory had not illuminated their early days, they knew little of the stifling reign of Charles X, and the Revolution of 1830 took place when they had only a little while outgrown the nursery. By the time they grew up the complexion of affairs in Paris wore a more even tone. Assisted by Guizot, Louis Philippe had found the *juste-milieu* to his people's satisfaction, revolutionary tendencies had been checked or diverted into harmless channels of humanitarian reform, the *bourgeois* had firmly grasped his power and built up an already solid bulwark of commercial interest. In the artistic world, too, things were quieter. "Hernani," once a scandal, had become a classic, and there was no further need of red waistcoats and furious *claques*. Romanticism, indeed, had become so workaday that a successful little excitement was aroused by a reaction against it in what was called "l'école de bon sens," whose chief poet, Ponsard, gained quite a celebrity for a short time with his classic drama "Lucrèce." Beyond the gadfly of artistic impulse and the natural fermentation of the adolescent mind, there was little to rouse a young man's passions or send his blood coursing faster through his veins; there was no particular idol to worship, no hobby-horse to ride, as a Gautier or a Borel had worshipped Hugo and mounted the gallant steed called Middle Ages. The creed of Romanticism was so thoroughly established that there was nothing left to make any fuss about, with the natural consequence that its early extravagances had fallen out of fashion and there was no further need to be satanic or profess excessive sensibility. Literature was feeling its way to the austerer Romanticism of Flaubert and the Goncourts, as painting towards the "realism" of Courbet, but the growth was still below ground and the surface as yet seemed undisturbed. The generation of Rodolphe and Schaunard found, therefore, in Paris no eager band to whom they could ally themselves and to whose educative influence they could submit. Driven by their impulses towards the arts, with souls naturally romantic, as most young men's souls are, they found no cause which they could immediately embrace in the manner of the second *cénacle*. They missed that valuable education which is the idolization of a great man, and were confined instead to fighting their own battle, a very much less distinguished affair, which allowed many little dishonourable compromises with indolence and in which victory meant no more than individual success. This explains, to some extent, the absence of intellectual fecundity in Murger's heroes, which even their most devoted admirers cannot deny. Rodolphe's poems are indeed only pale imitations of Alfred de Musset, who was an almost inevitable model for any lyric youngster of the day; his more serious effort, a drama called "Le Vengeur," good enough to burn for warmth in a draughty garret, is not vouchsafed to us in quotation by Rodolphe's creator. Marcel was obviously not a very gifted painter, in spite of his famous *Passage de la Mer Rouge*, which was sent up in a different guise to each Salon and inevitably rejected, and when this great work was sold to become a shop-sign the artist's pride was not in the least revolted. Schaunard never gives any signs of musical inspiration till at the close he publishes a successful album of songs, and Colline, polyglot philosopher as he is dubbed, abandoned his career before anything tangible had been achieved to make an advantageous marriage and give musical evenings. It would, of course, be pedantic to insist upon these considerations in the case of a book of short stories which aims chiefly at amusing, but it is impossible not to be struck in reading the "Scènes de la Vie de Bohème" by the absence from the conversation of the characters of any indication of their artistic ideals. Save when Schaunard tells the sugar-merchant that he was a pupil of Horace Vernet, murmuring to himself, "Horreur, je renie mes dieux," and Marcel makes a scornful allusion to the "école de bon sens," the only proof that they are true artists lies in their creator's own assertion, of which he is not entirely mindful in the *dénouement*. The worst sinner of all is Colline, for this mine of knowledge, throughout the book, is made chiefly remarkable for the composition of dreadful puns. This may be partly due to that want of "a little more art and a little more poetry" of which Janin accused Murger, but the fault was not only personal. The second *cénacle* and the brotherhood of the Impasse du Doyenné were, without doubt, just as commonplace in their ordinary conversation, but what lifted them off the ground was the enthusiasm of a hotly waged artistic struggle, which by Murger's day had died down. His four heroes are Romantics in general, but in no sense champions of any cause.

Another unmistakable fact about Rodolphe and his friends is that they were inconspicuous. True, they made the Café Momus unbearable to its more peaceful customers, and were not unknown at the Chaumière, but the Café Momus was in a back street, and the Chaumière was certainly not the Bal de l'Opéra. They were miles away from the *viveurs* upon the boulevard, and their connexion with the prominent writers and artists of the day was extremely remote. They made no public appearance, they were not a force to be reckoned with. They kept up the form of defying convention, but it was now no more than a convenient form for the impecunious. Art and the *bourgeoisie* were beginning to play into one another's hands; the former had gained its liberty to a great degree, while the latter by the gilded pill of commercial success had purged artistic demonstration of its crudities. The time when eccentricity was a symbol had passed; now it was only a skin to be sloughed, as Marcel saw when in a very sensible lecture delivered to Rodolphe he said:

"Poetry does not exist only in a disordered life, in improvised happiness, in love affairs that only last as long as a candle, in more or less eccentric rebellions against the prejudices which will for ever be the sovereigns of the world: a dynasty is more easily overturned than a custom, even a ridiculous one. To have talent it is not sufficient to put on a summer overcoat in May; one can be a true poet or artist and yet keep one's feet warm and have one's three meals a day."

Their Bohemia, in fact, was a kind of undergraduate existence, in which all sorts of disorder and youthful folly might be excused on the plea that youth must be served, but which could in no sense be regarded as a part of civic life, much less as the best part, the most truly disinterested and artistic. This is a significant change of attitude from the days of *la Bohème galante*, which was one of the centres of Paris. That, indeed, was transitory and presupposed youth, but it was not obscure and its inhabitants had no misgivings. It was not they who gave it up as the writer of Ecclesiastes put away childish things, for they gloried in it all their days as the best part of their life; it was that the world claimed them for its business in spite of themselves. In their disinterested love of art they had made themselves valuable, and when the command went forth "Come and be paid" they were forced to go. To guard against any accusation of misunderstanding Murger, it may be admitted that he calls his heroes only a small section of Bohemia—they moved, to use his phrase, in the *troisièmes dessous* of literature and art—but there is no indication that Murger conceived a Bohemia which had its part in any higher sphere. When Rodolphe gets a lucky present of five hundred francs the determination he avows is not to suffuse his little corner of Bohemia with a more worthy splendour, but to become, like every other successful man, a *bourgeois*. "These are my projects," he cries to an astonished Marcel. "Sheltered from the material embarrassments of life, I am going to work seriously; I shall finish my great work, and gain a settled place in public opinion. To begin with, I renounce Bohemia, I shall dress like everybody else, I shall have a black coat, and I shall frequent drawing-rooms." Such a speech would have fallen like a thunderbolt in Camille Rogier's Pompadour *salon*, and its author considered charitably to be in the first stages of lunacy. Marcel, however, falls in at once with the ambitious scheme, and they are only saved by their Bohemianism being stronger than their resolution. Both in the stories and the preface to the "Scènes de la Vie de Bohème"—where Murger speaks with a picturesque seriousness—there is no sign of that former joy in Bohemian life as the life which was alone worth living by poets and artists. Throughout he regards it as a necessity conditioned by the artistic impulse combined with poverty, to be borne with the courage and gaiety of youth, to be regretted "perhaps" from the vantage-point of subsequent prosperity. The true Bohemia—as distinct from the Bohemia of mere idealists, incapables, and amateurs—he regards as a narrow, stony path leading up the sides of an arduous mountain, beset by the chasms of doubt and misery, but making for a possible goal, the goal of a sufficient income. Divested of all its *agréments*—resourcefulness, humour, courage, extravagance, which are properly attributes of youth, the real illuminant—Murger's Bohemia is laid bare as a merely economic state. The true Bohemians, he says, are known upon the literary and artistic market-place, where their wares are saleable, but at moderate prices; "their existence each day is a work of genius"—"preceded by a pack of ruses, poaching in all the industries connected with the arts, they hunt from morn till eve that ferocious animal which is called the five-franc piece." To Murger, who wrote of what he knew, the man who had the means to live a stable existence, howsoever retired, was a fool if he remained in Bohemia: to the inhabitants of *la Bohème galante* it was the not being entirely destitute which made their life peculiarly worth living. If Colline ever speculated with any profundity he may have seen that his friends and he lived really in a prison of which poverty, prodigality, and idleness were warders. The Bohemia of Gautier, Gérard de Nerval, and Houssaye had all the glory of a voluntary protest, a passionate assertion of liberty, a revivifying of life in accordance with new artistic ideas.

The difference is not simply one of degree. The brotherhood of the Impasse du Doyenné were less destitute and more talented than Rodolphe and his friends, but that is not a point that at this moment requires stress. The important fact is that in a few years Bohemia had undergone a great change; that, whereas a few years after 1830 young men with a little money and some talent deliberately chose to make their life more picturesque than that of ordinary citizens and to escape from the suffocating atmosphere of commerce and officialdom, a few years after 1840 the ideal of struggling artists was to become as soon as possible successful merchants and to escape from the possibility of that picturesqueness which they welcomed as an alleviation of a state of transitory discomfort. It would be quite beside the mark to regard Bohemia as guilty in this of self-degradation; so far, indeed, as the change was conscious, the majority of mankind must logically find it praiseworthy, for all human effort is judged by its tendency to well-being. The change, however, was none of Bohemia's doing, but was due mainly to the fact that art was beginning, in the modern sense, to pay. The beginnings were small, but they were quite evident, especially in the increased profits from journalism and illustration. The old Bohemia of the golden age rested on the supposition that the artist worked primarily to please himself, and that money, source of enjoyment as it was, remained a secondary consideration. The supposition, in the first forward rush of commercial prosperity, was bound to become untenable. Writers and artists of obvious talent were too valuable commercial assets to be left to their careless selves; they had to be tempted into the cage—an easy task, for, if money be regarded as a means of more enjoyment, why should a Bohemian resist it? It was unimportant if individuals held out, or were too uncompromising to suit the market; the fact remained that there *was* a market and a list of quotations, and this fact was the disruption of Bohemia. Whereas it had been a true fraternity in which art was all-important and individual celebrity a thing of so little moment that there was complete equality of intercourse, it now included the last two sections of a trisected world of artists—the well-paid, the ill-paid, and the not paid at all—and where money intervenes all equality ceases. The majority of the well-paid were kept too busy even to see they had lost the old freedom; they were tempted to live as other people in decent rooms and decent coats, and as their vanity kept them from complaining, the ill-paid and the not paid at all naturally envied their state, striving and jostling for an equally happy captivity, or at least intending to do so as soon as their irrepressible blood took a staider course through their veins. The charm of Murger's merry crew is that their blood was too strong for their business instincts; the Bohemian spirit snatched them along in spite of Mammon, for Mammon, incomplete as his hold has always been over youth, was in those days but just learning his strength. Where youth and art combine the Bohemian spirit is always there; only the possibilities of Bohemia have in the course of time been crowded out. But in Murger's Paris Bohemia, shorn of earthly glory as it was, without lot in the brilliance of the boulevard, cut off from the more thriving traders in the artistic market-place, was still a possibility because the Bohemian tradition was still fairly strong, and because Paris was still a small city, its life little disturbed by a floating population of aliens and its interests completely self-centred.

The Bohemia described by Murger certainly corresponded in one respect with the general conception of Bohemianism to-day in that it was devoid of any material splendour. Neither Rodolphe nor Marcel indicates any desire for the old furniture, damasks, and other decorations which so glittered in the eyes of the early Romantics, but at any rate such things would have been beyond the capacity of their purses. They were unequivocally poor. When Rodolphe was in funds he could afford a hundred francs a year for a garret in the Rue de la Tour d'Auvergne; when Providence was less kind he lived "in the Avenue de Saint-Cloud, on the fifth branch of the third tree on the left as you leave the Bois de Boulogne." As for entertainments, they came a long way behind the costume ball of the Impasse du Doyenné. At Rodolphe's Wednesdays in the Rue de la Tour d'Auvergne, it was said, one could only sit down morally and was forced to drink badly filtered water in eclectic earthenware. Even the grand *soirée* given by Rodolphe and Marcel, which began with a literary and musical entertainment and ended with a dance prolonged till sunrise, only cost the hosts fifteen francs—miraculously acquired at the last moment—in addition to a set of chairs which fed the stove from midnight onwards, though, as these belonged to a neighbour, they were probably not paid for. Their wardrobes were not conspicuous for any particularly Romantic or medieval effect, but simply, except in times of exceptional windfalls, for extreme dilapidation. Schaunard's chief garment was an overcoat worn to a state of utter baldness; Colline's ulster, crammed with books and papers, had the surface of a file; Marcel's coat was called "Mathusalem," but he must have acquired it subsequent to the sugar-merchant's momentous visit, for at that time, after an hour's search to discover a costume fit to dine out in, the net results were a pair of plaid trousers, a grey hat, a red tie, a (once) white glove and a black glove. To dine sufficiently at a small restaurant was for them no ordinary luxury, and as for entering the *Rocher de Caucale*, they might as well have aspired to membership of the Jockey Club. Why, Schaunard had never seen a lobster till the old Jew gave them all a feast after buying Marcel's *Passage de la Mer Rouge*. Some days they dispensed with dining altogether, on others the staple dish was pickled herrings; so it is hardly surprising that on the proceeds of Marcel's picture they remained at table for five days, the room filled with a Pantagruelic atmosphere and a whole bed of oyster-shells covering the floor. It was not that they took up any quixotic attitude of art for art's sake, like the society called *Les Buveurs d'Eau*, whom Murger describes in one of his stories and whose principle was not to make the slightest concession to necessity. They were imperfect journeymen, indolent, careless, too easily distracted, but they were among those who were ill-paid rather than those who never tried to be paid. Rodolphe edited a small fashion paper, *L'Écharpe d'Iris*; Marcel painted ruined manors for a Jew dealer and portraits of the lowliest possessor of a few spare francs; Colline gave lessons in the same range of subjects as Pico di Mirandola professed to discuss; and Schaunard, besides exhibiting a special ability as a borrower, put music to bad poetry for hard-hearted music-publishers.

In comparing this Bohemia with that of Gautier and Gérard de Nerval, it is easy to see the justification of Lepelletier's epithet "carottière." The graceful adjuncts and by no means contemptible achievements of a former day had vanished as completely as its enthusiasms. The presence of Roger de Beauvoir and Nestor Roqueplan in the Rue de la Tour d'Auvergne is as difficult to imagine as the composition of "Mademoiselle de Maupin." Yet Rodolphe and his friends were at least as well off in one respect, that is, in their affairs of the heart, if, indeed, they had not some advantage. The divinities of the Impasse du Doyenné, Cydalise excepted, seem to have had their home in the *corps de ballet*, a body not notable for the tenderness or constancy of their attachments. Murger, who, like his Rodolphe, was an amorous sentimentalist, gave some poetic value, if not as much as he intended, to the figures of Mimi and Musette, the idols of Rodolphe and Marcel, who play such a prominent part in the "Scènes de la Vie de Bohème," that it would be an affectation not to speak of them, although an Englishman must always do so with some reserve. In spite of all that may be said against them—indeed, *is* said by their very creator—there is a charm about Mimi and Musette which must always hold the reader of these stories, a charm which includes Francine, who died holding the muff bought for her by her lover, and the vulgar Phémie Teinturière, who shared the lot of a no more refined Schaunard. Without sympathizing, at least temporarily, with all the blend of mystery and frankness which a Frenchman breathes into the word "amour," it is useless to read French literature. To him love is the highest emotional value—emotion being in its turn the highest value in life—so that a union, whether it be celebrated in the Madeleine or in the *mairie* of the notorious thirteenth *arrondissement*, is equally sacred and equally interesting. We in England look at love differently and, as we naturally think, better, but we are not hindered, nevertheless, from abandoning our view occasionally. We do so implicitly when we shed tears over "La Dame aux Camélias," over "Madame Butterfly," and over Mimi herself in Puccini's "La Bohème." To be honest, then, we must accept Murger's view, if we enjoy his book, as there is very little doubt that we do. We applaud Musette when she surreptitiously waters the flowers whose duration is to measure that of her love for Marcel; we forgive her fickleness because she follows her fancy without calculation, even though on leaving the rich young nobleman to visit Marcel she takes six days on the road; we warm to Mimi because Rodolphe really loved her and she him, though his jealousy and her love of luxury made their days a burden and their rupture certain; and if we join heartily in Marcel's ironical tirade against Mimi the fine lady, we cannot restrain our sadness at Mimi returning to her old love to die. The life of the Impasse du Doyenné was so joyous, strong, and full that its *amours passagers* can be taken for granted, happy fantasies without regrets; but Murger's Bohemia, with its frequent moments of despondency and hardship, was forced to rely upon its heart to supply that relieving colour which its surroundings could not give. Mimi and Musette, Phémie and Francine, even the little *giletière* who corrected Colline's proofs and never appeared, meant so much more than Lorry or Victorine. So long as their attachment lasted they made a home out of the barest garret, doing for their men those thousand little things which men are too lazy or preoccupied to do for themselves. Besides, they opened a field for the exercise of unselfishness—a valuable service in itself. In this connexion I need only cite one delightful little story, to which I have already referred, entitled "La Toilette des Grâces," an idyll which no afterthought can spoil. It tells how Rodolphe, Marcel, and Schaunard, having earned a little money by making their respective arts serve the humblest of commercial purposes, decided to surprise their mistresses by giving them new dresses. One fine morning Mimi, Musette, and Phémie were awakened by the entry of a procession headed by Schaunard, in a new coat of golden nankeen, playing a horn, and close behind him a shopman bringing samples. They nearly went mad with joy. Mimi jumped like a young kid, waving a pretty scarf; Musette, with each hand in a little green boot, threw her arms round Marcel's neck and clapped the boots like cymbals; as for Phémie, she could only sob "Ah, mon Alexandre, mon Alexandre!" The choice was made, the bills discharged, and it was announced to the dames that they must have their new dresses ready for a day in the country on the morrow. That was a trifle; for sixteen hours they cut and stitched, and when next day the Angelus sounded from the neighbouring church they were already taking their last look into the looking-glass. Only Phémie had a little sorrow. "I like the green grass and the little birds," she said, "but one meets nobody in the country. Suppose we made our excursion on the boulevard." But they went to Fontenay-aux-Roses instead, and when they returned late at night there were only six francs left. "What shall we do with it?" asked Marcel. "Invest it in the funds," said Schaunard.

There are, doubtless, artistic *coteries* to-day in whose existence parallels may be found to the "Scènes de la Vie de Bohème," but reproduction is impossible, for Murger's Bohemia, no less than *la Bohème galante*, was conditioned by its time. The conditions include a Paris of provincial narrowness, greater simplicity together with less conspicuous uniformity in ordinary life, less elaborate amusements, no Montmartre *cafés*, no swamping proletariat beside whose *mœurs d'Apaches* the eccentricities of Bohemia seem mild and unimportant, a tiny fraction of the present opportunities for advertisement and publicity, and a lower standard, perhaps, of general education. To these one other condition may be added—the existence of Musette and Mimi, who were the last of the *grisettes*. Murger himself, in a passage which I cannot do better than quote in the original, points out clearly their transitoriness:

"Ces jolies filles moitié abeilles, moitié cigales, qui travaillaient en chantant toute la semaine, ne demandaient à Dieu qu'un peu de soleil le dimanche, faisaient vulgairement l'amour avec le cœur, et se jetaient quelquefois par la fenêtre. Race disparue maintenant, grâce à la génération actuelle des jeunes gens: génération corrompue et corruptrice, mais par-dessus tout vaniteuse, sotte et brutale. Pour le plaisir de faire de méchants paradoxes, ils ont raillé ces pauvres filles à propos de leurs mains mutilées par les saintes cicatrices du travail, et elles n'ont bientôt plus gagné assez pour s'acheter de la pâte d'amandes. Peu à peu ils sont parvenus à leur inoculer leur vanité et leur sottise, et c'est alors que la grisette a disparu. C'est alors que naquit la lorette."

A Grisette

The *grisette* made love for love: like a wild rose, she had to be plucked, and when men came to prefer buying bouquets in shops, she naturally died away. Money already tainted Bohemia, even here, in its heart. The opportunity of luxury tempted both Mimi and Musette to be unfaithful, but since caprice was ever stronger with them than self-interest they were not undeserving to be called the last of the *grisettes*. They were necessary adjuncts to Bohemia, and satisfactory adjuncts, in spite of their caprices, for the last thing which Bohemian man required was the Bohemian or—to use an obsolete phrase— the "emancipated" woman. Too ignorant to meet their lovers, even had they wished, upon their own ground, they held their place by keeping to their natural advantage, the woman's desire to please. So they passed through life, making the feast more festive and the fast less desolate, filling a void and mending a sorrow as light-heartedly as they darned a sock or patched a ragged coat. Mimi and Musette were the true counterparts of Rodolphe and Marcel, and it is with regret that we see them disappear into an epilogue of prosperity and propriety. Yet it was all they could do, for what I have called the Bohemia of common mortality became dangerous long before the age of thirty years. Rodolphe could not have written in middle age to Marcel as Bouchardy did to Théophile Gautier; only hypocritically could he have said "nous étions ivres du beau." Murger escapes any false effect of that kind in his conclusion:

"'We are done for, old fellow,' says Marcel, 'we are dead and buried. Youth only comes once! Where are you dining to-night?'

"'If you like,' answered Rodolphe, 'we will go and dine for twelve sous at our old restaurant in the Rue du Four, where the plates are of village earthenware, and where we were always so hungry when we had finished eating.'

"'Good heavens, no. I don't mind looking back at the past, but it shall be across a bottle of decent wine and seated in a good arm-chair. It is no use, I'm corrupted. I only care now for what is good!'"

X

MURGER AND HIS FRIENDS

Si on excepte quelques natures fortement trempées qui se tirèrent des impasses de la Bohème, le reste fut condamné à vivre difficilement en face d'un idéal borné et sans avenir. Ni études, ni loisirs, ni aisances ne permettaient à ces aspirants à l'art de s'élever et de conquérir un nom.

CHAMPFLEURY:
"Souvenirs et Portraits de Jeunesse"

IN order to catch at a glance the result of a lapse of years I lingered in the last chapter over Rodolphe, Mimi, and their friends, figures drawn from the moving scene of contemporary life, yet snatched from the changes of time as permanently as those on Keats's Grecian urn. The "Scènes de la Vie de Bohème" show, as it seems to me, more clearly than any other kind of record, the decadence of Bohemia, regarding the degree of its approach to an ideal of complete artistic existence, since the great days that followed 1830. This might, indeed, be a warrant for not returning to more documentary facts at all, but there are always those to be considered who view Fiction as a sprite so far divorced from actuality that they are unable to place any trust in her indications. The teller of stories, in their apprehension, is always on the look-out for a good effect, to which end he will minimize the essential and magnify the unessential, distorting sober fact at the call of his individual imagination. They are the people who read novels, as they say, for relaxation, while finding wisdom alone in biographies and memoirs bristling with dates and packed with quotations. The question, "What, after all, is sober fact?" is sufficient to put them into confusion, but to propound that ancient problem would be here beside the mark, for in a book that honestly professes to be as sober in fact as any it would be unbecoming unduly to press the point on behalf of fiction. The warrant, therefore, will be allowed to pass, and we return to those tales which men have told about themselves and their friends under the names which they bore at baptism, duly signed and dated. Such information as they give concerning the later years of Bohemia is, at best, fragmentary, but the fragments have some appearance of falling together in the light of Murger's picture. A more diligent research might have produced a more detailed record, but it may be questioned whether the total effect would have been any clearer. There were scores of obscure persons in Bohemia, but their daily uprising and lying-down were not so very widely different. At least this may be asserted, that after a certain number of facts it is safer to use the imagination for the rest.

Murger and his friends were the legitimate successors of *la Bohème galante*, and in view of their fictitious counterparts already introduced the main interest of this chapter lies with them. Yet before they appear there are some byways of Bohemia that call for inspection as an illustration and a contrast. Bohemia was, of course, always bordered on one side by the student life of the Quartier Latin, the freedom and licence of which were both different and older in origin, going back to the days of the schoolmen, when indigent scholars of all nations filled the great university cities of Europe, forming in each a picturesque but turbulent community. Even in most prosaic days the students of Paris have kept up the medieval tradition, but particular manifestations would naturally be influenced by the manners of the day. It is, therefore, not surprising that the student quarter was profoundly affected by the Romantic movement, and reflected its battles and its extravagances with a hilarious distortion. The motley world of the Quartier Latin and those who, though no longer students, remained attached to it had their "local colour," their Gothic enthusiasms, and their orgies. They had dining clubs with fantastic names, such as "Les 45 jolis cochons," which indulged in something very like bump-suppers, with loud singing in the streets, window-breaking, and practical joking to follow. The campaign of "Hernani" was imitated in the Salle Chanteraine—a theatre for amateurs—where there was nightly a *fracas* with fisticuffs between the various factions. Elaborate farces were organized to mystify the good people of Paris, of which Maxime du Camp gives a good example in his "Souvenirs Littéraires." It was called "La grande chevauchée de la côtelette aux cornichons." Thirty young men, dressed in velvet waistcoats and nankeen jackets, with long hair and beards, headed by a certain young teacher of history waving a stick, marched solemnly in serried single file with a halting step, dangling their arms at the same time, from the Place Pigalle over the Pont Royal, crying in unison, "Une deux, une deux, le choléra, le choléra!" At the end of the Pont Royal they turned round in a body and shouted, "Connaissez-vous le thermomètre de l'ingénieur Chevalier?" Solemnly facing about again, they proceeded as before to Sainte-Mandé, where they lunched off pork cutlets.

The special home of the wildest jokers and most desperate caricatures of the new spirit was a certain tumble-down barrack, No. 9 Rue Childebert, a street on the south side of that beautiful old church Saint-Germain-des-Prés, and now merged in the Boulevard Saint-Germain. This house, familiarly called "La Childebert," was five or six stories high and thoroughly decayed, for its owner, a Madame Legendre, refused to carry out any repairs. She was justified in this attitude to some extent by the fact that few of her tenants paid any rent. Indeed, according to one witness, no man in his senses would have paid any rent for a room upon the top floor from 1837 onwards. One student, however, an ingenious fellow called Lepierre, who both lived on the top floor and paid his rent, succeeded in forcing the stingy lady to repair the roof.

Having been drenched one night during a hard storm, he took his revenge by removing a portion of his flooring, and hiring all the peripatetic water-carriers that could be found to pour water down the hole. The *concierge* remonstrated, but in vain, and Madame Legendre was sent for in hot haste. When she arrived in a cab she was gaily serenaded by the inhabitants, and on proceeding to the flooded room she was horrified to find Lepierre in the costume of Adam before the Fall, who claimed a right, he said, to have a bath at his *own* convenience. Madame Legendre fled, but the roof was repaired. The gay desperadoes of La Childebert were capable of carrying through any *charge*, howsoever lurid. One of the most successful was known as "le nez de Bouginier." Bouginier was an artist, the size of whose nose inspired his friend Fourreau with the idea of an exaggerated caricature in which this feature was made enormous. A stencil was cut and copied, and for many days Bouginier's nose appeared on all the walls in Paris. It is even alleged that two parties of students, about to travel in the East and wishing to meet on the voyage, hit on the simple plan of following Bouginier's nose. The party starting first took a stencil with them, so that the second party, leaving a fortnight later, were able to track them to Marseilles, Malta, Alexandria, and Suez. In a certain medallion in the Passage du Caire, just south of the Boulevard Bonne Nouvelle, Bouginier's nose is still immortalized. La Childebert was always "up to" something, but a certain fancy-dress *conversazione* completely convulsed the neighbourhood. The schools of art and poetry dressed according to their views, and by universal consent the Romantics, for all they could do in pourpoints, doublets, and general local colour, were easily beaten by the Classicists. Romulus and Remus with their wolf and Hercules with the Nemean lion created a *furore*; so great was the real consternation of the district at the apparition of these wild beasts that the commissary of police had to intervene. The wolf and the lion suffered themselves to be led with great docility to his office, where they turned out to be a great Dane and a mastiff respectively, painted and padded with diabolical cleverness.

La Childebert was strongly represented in a revellers' club called "Les Badouillards," that flourished between 1835 and 1838. In "Paris Anecdote" Privat d'Anglemont, who is the chief authority on the Childebertian doings, describes the qualifications of a perfect Badouillard. He had to pass a regular test before entering the bacchic brotherhood; he had to be strong and agile, a clever and ready boxer, fencer, and wrestler, he must have proved his courage in several encounters, shown a fine taste in choreographic fantasy at the Chaumière and an ability to engage in a duel of slang with any chance person, and have sworn eternal feud against the sleep and peace of mind of all *bourgeois*. The initiation was a solemn and trying ceremony. It began with a copious dinner, followed by a ceaseless absorption of various liquors till the time came for going to the ball. Here the candidate stayed all night, behaving as outrageously as possible. He then adjourned without sleep to breakfast, and passed the rest of the day in the *cafés* of the Quartier Latin, drinking, playing billiards, and flirting. At night the programme was repeated, and if by the third night he had accepted every challenge, never fallen asleep, nor tumbled under any table, he was allowed to seek his bed a perfect Badouillard.

For all its light-hearted absurdities La Childebert was not Bohemia, for its existence belonged rather to that of irresponsible students than of artists. I only mention it by way of contrast, as I now mention again Privat d'Anglemont, the author of "Paris Inconnu" and "Paris Anecdote," legendary as a Bohemian, but of a very different type. These two curious and valuable books are a complete study of the seamy side of Paris during the latter part of Louis Philippe's reign. The life of the porters in the Halles, the *chiffonniers*, and all the pliers of obscure trades, with their customs, their dwellings, and their manners, is most faithfully reproduced in them in a manner which could only have been made possible by a complete identification of the author with the subjects of his observation. Such, in fact, was the lifework of Privat d'Anglemont, a Creole born in Guadeloupe. He became the legendary *noctambule* of Paris, realizing, as Charles Monselet says in his preface to "Paris Anecdote," the popular idea of a Bohemian—that is, simply an eccentric vagabond. In the sense of the word as used in this book, he was not a Bohemian at all, for, though he wrote articles and books upon his experiences, he was in no sense an artist, nor was he striving to make his life conformable to artistic liberty. He was animated simply by a gipsy passion for roaming, combined with a taste for mystery and romancing. Faithful as his books were, he hardly ever *spoke* the truth: twenty times he told Théodore de Banville the history of his life, and each time it was different. Still, he merits a word here on account of his reputation as the complete Bohemian, a reputation increased by his being an easy peg on which to hang any fantastic story that came into a journalist's brain. Théodore de Banville, who first met him in 1841 and, according to Monselet, idealized him absurdly, gives some curious recollections of him in "Mes Souvenirs." He was a handsome man, dark, tall, and slender, rather resembling the elder Dumas. He passed most of his life wandering about the low quarters of Paris in complete poverty, often begging a meal from one of the *cabaretiers* of the Halles, who all loved him. Yet, de Banville avers, he was not really unprovided for, since at irregular intervals a relative used to send him about £200 from America in gold pieces. But Privat d'Anglemont preferred to live without money, so that he never hesitated in getting rid of this burden as soon as possible by standing a dinner to all the poor and hungry women he could find in the tiny inn called the "Bœuf Enragé," at the bottom of the Rue de la Harpe. Like Gérard de Nerval, he would set out on a voyage at a moment's notice and without a moment's preparation, and such was his charm that he had affectionate friends in the lower quarters of many a French town. Once during his nightly wanderings he was stopped by some robbers. "But I'm Privat," he said, roaring with laughter. At which the robbers joined in the laugh, and invited him to supper. By a ruined hut they sat down to drink the best champagne in the light of the stars, to smoke, and to tell stories. Privat delighted his hosts, who invited him to meet them again; but he shook his head, saying, "N'engageons pas l'avenir."

Privat d'Anglemont, who eventually died of consumption, did little more than carry on the traditions of the "noctambules," less mischievously than their founder, Rétif de la Bretonne, less modestly and artistically than Gérard de Nerval, but so much more seriously than either of his predecessors that he left little scope for a new departure to his own successor, Alfred Delvau. He was not, in the truest sense, a Bohemian, though he led an existence ever bordering on the confines of Bohemia. The same may be said, in a more transitory sense, of Flaubert, the great renovator and refiner of Romanticism. Most of his life was spent in the country, but there was a short period when he came to study law in Paris, which, if it were not mentioned, might justify a challenge from readers familiar with "L'Education Sentimentale" or Maxime du Camp's "Souvenirs Littéraires." So far as the first of these books is concerned, little time need here be spent in finding relevant points of comparison. The last thing which Flaubert desired to portray in that depressing picture was an existence in any sense artistic. His hero is a provincial youth who, during his student days in Paris, drifts aimlessly and indolently through a variety of second-rate experiences in company with second-rate friends. Flaubert's own experiences are, no doubt, frequently worked into the material, but "L'Education Sentimentale" is nothing so cheap as autobiography served in a thin sauce of fiction. It is a novel in which the author has with the highest exercise of penetrative imagination treated what Mr. Henry James would call the "germ"—the dreary wastefulness, that is, of such a life in case of such a young man as Frédéric Moreau, who with Madame Bovary is Flaubert's contribution to the pathology of *le mal romantique*. Flaubert himself, with all his excitability and extravagance, was of a much stronger stamp; the strength of his artistic conviction saved him from all such flabbiness. He came to Paris to study law, but, having failed to pass his examination, returned to his home in 1843. If he had stayed he might easily have become one of the leading figures, certainly a powerful influence, in that Bohemia which Murger knew. Maxime du Camp, who made his acquaintance early in 1843, shows him as a young man living always at a high pitch with the flamboyant vitality that would have done no dishonour to the Impasse du Doyenné, so far was he from being the victim of Frédéric's weak-kneed desolation. He passed his days in an alternation of prodigality and poverty, spending fifty francs on his dinner one day and feeding on a crust and a slab of chocolate the next. He lived in a kind of intellectual tornado, both frantic and noisy. He went into ecstasies over mediocre works in which he perceived beauties hidden from the rest of the world, but which he loved to point out stridently to his friends, intoning the prose, roaring the verse at the top of his voice, repeating incessantly any word which took his passionate fancy, and filling all the neighbourhood with his din. He would wake up a friend without compunction at three in the morning to show him a moonlight effect on the Seine; one moment he would be inventing sauces to make brill appetizing, and the next he would be plotting to smack Gustave Planche's face for having spoken slightingly of Victor Hugo. The *cénacle* composed of Louis de Cormenin, Le Poitevin, Du Camp, and himself often dined at Dagneaux's, one of the better restaurants of the Quartier Latin, and stayed talking ceaselessly till the doors were closed. Their ambitions were as wild as their conversation; Flaubert and Du Camp seriously determined to learn everything between the ages of twenty-one and thirty, to produce great works till forty, and then to retire into the country. Except for the fact that, according to his friend, Flaubert disdained the women whom his beauty attracted, this was a promising beginning for Bohemia. As the world knows, fate decreed otherwise, and he retired to develop in that close intellectual atmosphere with Louis Bouilhet and Du Camp, of which the latter says: "Living as we did, in solitude, we exchanged only the same set of ideas apart from all criticism, so that things in general lost their right proportion in our minds."

Flaubert's life in the Rue de l'Est was, at best, only a tentative pathway in Bohemia, like one of those tracks in a suburb that give hope of leading somewhere, but change their mind *en route*. It is too small a digression to be distracting, and I entered upon it, among other reasons, because its little adventure coincides in date with those movements in the central market-place yet to be touched on. One more alley, however, must be taken on the way, for it is, indeed, only just off the market-place. The name upon its wall is that of Charles Baudelaire, a well-known figure whose exact relation to Bohemia is, nevertheless, not so easy to determine. He began very much in the manner of Flaubert, coming as a student to the Quartier Latin and residing at a not very strictly kept *pension* near the Panthéon between 1839 and 1841, his eighteenth and his twentieth years. I need not repeat the distinction made between student life—*das Burschenleben*—and out-and-out Bohemianism. Baudelaire filled his days to their fullest extent, mixing together indiscriminately the enjoyments of student, dandy, and *viveur*, so far as his means allowed. It was only at the end of this time that his determination to take up literature scandalized his stepfather and caused his enforced sea voyage. When he returned in 1842 he had come of age and possessed a capital of 75,000 francs. He set about spending this money with a gusto and in a manner not unworthy of the golden age of Bohemia. He had various lodgings till he settled for two years in a beautiful apartment in the old Hôtel Pimodan on the Île St.-Louis, where his comrade was the painter Boissard, a good artist who, as Gautier said, exhausted himself in enthusiasms, and in whose wonderful Louis XIV salon the society of *hachischiens* met. Had Baudelaire been a true Bohemian at heart he might have instituted a second *Bohème galante*, but he was wanting in that simplicity and goodfellowship which are signal qualities in the Bohemian character. He wished to make his life, like his art, a study in exquisite intensity, so that in the days of his splendour his mode of living was rather that of a "dandy" than anything else. He dressed with immense care, but in a bygone fashion; he pursued every kind of sensation, frequented every kind of society, and became the leader of a set who carefully cultivated eccentricity for its own sake, an eccentricity too *posé* to serve as a type of Bohemian manners. To make himself a subject of astonishment was his chief amusement, to which end his devices—such as entering a restaurant with a friend and feigning to begin a story with the loud exordium: "After I had murdered my poor father——"—were innumerable. So much may be said with a certain pity or amusement, but it must also be admitted that a certain refinement, both social and intellectual, kept him from associating himself entirely with the not over-discriminating Bohemia of his generation. It is all the more fair to say this because after 1844, when his stepfather got a guardian appointed to take charge of his remaining capital and he was reduced to eking out a reduced income by journalism, with all its attendant disappointments and hardships, he chose with some discrimination the extent to which he would throw in his lot with the Bohemian life for which he had by that time every qualification. He became a friend of Murger and many other complete Bohemians, and there is a story of his asking the original of Schaunard to dine and giving him a piece of Brie cheese and two bottles of claret, asking him to imagine that he was enjoying the dessert after a good dinner. Yet his real intimates were a band of young men, Théodore de Banville, Charles Monselet, Villiers de l'Isle Adam, and Leconte de l'Isle, who chose to maintain a certain amount of order in the midst of eccentricity and found boisterous joviality less to their taste than the more delicate affectations of wit. Here again I hold no brief for the complete Bohemians. They had their compensating virtues, but it is hardly doubtful that Baudelaire and his friends were the better educated and the more truly artistic set of the two. This, perhaps, was the greatest tragedy of Bohemia's decline, that its spiritual distinction faded with its material well-being. At any rate, for a combination of reasons, laudable and the reverse, Baudelaire's set was not Bohemia, and if, as I leave them, I may insist particularly on one of the less laudable reasons, it is that pose, which is another form of convention, must by the very conception of Bohemia be excluded from its characteristics. Nadar hits the difference when, in his curious little book on Baudelaire, which is written in an idiom describable as a French version of that elliptical quaintness associated with our own *Pink 'Un*, he writes: "Avec ces épileptiques, combien loin du sans façon tout bonhomme, de la simplesse à la bonne franquette de mon autre bande de Bohème, 'la bande de Murger' et de notre 'Société des buveurs d'eau.' ..."

We return, then, to the author of "Scènes de la Vie de Bohème" at the end of a rather circuitous route. In speaking of the Bohemia which he immortalized I have called it, in distinction from certain modifications or superficial resemblances, the central market-place, but no more need be sought in that phrase than an effort to represent it by a handy image as exhibiting the main civic qualities and manners implied in the generic name. Compared with earlier days, a far less proud and bustling burgherdom trod its rather muddy paving-stones, for it had suffered as some agricultural centre when railways were beginning. Yet any pride of succession which they may have had was legitimately theirs, for, if they were less materially and intellectually endowed, if the peculiarly happy circumstances of their civic foundation had passed to make their ultimate disruption certain under the changed conditions of all that is included in social development, they still preserved the Bohemian character, with its simplicity, gaiety, humour, and courage. To labour the point further is unnecessary, for if it is not already clear, the fault is too remote to be here corrected. In the "Scènes de la Vie de Bohème" all the daily comedy and tragedy of this Bohemia of common mortality finds expression: the life there described so intimately and humorously stands or falls by its artistic truth, to which no amount of possible documentary corroboration adds an iota. Nevertheless, the professed concession to a desire for ascertainable "facts" with which this chapter opened must be made, at the risk of seeming to expose the vanity of the researcher as the real object of indulgence. Since, in the garrulous world of to-day, nobody can make the least incursion into the public eye, much less produce a successful book or picture, without the appearance of a crop of "personal notes," so Murger's picture may be taken for granted, and what follows may appear in the light of "personal notes," claiming no more connexion than a general relation to the picture.

Murger[28] was no son of a landed proprietor nor even sprung from a middle-class family, as most Bohemians naturally were, for the whole life of Bohemia presupposes a more or less literary education seldom vouchsafed to the children of lower social order. His father was a German tailor in the Rue des Trois Frères, who wished, not without reason, that his son should succeed him in his trade. Murger's early education was therefore confined to the rudiments, and his deficiencies in that respect were a burden upon him all his life. The career of a tailor, for all that, aroused his utmost aversion; through his two friends, Emile and Pierre Bisson, who became clerks, he acquired a violent taste for poetry, with the composition of which he judged the shears incompatible. His father took the rebellion hardly, but got him a place, since he liked pens and paper so much, as errand-boy to an *avoué*, an occupation in which he continued to cultivate his poetic inclinations. When seventeen years old, in 1839, through the interest of M. de Jouy, a critic and member of the Academy, he was appointed secretary to a Russian diplomat, M. de Tolstoi. His salary was only 40 francs a month, out of which he had to pay a small *pension* to his father for board and lodging; still, he was happy. His duties were very light, and his employer, who also had a literary turn, took a certain amount of interest in him and gave him occasional presents of money. During the next two years he made the acquaintance of that group of friends on which he drew for his stories of Bohemia, and experienced two love affairs. The first object of his affections was "la cousine Angèle," the heroine of a chapter in "Scènes de la Vie de Bohème," in which Rodolphe in his draughty garret, by dint of burning his great tragedy in the stove, warms himself sufficiently to write the commemorative poem for the tombstone of a defunct *bourgeois*, buying with the proceeds a bunch of white violets for his disdainful cousin. The second was a certain Marie, who eventually ran away with one of his friends—a tragedy which he relates in "Scènes de la Vie de Jeunesse." By this time he had become a thoroughly developed Bohemian, intolerant of all restraint. He left his father's home, and even for a time gave up his post with M. de Tolstoi.

It was then that Henry Murger's Bohemia was definitely formed, a society described by one of them as "ce demi-quarteron de poètes à l'outrance, mais absolument inédits, réunis dans un tas, sans vestes ni semelles, ne doutant de rien, ni de leur lendemain, ni de leur génie, ni du génie de leur voisin, ni de l'éditeur à venir, ni du succès, ni des belles dames, ni de la fortune—de rien, si ce n'est de leur dîner du soir, trop convaincus, d'ailleurs, quant à la question de leur déjeuner du matin." Their names were the brothers Bisson, Lelioux, Noel, Nadar, Guilbert, Vastine, the brothers Desbrosses, Cabot, Villain, Tabar, Chintreuil, Pottier, Karol, Schann, and Vernet. They called themselves the "Société des Buveurs d'Eau," but they were by no means so quixotic as Murger draws that society in "Scènes de la Vie de Bohème." It was simply a union for mutual help, the rules of which did not bar any commercial occupation. The members lived as they pleased or as they could, and water was only a compulsory beverage at the official monthly meetings, when they all submitted their work to the criticism of their brethren. Their ordinary occupations were various enough. Noel gave drawing lessons; another was a judicial stenographer; Jacques Desbrosses, nicknamed Christ—the original of "Jacques D——" in "Scènes de la Vie de Bohème"—and Cabot drew designs for monumental masons; the other Desbrosses, called Gothique, earned a little money by painting door-signs for midwives; Schann, the original of Schaunard, was a musician, and Wallon, Murger's Colline, who joined the society later, eked out his barren philosophy by giving lessons; Chintreuil, afterwards to become a well-known artist, was then a bookseller's assistant, with Champfleury for his colleague; and Nadar, otherwise F.

Tournachon, whom Alphonse Karr describes as "a kind of giant with immense legs, long arms, a long body with a shaggy head of red hair above it, and staring, intelligent, flashing eyes," was the poet and journalist who became a celebrated balloonist and an immensely successful photographer. His caricature hangs in the section of the Musée Carnavalet devoted to early aeronautics in Paris.

We may take it from Murger that the shortcomings of fortune were borne with humorous fortitude on the credit of her occasional smiles, but there was no illusion about the privations. Nadar, Champfleury, and Delvau all agree that a bitter wind blew upon them. It was not so bad, in Nadar's opinion, so long as they lived more or less together, and this they did for a short time in an old house by the Barrière d'Enfer, which looked like a farm with a farmyard inhabited by hens. Champfleury made their acquaintance at this time in a little dairy where they sometimes took their meals. It was a strange society. Some wore blouses, others Phrygian caps, while the brothers Desbrosses had large sky-blue overcoats, turned back with pink satin and fastened by huge mother-of-pearl buttons. These two brothers were the originators of the colony at the Barrière d'Enfer, and its chiefs "surtout par leur misère." They harboured some of the others, who found a resting-place for the night in two hammocks slung in their small room. Murger was among them, the art of painting being for the moment his preoccupation. Fine days were spent lounging on the roof and contemplating the then rural surroundings. Anybody arriving with five francs in his pocket would have been regarded as a millionaire; indeed, they were happy enough when they could afford a few fried potatoes for dinner. Yet they would not have exchanged their hovel for the Garden of Eden, and they fed upon their dreams with inexhaustible confidence. Privation was still worse when the society broke up. One Bohemian lived a whole week on raw potatoes brought by his poor mother from the country; another went three days without food; another passed a winter shirtless in a calico blouse and a lasting waistcoat; another, as a device to keep himself warm, used to carry a log of wood up to his high garret, drop it over the banisters, and run down to fetch it again; an older Bohemian who heard of this manœuvre exclaimed: "Spendthrift, why the log?"

Henry Murger himself, who had abandoned painting and definitely adopted the vocation of a sentimental poet, went to live with his friend Lelioux, first in the Rue Montholon and then in that garret at £4 a year in the Rue de la Tour d'Auvergne where Rodolphe's friends "drank badly filtered water out of eclectic earthenware" at his Wednesday receptions. He had resumed his employment with M. de Tolstoi, but he was too improvident to keep out of misery for many days together. More than once he became so ill with purpura, an eruptive disease due in his case to the abuse of coffee, that he had to go to the hospital. Some extracts from his letters during these years will give an idea of his destitution. On December 14, 1841, he writes:

"Les Desbrosses passent la moitié de la journée à ne pas manger et l'autre à crever de froid. Les chats se méfient d'eux, et, en fait de chéminée, ils ne possèdent que leurs pipes—bien des fois sans tabac."

March 6, 1842:

"Sans le Christ, qui m'a donné à dîner et à déjeuner quatre fois la semaine, je ne sais pas ce que je serais devenu. Ce garçon n'a pas volé son surnom."

April 25, 1843:

"Nous crevons de faim; nous sommes au bout du rouleau. Il faut décidément se faire un trou quelque part ou se faire sauter la cervelle."

March 17, 1844:

"De Charybde en Sylla, mon cher ami! La misère est plus horrible que jamais chez moi et autour de moi. Ma place au *Commerce* n'a pas eu de suite; je suis de nouveau sur le pavé. C'est horrible! Aussi le découragement m'a-t-il pris et tout à fait submergé. Encore quelques jours de cette position et je me fais sauter la cervelle ou je m'engage dans la marine.—Pardonne-moi ces plaintes! C'est le cri de la *fin*."

Like Colline, he punned even in his misery.

Letters of this doleful nature do not throw a very gay light upon the Bohemian market-place, where there was high competition for a small custom and prices ruled low. They contain a truth which no consideration of Bohemia can omit, but it was not the whole truth, as Murger himself testifies in his stories. It was a life of good days as well as bad, even in the leanest years, or "Scènes de la Vie de Bohème" could never have been written. Murger himself had already begun to hand some small wares over his counter. Rodolphe, the poet, it will be remembered, did not disdain to edit a small fashion paper called *L'Écharpe d'Iris*, in which, to Colline's extravagant delight, he inserted the philosopher's articles on metaphysics. This was a direct touch from life, for Bohemia in more than one instance lent its pen to trade. There was a certain Charles Vincent who edited two papers of the leather trade, *Le Moniteur de la Cordonnerie* and the *Halle aux Cuirs*. In his editorial capacity he retained all the new pairs of boots and shoes sent in by advertisers, and with these he often paid his contributors. Murger in 1843 edited *Le Moniteur de la Chapellerie*, the industrial fruits of which were, no doubt, less profitable, but even a few hats and a few francs a month were of considerable value in Bohemia. They were, of course, nothing like the editorial profits of to-day. Receipts were extremely precarious, when, even on a well-written literary paper like *L'Artiste*, the application of a contributor for payment caused a considerable rummaging in tills and pockets before twenty-five francs could be found *dans la boutique*.[29] Yet small change was enough to stand a Bohemian holiday, and Murger's gloomy letters must be discounted by balancing them against Rodolphe's expedition to Versailles with Mademoiselle Laure after he had ransacked Paris for the five francs necessary to do that expedition in sufficient style. It would be absurd to suppose that Murger, with Nadar, Schann, and a *grisette* or two, did not sometimes invade the Chaumière in a joyous band or wake from sleep the serious inhabitants of the Rue de la Tour d'Auvergne.

At the same time, howsoever the balance of pleasure and pain be struck, it is clear that happy memories of this Bohemia could only remain to those for whom it was only a necessary stage in life and not a death-trap. This tendency to poetic melancholy and the painful slowness with which he worked might have caused Henry Murger to sink for ever like many of his friends. He was saved, in the first instance, by Champfleury, who, when he was finally sold up in the Rue de la Tour d'Auvergne, took him to live in the Rue de Vaugirard and induced him to abandon poetry for prose. Jules Husson-Fleury, who was born at Laon in 1821 and became a well-known writer under the name of Champfleury, a great collector of prints and porcelain, on which he wrote some valuable monographs, and finally the director of the Sèvres manufactory, passed through Bohemia during the same years as Murger, and in his "Souvenirs et Portraits de Jeunesse" records many lively experiences. He first came to Paris as shop-boy and assistant in a bookseller's shop where, as I have already said, the future painter Chintreuil was in the same service. Champfleury lost his place for reading the books on his errands instead of delivering them to the customers, but during this year 1839 he saw something of Murger and the colony of the brothers Desbrosses. He then left Paris for a year or two, and returned when Murger was living in the Rue de la Tour d'Auvergne, though the acquaintance was not at once renewed. It was approximately in 1845 that they went to live together in the Rue de Vaugirard, after Champfleury had met Murger again in the hospital. They did not by any means leave Bohemia; in fact, there is reason to suppose that to some extent the character of Marcel was drawn from Champfleury. They wrote a vaudeville together which was never accepted, and attacked the difficult art of writing stories. Murger was able to place some of his work in *L'Artiste*, the editor of which was Arsène Houssaye, and in 1846 the "Scènes de la Vie de Bohème" began to come out in *Le Corsaire*. They were poorly enough paid at the time, but their dramatisation by Barrière in 1849 proved a huge success, and from that time onwards Murger settled down to more serious work and a less disorderly life.

But I am anticipating Champfleury's memories of the last days of Bohemia. In his view, at any rate so far as Murger and he were concerned, the indolence of Bohemia has been much exaggerated. "In reality," he says, "work was the basis of our life." They had a joint library, to which Murger supplied the poets and Champfleury the prose-writers. The latter read voraciously to educate himself, but Murger chiefly thumbed the pages of Victor Hugo and Alfred de Musset; he took regular doses of Shakespeare in a French translation, traces of which appear in "Scènes de la Vie de Bohème," but he had little knowledge of other classic authors. He worked with extraordinary difficulty; a page of prose cost him a night's work and intense intellectual labour, for "Murger n'était plein que de son cœur." Champfleury, for all his friendship, was a shrewd critic when he observed that his whole vision was introspective: "He swept the same chimney so often that in the end the plaster came off and the bricks fell down"; or again: "Besides his little library, his belongings consisted of worn white gloves, a velvet mask, and a withered bouquet hung on the walls. All Murger's work lies in his memories—some faded flowers, a meeting at the Bal de l'Opéra, a heart-ache."

Certain disorders of Bohemia are not excused by Champfleury, particularly that of not paying debts. His friend Fauchéry, an engraver who afterwards went to seek his fortune in Australia, induced him at first to accept the Bohemian code, which was:

1. Never to pay one's rent.

2. To conduct one's removals by the window.

3. To consider all bootmakers, tailors, hatters, and restaurant-keepers as members of Mr. Credit's family.

Some went so far as to maintain that after a clandestine removal through the window no piece of furniture which had passed the gutter in the middle of the street could be reclaimed by the proprietor. This less creditable attitude of Bohemia, which is sufficiently prominent in "Scènes de la Vie de Bohème," was repudiated with some shame in after years by many of Murger's friends. In the book Rodolphe pays his debts when he settles down, and we have it on the authority of Delvau that Schann (Schaunard), who eventually kept a respectable toy-shop, and the original of Musette, who married a chemist, took in their later days a more usual view of money matters. Champfleury confesses that he himself was saved by an amiable girl, who for a time became the divinity of his garret. Unlike Mimi and Musette, she had a horror of debt and vagabondage and inspired him with a pleasure in his own humble hearth, so that he gradually detached himself from his comrades, who were for the most part so ill provided for in the matter of lodging that their chief workroom was a *café*, where they arrived at nine in the morning, to leave at midnight. They read the newspapers, played at dominoes or *tric-trac*, and occasionally did a little work. Fauchéry, in particular, caused considerable surprise among the regular customers by bringing his whole engraving apparatus and solemnly setting to work. Some respect certainly is due to the proprietors of these little eating-houses who so gallantly put up with and gave credit to this noisy and not very profitable *clientèle*, who were capable of perpetrating all the outrages committed by Rodolphe and the rest in their constant asylum, the Café Momus.

Champfleury says little of the amiable goddess who rescued him from vagabondage except that she left him, like Mimi, because she grew tired of cheap muslin, but in another chapter he gives some account of two other idols of Bohemia whom he calls Mademoiselle M. and Mademoiselle P. Mademoiselle M. was dark and merry, a thorough coquette who laughed at wounded hearts; Mademoiselle P. was fair and melancholy, always in tears for the last lover who had left her. A generation of Bohemians were their lovers, poets and painters especially. As the generation grew up the divinities grew wiser, and Mademoiselle M. was the first to do a little mental arithmetic. For her own friends who had a future the days of idleness were over; there was no future for her either among the stranded remainder or in a new generation. Accordingly she departed to more profitable spheres. Mademoiselle P. stayed a little longer, still loving her poets, and weeping *toutes les larmes de son corps* to find that she had a too formidable rival in the desire for fame which watched at the door of her lovers' hearts, till finally she found a worthy man who was no poet to love her and eventually to marry her. Mademoiselle M., meanwhile, had made by her conquests quite a respectable capital, with which one fine day she set sail for Algiers. Unhappily she left Marseilles in a steamer which sank with all hands, so that she and her gold came to rest at the bottom of the sea—a sad story from which Champfleury in an unworthy moment makes some show of drawing a moral. Neither of these young women can be identified with Murger's heroines. Musette, as I have said, married a chemist; Phémie Teinturière, Schaunard's choice, was according to Delvau, a not over-respectable person resembling a heroine of Paul de Kock; as for Mimi, Delvau asserts that Murger loved her while he wrote the "Scènes de la Vie de Bohème," and that her life and wretched death are matters of fact. However, that we may not be too lugubrious let me add that I have read in the French equivalent of "Notes and Queries" a statement that she cheerfully lived to keep a stall in the market.

One more bead in this string of scattered "facts," and the hungerers for documentary evidence must go away satisfied. The disorder of Bohemia requires no emphasis, but it is curious to note that the persons in whom its more orderly elements were incarnated were Champfleury himself and the original of that odd figure, Carolus Barbemuche, the solemn young tutor who in Murger's story glances so enviously at the *cénacle* of Rodolphe, Schaunard, and Marcel in the Café Momus, who saves them from disaster by paying for their reckless Christmas Eve supper, who demands so humbly the privilege of being admitted to the clan, who serves so long and expensive an apprenticeship and gives such a splendid festival on his reception, even to the length of lending all his own presentable clothes to his guests for the occasion. Carolus Barbemuche was drawn, much to his disgust, from Charles Barbara, an obscure writer of fantastic stories, who joined Murger's Bohemia after acting as tutor to two boys. He had a face like a sphinx, rarely smiled, and seemed to be afraid of the wild jokes of his friends. Unlike the rest, he lived almost a hermit's life, receiving nobody in his garret, and retiring there every night neither to read nor to write, but to think, a queer occupation for a Bohemian. Of him Champfleury writes:

"He and I represented order in a group doomed to disorder; we were the *bourgeois* of Bohemia, as much by our ambitions as our manner of living. The details of one day of our life, which continued in the same way for ten years, will show the succession of our studies and our labours. Rising very early, dashing from my bed to my table, I used to write till nine o'clock. An hour sufficed me for breakfast and a walk to the library, where I worked till twelve; there I used to meet Barbara, whom I took to the public lectures at the Collège de France, the Sorbonne, or the Jardin des Plantes. Two lectures, an hour each, exhausted our attention, and, resuming our walk, we arrived at Schann's temple of music, exclusively consecrated to quartets. Two hours of music every day, without counting piano trios three times a week at another house, made us able to read all the chamber music of the German masters.... Barbara was the finest instrumentalist in our band; son and brother of distinguished musicians, he had received in early youth excellent violin lessons, the fruit of which was not lost later, and he brought to the leading of a quartet a restrained emotion which is to be found in some pages of his writings."

It is an unexpectedly pretty glimpse into a part of Bohemia where Murger was not at home. When the quartets took place in a little square of the Quartier Latin, students and *grisettes* came to listen before the open window, and workpeople on every story put out their heads to watch for the arrival of the musicians. Murger's disreputable Schaunard, with his symphony on *L'influence du bleu dans la musique*, was always, I must confess, my favourite; but to discover that he played the quartets of Haydn, Mozart, Beethoven, Schubert, and Mendelssohn for two hours a day with Barbemuche and Marcel—well, it was an intoxicating vision. Schaunard, who had a passion for lobsters, the composer (in his fleshly form of Schann) of a famous drinking song, as second violin in a Beethoven quartet—oh pleasant, pleasant fellow, who truly deserved to come into the comfortable harbour of a toy-shop!

Marcel, so far as he was Champfleury, found a haven too, and lived till 1889. Colline retired to found a new religion in Switzerland, and Rodolphe-Murger, though he lingered for some years in the band of artists and writers who haunted the *brasserie* where Courbet raised the temple of realism, finally turned his back on dissipation and settled at Marlotte, even now a charming village near Fontainebleau. His chief recreation there was hunting, an occupation quite innocuous to the game, if it be true that a certain hare survived his attentions for a whole season, and when an unwary keeper shot it one misty afternoon, he exclaimed with genuine compunction, "Tiens, c'est le lièvre de M. Murger!" In 1861 he came to die in Paris of arteritis, and all the literary world visited his bedside. He died two days after his admission to the hospital, exclaiming, "Pas de musique! Pas de bruit! Pas de Bohème!" Bohemia, indeed, had long been dead, and in his last moments he may have recognized that it was well. There was no longer room for it in a busier, a better-swept world. In its golden age Bohemia did no more than share the imperfections of all human institutions. It had virtues, a liberty, a pride, and an ideal of its own. Murger had seen the beauty become a slattern, pretty no doubt beneath her smuts, gay in the midst of her sorrows, but free by tolerance, not by protest, her pride almost in the dust and her ideals in the possession of others. In the words which Théodore Pelloquet spoke over his grave, Murger belonged to an evil generation:

"Il appartenait à une mauvaise génération, à une génération vieillie avant l'heure, et, malgré sa vieillesse prématurée, sans expérience, sans enthousiasme et sans colère, ayant de la vanité et pas du tout d'orgueil, une vanité niaise, puérile, qui se manifeste surtout par l'affectation d'une ironie mesquine, en face de tous les enthousiasmes et de toutes les grandes causes; à une génération, en un mot, qui laissa périr dans ses mains le magnifique héritage que lui avaient légué les hommes de 1830."

XI

AMUSEMENTS OF BOHEMIA

THE pageant of 1830 has passed, and our gaze has been directed to its Bohemian ingredients with the purpose of noting the particular marks and qualities which distinguished Bohemia, and how their particular manifestations were conditioned and varied by the progress of the years. Looking out of the window of the present, we have been unable at any moment to call a halt, lest we should lose a comprehensive view of the main development. Now that this view has been gained it will do no harm to send the procession once more before the mind's eye, that we may fix at leisure any less important details which may seem in themselves attractive. One of the most happy qualities of the Bohemian nature is its capacity for amusing itself. Real boredom and lackadaisical idleness do not come into the list of its shortcomings. The passionate Romantics, indeed, fashionably suffered from "spleen" and "ennui," they proclaimed a "cœur usé comme l'escalier d'une fille de joie," but the Bohemian, so far as he indulged in these peculiarities, was amusing himself. To him "spleen" and "ennui" were part of the game which he embraced with enthusiasm and in which he desired to excel; yet they were parts to which, as a general rule, he did not pay too much attention, preferring the more positive and assertive sides of Romanticism. Neither Gautier nor Gérard de Nerval nor Rodolphe nor Schaunard presents himself to the imagination as suffering from boredom. An unfailing capacity for amusing oneself and finding amusement in one's fellow-men is an essential Bohemian *trait*. The preceding chapters have not been wholly devoid of indications as to the way in which these talents were exercised by the Bohemian clans, but it was necessary to insist rather on the diversions which characterized the *particular* spirit of each brotherhood than on the general opportunities which they all enjoyed with slight variation. The field is now open without restriction, and it will not be amiss to take a glimpse here and there at the Bohemian enjoying his leisure, if only to add a few vivid touches that will enliven the background of the picture. The work of Bohemia can always be taken for granted; artistic endeavour, whether actively or indolently pursued, varies but little in external feature; the change, the colour, the tragedy and comedy are only to be found within the artist's mind; but the amusement of Bohemia, so far from being hidden, courts publicity. It takes its colour, too, so largely from the changing world around that there is great pictorial value in its easily observable vicissitudes. For that reason I devote this chapter to the subject of its title without further apology, but only with the caution that here the accidents rather than the essentials of Bohemia are regarded. The privilege of amusement is open to everybody, but to see what

Bohemia made of its privileges in that respect is, perhaps, to quicken it for the imagination by an extra spark.

Precisians might say that dress hardly comes under the head of amusements and that on certain views it is more properly included in the category of necessities or of nuisances. Yet there is no doubt that for all women—and for more men than would admit it—to be well dressed is an enjoyment, a term only differing from amusement by a smaller suggestion of possible frivolity. It is quite a sufficient warrant, at all events, for giving dress a small part in this chapter; besides, the costume of any individual or society is both a sure indicator of qualities and an apt focus for judgment. In England, the very home of illustrated books and papers, it is not necessary to say much in evoking the costume of a past age, so that the subject may be treated quite shortly, especially as regards the men of Bohemia, whose dress was too often a deplorable tragedy. When Marcel went to Musette's party with "Mathusalem" buttoned up to the neck over a blue shirt dotted with the figures of a boar-hunt he was, as Murger says, "dressed in the worst taste possible." In such a case there is no more to be said; his appearance would vary little from age to age. To the Bohemian in his lean days, certainly, it would be an insult to impute enjoyment of his tattered wardrobe. Those who most enjoyed dressing, without a doubt, were the Bohemian generation who cheered "Hernani" with such frenzy, for they made their *pourpoints*, felt sombreros, Robespierre waistcoats, and Phrygian caps effective details in the general Romantic demonstration and, as such, matters of intense pleasure. But these extravagances have already caught our attention; they were part of that frantic desire for novelty and colour which was a symptom of *le mal romantique*; their proper complement was that rage for fancy-dress balls which broke out shortly after 1830 and laid every nationality and period under contribution for picturesque costumes. So far as the men are concerned, it need only be pointed out that the general dress of the time—against which Bohemia stood out at first and into which it gradually faded—was that of tight pantaloons with straps, long coats with full skirts and accentuated waists, full cravats, lavish jewellery, and high hats in a bewildering variety of shapes, cylindrical, conical, inverted conical, curly, straight, with broad brims and with scarce a brim at all—the civilian uniform, in fact, of our own late Georgian and early Victorian era. It was a dress that only a few could wear with distinction; on the rest it wrinkled and puffed in inevitable ugliness. A Roger de Beauvoir could look immaculately moulded, but one has only to glance at the caricatures of Traviés, Monnier, Daumier, and Gavarni to see how unequivocally hideous were the clothes of an average man. To be out at elbows in this exacting fashion was indeed to be a sorry sight, and one can well imagine poor Lucien de Rubempré to have been in his provincial attire fair game for the sneers of Rastignac and de Marsay. Still, even the Bohemian had a new suit at times, and it lights the memory of Arsène Houssaye, Camille

Rogier, Murger, Champfleury, and the rest to recall that it was not for comfortable lounge suits and flannels that they got into debt, but for correct suits of "tails," flowery waistcoats, top-hats, and patent leather boots. It gives a quaint touch of decorum to the picture of their wildest excesses.

Women entered Bohemia as guests rather than as inhabitants, and to the fair visitors conformity to fashion was anything but a trifle. To deck themselves fittingly was their constant amusement, and one in which they took good care that their swains should be sharers. The female dress of the time is well known to us from early pictures of Queen Victoria and the paintings of Winterhalter; there are few, too, who at one time or another have not seen some of Gavarni's beautiful fashion plates. The Empire style had entirely disappeared, and the accent was in 1830 laid chiefly on the waist. The shoulders were sloping and wide, the sleeves so voluminous that by 1836 they were like miniature balloons, the skirt very wide and full, ending above the ankles. The waist and head were made to seem very small in proportion, so that two loaves placed one on top of the other would have made a very good caricature of a woman's figure at any time during the golden age of Bohemia. The hair was elaborately done to frame a pretty face daintily under a large poke-bonnet. It was pre-eminently the day of "fragile" women: nothing in their costume seemed made for hard wear. Cydalise or Victorine, as she swung in the hammock among the gallants of the Impasse du Doyenné, would have kicked a little cross-laced foot out from ethereal folds of flowered muslin, and gathered a gauzy scarf enticingly round bare shoulders. Fashions were indeed expensive for a fond lover's pocket, but at least he was never at a loss what to buy for his mistress, so many were the little accessories to the Graces' toilet. He was never wrong, for instance, in offering a piece of gay ribbon, for there were bows everywhere, on the bosom, on the sleeves, and, with long dazzling streamers, round the waist. There was no end to their variety and combination of colours, brilliant and pale; even the crudest Scottish tartans were not considered amiss, as a certain dress in the London Museum will show the incredulous. If ribbon was too paltry, a man in a really generous mood would present a cashmere shawl, an expensive and much appreciated luxury. The manipulation of shawls on frail, rounded little persons, who, in England at least, still fainted at will and indulged in the vapours, was a matter of some art. Balzac, in one of his short stories, asserts that a *femme du monde* could be distinguished from the actress or the *grisette* by the handling of her *cachemire* alone. There was only one great change in woman's dress between the earlier and later days of Bohemia, and that was in the sleeves, which dwindled suddenly as if the balloons had been pricked, and became either closely fitting or almost disappeared into two little frilly bands. In fact, during the forties, before skirts began to be exaggerated on horse-hair paddings and verge upon the crinoline, female costume was as nearly natural as it can be if corsets be granted. Nothing can be more charming than the appearance of the Queen of the Belgians in her portrait by Winterhalter which hangs in the gallery at Versailles. She wears a red velvet dress, cut simply as to the *corsage*, with the skirt reaching the ground in full, stately folds: there is no extravagance of bows and frills, only a little lace at the bosom and sleeves. So, if we would picture Mimi or Musette, as they were dressed for that memorable day at Fontenay-aux-Roses, in the new muslin frocks made by their own hands, we must imagine dainty little women, looking as if a breath would blow them away, their pretty cheeks showing between two bewitching clusters of ringlets, straw bonnets with not too large brims upon their heads, tied with a coquettish ribbon, gowns of flowered muslin, light, simple, and flowing, and scarfs pinned round their sloping shoulders or held in place by mittened hands. Gavarin drew them to the life time and time again, and they were considerably more attractive than any would-be *Bohémiennes* of our time in their rough, untidy tweeds or amorphous "rational" dress.

From the amusement of clothing the body it is an easy transition to that of refreshing it. Eating and drinking, like dress, may from a certain point of view come under the head of necessities, but indulgence in good cheer when possible is a habit of young people of which a Bohemian was by no means contemptuous. A word, therefore, about his particular haunts among the thousand *cafés* and restaurants of Paris will not be out of season. After 1830 the great houses in the Palais Royal had fallen out of fashion, and the four leading restaurants of Paris were on the boulevard. Bohemians, it is true, were not often to be found within them, but in the golden age, when Bohemia was nearer to the dandies and *viveurs*, it would at least have been possible that in a moment of extravagance some Bohemian friend should have accompanied Roger de Beauvoir into the Café de Paris, the Café Riche, the Café Hardy, or the Café Anglais. The Café de Paris was opposite Tortoni's, which stood at the end of the Rue Taitbout. Besides being the home of the aristocratic *petit cercle*, it was renowned for its witty conversation and its general air of luxury. Since it was favoured by the aspirants to smartness, as well as the perfect examples, its society was less select than that of the Café Riche, at the corner of the Rue Lepeletier, or the Café Anglais, which still remains in its old position. There was a quiet solidity about the Café Anglais, in particular, which gave it a peculiar air of distinction, though its company was gay enough at supper-time. It was especially famous for its roast meat and its grills, though in these matters the Café Hardy, at the corner of the Rue Laffitte, ran it close. Hardy was an English cook who invented the *déjeuner à la fourchette*, and popularized it by setting up the first silver grill in Paris. Customers chose their own cutlet or steak and saw it cooked before their eyes. At all these four the prices were very high, and with regard to two of them it was said: "On doit être riche pour dîner au Café Hardy, et hardi pour dîner au Café Riche." However, the chief haunt for Bohemians with money to spend was the

Rocher de Cancale, where it was easier to be uproarious without offending the proprieties. This famous restaurant still stands in the dirty, provincial Rue Montorgueil, in the midst of small shops whose wares overflow on to the pavement. The stately ornamentation of dark painted wood is still visible on its upper stories, but the specimens of edibles in its ground-floor windows tell too plainly to what depths it has sunk. It is no longer a possible home for Rastignac and his boon companions, nor would it tempt Arsène Houssaye to entertain there the brethren of *la Bohème galante*, for it merely plies the trade of the convenient *marchand de vin* in a rather squalid quarter. The Rocher de Cancale had declined already during the later days of Bohemia, and in Murger's day they repaired on *jours de liesse* to the Café de l'Odéon, Hill's Tavern in the Boulevard des Capucines, or the Cabaret Dinochan at the corner of the Rue de Navarin. The first of these was, in particular, the haunt of Baudelaire and his friends, where the unfortunate Hégésippe Moreau made his brief acquaintance with the main stream of Bohemia towards the end of his days, which had been mainly passed in a backwater. Hill's Tavern was one of the many chop-houses in the English style that flourished in Louis Philippe's Paris—only the Petit Lucas, a charming place for a quiet dinner, remains to-day—to cater for the down-at-elbows Englishmen, jockeys, and trainers, of whom there was always a certain number. At supper-time, however, it was invaded by Bohemia, and was often so full that its doors had to be closed. One of its peculiarities was that its private rooms were named after Shakespeare, Byron, and other great poets. The Café Dinochan, according to Delvau,[30] was the ground on which a great many small papers of the day were started. Monselet, Nadar, Fauchéry, and Champfleury were among its customers, and Murger died in debt to its proprietor for twelve hundred francs, for it was said of this worthy creditor: "On dîne très-bien chez lui quand on a quarante sous dans une poche—et dix francs dans l'autre." Yet the full apparatus of a restaurant was not necessary to the gaiety of Bohemian suppers, for in scanty days they made just as merry in the shops of one or two bakeries on rolls and warm milk. The Boulangerie Cretaine in the Quartier Latin was famous for its milk rolls and for the brilliant conversation of Privat d'Anglemont, who, though it was against his principle to get into debt, ran up a bill there for halfpenny rolls of six hundred francs. The other famous baker was the *pâtissier* Pitou, by the Porte Montmartre, where a crowd of Bohemians used to congregate after the midnight closing of the *cafés*. In the back shop was a table running round three sides of the square, and at this "piano," as it was called, the quaint figure of Guichardet presided. Guichardet, whose "nez vermeil et digne" was celebrated in one of Banville's triolets, was a Bohemian of the type of Balzac's Comte de la Palférine, one who had voluntarily dropped out of the race of life while preserving all his dignity and pride. He passed his days in amiable vagabondage, but preserved "a perfume of exquisite politeness and witty impertinence which made him the most delightful companion in the world." So says Delvau, according to whom he was the only man left in France who really knew how to say "Femme charmante!"

So far I have mainly mentioned the haunts of Bohemians with the means and inclination for a certain amount of self-indulgence. But in Bohemia occasions preponderated when indulgence in anything beyond bare necessities was an impossibility. The left bank swarmed with cheap refuges for those who had hearty appetites and only a few pence. There was Viot's for the poorest of the poor; Dagneaux's or Magny's in the Rue Contrescarpe-Dauphine—rather superior houses where it was possible to procure a semblance of good cheer; and the Cabaret of Mère Cadet outside the Barrière Montparnasse, where Schaunard had his first meeting with Colline over the stewed rabbit with two heads. This last had a garden which ran along the Montparnasse cemetery, and under the shade of its dusty shrubs not only literary Bohemians but nearly all the young actors and actresses of the Théâtre Montparnasse and the Théâtre du Luxembourg made their scanty meals. You might as well have asked for sphinx there as chicken, says Delvau, the staple dishes being stewed rabbit and *choucroute garnie*. To give a longer catalogue of such places would be neither instructive nor amusing, and their types are easily enough found in the Paris of to-day. There are two, however, that call for special mention, for fiction has carried their fame beyond the days of their material existence. No reader of Balzac's "Illusions Perdues" can have forgotten the description of the cheap eating-house at the corner of the Place de la Sorbonne and the Rue Neuve de Richelieu, with the small panes of glass of its front window, its comforting announcement of *pain à discrétion*, its long tables like those of a monastic refectory, its varieties of cow's flesh and veal, and the hurried air of its diners, who came there to eat and not to loiter. This famous house, where a dinner of three dishes with a *carafon* of wine or a bottle of beer cost ninepence, where Lucien de Rubempré met Lousteau and made the acquaintance of d'Arthez and his virtuous friends, was the restaurant of Flicoteaux, no product of Balzac's imagination, but a name known to all the strugglers for fame and fortune. It was a sure ground on which to observe Bohemia, not indeed in its greatest indigence, but on the days when there was at least no margin. Thackeray mentions it in his "Paris Sketch-Book," and there is a passage in Lytton Bulwer's "France" which vividly gives the impression produced by Flicoteaux on an English eye:

"Enter [he says] between three and four o'clock, and take your seat at one of the small tables, the greater number of which are already occupied. To your right there is a pale young man: his long hair, falling loosely over his face, gives an additional wildness to the eye, which has caught a mysterious light from the midnight vigil; his clothes are clean and threadbare; his coat too short at the wrists; his trousers too short at the legs; his cravat of a rusty black, and vaguely confining two immense shirt collars, leaves his thin and angular neck almost entirely exposed. To your left is a native of the South, pale and swarthy: his long black locks, parted from his forehead, descend upon his shoulders; his lip is fringed with a slight moustache, and the semblance of a beard gives to his meditative countenance an antique and apostolic cast. Ranged round the room, with their thin, meagre portions of meat and bread, their pale decanter of water before them, sit the students, whom a youth of poverty and privation is preparing for a life of energy or science."

Flicoteaux has long been swept away, and buildings of the Sorbonne now occupy its site. Gone, too, these many years, is the Café Momus, which stood in a back street by the old church of Saint-Germain l'Auxerrois, the hostelry celebrated by so many exploits of Murger's four heroes in "Scènes de la Vie de Bohème." It was here that Schaunard and Colline collected Rodolphe for the Bohemian brotherhood, and it became their home, not so much for meals, though it was the scene of their reckless Christmas Eve supper which introduced the saviour Barbemuche, but rather for the lighter *consommations* over which, by the French custom, they could spend unlimited hours—a precious privilege when a cold garret was the only alternative. There was nothing fictitious about the Café Momus; it was a real establishment serving some respectable shopkeepers of the quarter, when by some mischance, from the good M. Momus' point of view, it attracted the Bohemian horde of Murger, Champfleury, Nadar, Schann, Wallon, and many of the other "Buveurs d'Eau." Even on Murger's testimony, they must be admitted to have abused their privileges without shedding any very great glory in return, and we may take as fairly true the list of grievances which was drawn up by the proprietor against Rodolphe and his friends, from which it appears that they spent the whole day there from morning to midnight, making a desert round them with their strident voices and extravagant conversation; that Rodolphe carried off all the papers in the morning and complained if their bands were broken, and that by shouting every quarter of an hour for *Le Castor*, a journal of the hat trade edited by Rodolphe, the companions had forced a subscription on the proprietor; that Colline and Rodolphe played *tric-trac* all day, refusing to give up the table to other people; that Marcel set up his easel in the *café*, and even went so far as to invite models of both sexes; that Schaunard had expressed his intention of bringing his piano there, and that Phémie Teinturière never wore a bonnet when she came to meet him; that, not content with ordering very little, the four friends presumed to make their own coffee on the premises; and that the waiter, corrupted by their influence, had seen fit to address an amatory poem to the *dame du comptoir*. Murger puts a touch of exaggeration into this complaint, but it is to be feared, nevertheless, that no trifling *dossier* of misdemeanours could have been compiled against the originals of Rodolphe, Marcel, and the rest. We have it on Delvau's authority, at all events, that the profit of their custom was quite disproportionate to its assiduity, when he tells of their stratagem for obtaining asylum at small cost. The smallest possible order was a *demi-tasse*, which consisted of a small cup of coffee, four lumps of sugar, and a thimbleful of cognac; this cost five sous, a sum of importance in Bohemia. The practice, therefore, was that a certain student, Joannis Guigard, who was of the band, went in first, ordered a *demi-tasse*, and went upstairs to consume it. Murger would then arrive, ask if Guigard were upstairs, and run up. The rest followed in succession with the same question till the *cénacle* was complete and in a position to have a sip of coffee and some hours of warmth for nothing. After a short while Momus grew tired of these troublesome customers and formally gave them notice to quit. They accepted the intimation, but vowed revenge. Accordingly, a few days later, one of the band turned up with six wet-nurses in his train, while another brought six funeral mutes. The rest of the band then arrived, and the Bohemian spokesman, probably Schann, delivered a flowery discourse upon the affinity of life and death, with allusions to their guests' professions. He wound up by telling the mutes to bury the Café Momus and take the nurses as a reward. To make matters worse, he directed that the milk and beer which had been ordered should be warmed as a mixture. The mutes and nurses, furious at being thus deceived and insulted, broke into angry expostulations, and, aided by the jests of the Bohemians, the proceedings ended in a tremendous disturbance. Schann and two others were arrested, and the next day Momus sold his business.

The extent to which Bohemia, at its different phases, shared in the various pastimes of Paris cannot be determined with any accuracy, so much depended on individual taste and individual wealth. It is certain, however, that after 1837 gambling was not a Bohemian distraction, for in that year the public gaming-houses were closed. Before that time they were such a popular institution that the early Bohemia cannot be conceived to have entirely eschewed it. At the beginning of "La Peau de Chagrin" Balzac draws a powerful picture of the wretched crowd that haunted the Palais Royal, where Raphael de Valentin lost his last gold coin at a single coup. There were no less than four gaming-houses in the Palais Royal, Nos. 9, 113, 124, and 129, where the minimum stake was two francs for roulette and five francs for trente-et-un. Besides the Palais Royal, there were Paphos, Frascati, and the select Cercle des Étrangers. The popularity of gambling can be judged from the fact that the Treasury profited annually by it to the extent of five and a half million francs. Yet there is no record that the truly artistic members of Bohemia, like Gautier or Houssaye, so wasted time or money, while Murger and his friends were spared the temptation. In music, too, Bohemia played no very great part, in spite of the devotion of Champfleury, Barbara, and Schann to Beethoven's quartets. There was plenty of fine music to be heard in Paris during the time: Habeneck was introducing Beethoven's symphonies,

Berlioz was revolutionizing orchestration, while Liszt, Chopin, Paganini, Vieuxtemps, and de Bériot were among the soloists. Certainly those Bohemians of the golden age who had access to the *salons* of the Princess Belgiojoso or Madame de Girardin must often have heard these great artists, but it is not to be supposed that they were great supporters of concerts, unless it were of the Concerts Musard. These concerts, which won great fame through the personality of Musard, the conductor, began in 1833 in the Salle Saint-Honoré;[31] their programmes were excellent and the prices low enough to attract the least well off. Musard had a genius for making *pot-pourris* of operatic tunes and for introducing new effects, especially into dance music. His electric style of conducting made the Bals Musard far more popular than the great balls at the Opéra. He contrived a wonderful quadrille, for instance, out of "Les Huguenots," during which red lights were lit, tocsins pealed, tom-toms boomed, screams resounded, and the whole illusion of a massacre was thrillingly kept up. He also composed a *contre-danse* in the finale of which he broke a chair, and his triumph was a certain galop in which he discharged a pistol. This was thoroughly in keeping with the Romantic spirit, and after its first performance he was publicly chaired round the hall by the excited dancers. So far as pure music was concerned, however, it appealed most to Parisians in the form of opera. Meyerbeer's "Robert le Diable" and "Les Huguenots" produced frenzies of enthusiasm: no Romantic, consequently no Bohemian of Gautier's day, could afford not to have listened to them. Rossini's great vogue began at the same time, while Donizetti and Auber shared the honours of light opera till Offenbach appeared to carry all before him. Musical Bohemia was well educated, if not in composition, at least in execution, when it was possible to hear Duprez, Rubini, Lablache, Tamburini, Grisi, Mario, Persiani, and Pauline Viardot-Garcia. The ballet, too, with Carlotta Grisi, Taglioni, and Fanny Elssler, was an additional attraction at the Opéra. The devotion of *la Bohème galante* to the *corps de ballet* has appeared in an earlier chapter, and it was a devotion shared by most masculine society. Murger's Bohemia flourished after the greatest operatic enthusiasms, which its more classically inclined members probably despised; but their exchequers were not of the sort to allow for tickets at the grand opera, though they turned up in force at the light operas of the Théâtre Bobino. At this little theatre, more properly called the Théâtre du Luxembourg, there was a continuous uproar made by Bohemians and students. When this grew too unbearable the manager would appear in his dressing-gown and protest that the police would arrive if the respectable inhabitants of the quarter were disturbed; whereupon the whole audience struck up as one man Grétry's air "Où peut-on être mieux qu'au sein de la famille?" accompanied by the wheezy orchestra and conducted by the manager himself. At such a scene Schaunard and Marcel must often have assisted.

Nevertheless, in the eyes of Bohemia, the glory of the opera paled entirely before that of the drama. There was not one Bohemian with any literary talent who did not try to write a play—nay, many plays—tragedies in alexandrines, comedies, or vaudevilles; and when they were not writing plays they were haunting the theatres as dramatic critics, selling their articles simply for the sake of a free entry, unless, like Lucien's immoral set, they added the profits of blackmail. From the second *cénacle* to the end of Murger's Bohemia there was no end so generally pursued as dramatic composition. Bouchardy and Augustus Mackeat were dramatists, so were Ourliac, Arsène Houssaye, and Gérard de Nerval; Gautier was a dramatic critic; Murger and Champfleury failed as vaudevillists; and it is quite likely that Rodolphe's magnificent drama, "Le Vengeur," had its counterpart in reality. The "poète échevelé" and the humble *conteur* alike turned their eyes continuously towards the stage, besieging luckless managers without cease. The reason of this was partly, as may be supposed, that a successful play, then as to-day, gave far quicker and more splendid pecuniary returns for labour than any other form of literary composition. A concrete instance of that is the case of Murger himself, who was set on his legs entirely by the sudden vogue of the dramatized "Scènes de la Vie de Bohème." But there was another reason at least as strong, far deeper, and more honourable. The stage, as I have already pointed out, was the battlefield of the Romantic struggle. "Hernani" brought home the new truths to the public far more vividly than any novel or poem could have done; every night they were declaimed before compelled attention. It is not surprising, then, that the stage played so great a part in the amusements of Bohemia. It was, with one other, the chief of their pastimes. For them to listen to "Chatterton," the "Tour de Nesle," or "Antony" was not only a distraction, it was a frantic excitement which made their blood seethe almost painfully and sent geysers of hot eloquence from their lips as they munched the hot rolls of the Boulangerie Cretaine. These young enthusiasts were not stinted of good fare. Mademoiselle Mars, Marie Dorval, Rachel and Judith appeared at the Français during these eighteen years; at the Folies-Dramatique Frédéric Lemaître created with enormous success the part of Robert Macaire; while at the Funambules Gaspard Deburau was winning eternal fame as the incomparable Pierrot. There were a host of other theatres besides, the Variétés, Porte Saint-Martin, Odéon, not to mention smaller ones, managed for the most part by men of taste, supplied with plays by men with some pretension to talent, and criticized by unsparing critics, from Jules Janin downwards, who knew what they wanted and did not hesitate to speak when they did not get it. In the stage Bohemia found not only amusement and inspiration but part of its livelihood: it lived next door to that special world composed of actors and actresses. Yet, though Bohemians went to supper with Mademoiselle Mars, Dumas was very much at home with Marie Dorval, Roger de Beauvoir played pranks with Bache, and Rodolphe had a love affair with Mademoiselle Sidonie, the two worlds were definitely separated. In fact, the life of dramatic artists, whatsoever Bohemian flavouring it may have, has always had a mysterious taste of its own, incapable of mixture with any other blend of artistic life, so that, interesting as it may have been in Paris during these years, its omission from these pages has been intentional.

Bal Masqué à l'Opéra

The one other amusement—a pure pastime involving no material profit—which was particularly popular in Bohemia was dancing. In this respect Bohemia was no exception from the rest of Parisian society, for in all classes there was an inextinguishable passion for the dance. But the Bohemian, obeying only his own laws of social propriety, was in a more favourable position for taking full advantage of all public opportunities for this exercise and of all the *agréments* in the way of casual intercourse with both sexes which it implied. All the year round there were public balls given in Paris, at which the Bohemian was in his element, giving rein to his inventive humour, his high spirits, and his gift of seductive gallantry. During the first few years after 1830, the golden age of Bohemia, the balls at the Opéra were the most frequented, especially in the days of the carnival. There masks and dominoes covered dancers of every rank in society, for even the *femme du monde* slipped in unbeknown to her husband. This scene of utmost gaiety and brilliance, of which Balzac gives a picture at the opening of "Splendeurs et Misères des Courtisanes," was closely rivalled by the ball at the Variétés, at which a still more feverish excitement reigned. Or if the Bohemian preferred to make sure of a *grisette* as a partner he went to the Prado, the site of which was opposite the Palais de Justice, where, under Pilodo, the famous conductor, he could join Louise la Balocheuse, Angelina l'Anglaise, or Ernestine Confortable in the giddy whirl. The waltz was recognized at this period, but the quadrille easily held the place of honour, especially as it lent itself more freely to individual invention, such as Ourliac's magnificent variation depicting the grandeur and fall of Napoleon. It was through this licence in the figures of the quadrille that the *chahut* and the *cancan* were introduced by the rakish set among the *viveurs* which included Charles de la Battut, Alton-Shee, Monnier, and the famous Chicard—a leather-merchant who made a name by his grotesque costumes and wild dances, the term *chicard*, which degenerated into *chic*, becoming a general denomination for his imitators. I have not been able to arrive at the difference between the *chahut* and the *cancan*, but both were originally primitive dances indulged in by the lowest classes, quaint, but in all probability perfectly decent. The rage for extravagance during the early thirties changed them into formidable pantomimes of violence, if not always of indecency, which every complete reveller rendered with his own individual touch. Heine, in the course of one of his articles in the *Augsburg Gazette*, said of the *cancan*:

"It must be regarded simply as a pantomime of Robert Macairedom. Anybody who has a general idea of the latter will understand those indescribable dances, expressions of *persiflage* in dance, which not only mock sexual relations, but civic relations too, all, in fact, that is good and beautiful, every kind of enthusiasm, patriotism, uprightness, faith, family feeling, heroism, divinity."

Heine's view is rather too Teutonic, for the popularity of the *cancan* was due to the high spirits of the Romantic enthusiasm, and its degree of morality or immorality depended upon the individual dancer. Not much harm can be imagined to have dwelt in the dance-*persiflage* of the Impasse du Doyenné, whatever a Chicard or a Milord Arsouille may have made of it. The feature of public balls, however, was certainly a Dionysiac exaltation which culminated in the final *galop infernal*, as it was called, into which Musard particularly infused a special fury. It was less a dance than a stampede of maniacs, who rushed round the room, men and women, clutching one another anyhow, wigs flying, tresses waving, dresses rent from fair shoulders, all shrieking and shouting, brandishing arms, kicking legs, and stamping heedlessly on those who were unlucky enough to fall.

The Galop Infernal

The balls of the Opéra declined in attraction and became dull about 1836, but they were revived with still greater splendour two years later, when Musard was made conductor and members of the ballet were drafted in to enliven the company. Such balls, however, became too much public functions to suit the less splendid Bohemia of a later day, which found diversion more suited to its pocket and its manners at the Chaumière or the Closerie des Lilas on the left bank. It was at such places as these that Rodolphe and Marcel disported themselves, and Schaunard was arrested for "chorégraphie trop macabre." The Chaumière was a large garden on the Boulevard Montparnasse, a miniature edition of Cremorne or Vauxhall, with a primitive shooting gallery, a skittle alley, and switchback. It was open all day for students to promenade after lectures and make their addresses to the *grisettes* working under the trees. Its dances were very simple affairs; a few lamps and Chinese lanterns, a small orchestra, a bar for lemonade and *galette* were all that the management supplied, the fun, of which they had enough and to spare, being the dancers' contribution.

The Closerie des Lilas, though less generally popular than the Chaumière, was more particularly associated with Bohemia than the latter, for Murger, Vitu, Fauchéry, Théodore de Banville, and one or two others of that set frequented it regularly, as a French writer[32] says, "avec quelques comparses sans importance," among whom, no doubt, were Mimi and Musette. This little dancing-hall began in 1838 as La Chartreuse, being so called because it was on the site of the old Carthusian monastery in the Rue d'Enfer. It was in some sort the trial-ground for those of the fair sex who aspired to become stars of the Prado and the Chaumière. Privat d'Anglemont has described it in a rare pamphlet as it was in its early days under its extraordinary manager, Carnaud. As La Chartreuse it was the most primitive kind of *guingette*, the dancing-place being a large marquee, into which one descended by a steep flight of steps. On the left were an orchestra and *café*, and the only ornaments were nine plaster statues representing the Muses, which were handily adapted for supporting petroleum lamps on their arms. "There," says Privat d'Anglemont, "decent dress was not *de rigueur*; one came as one liked, or rather as one could—the women in bonnets or, in default of other adornments, covered simply by their hair, and the men in blouses. It certainly was the most original bar in Paris. It had a physiognomy of its own, strange, quaint, even a little burlesque, but it existed. Its population was to be seen nowhere else; it seemed to exist only at the Chartreuse and for the Chartreuse. Since this ball disappeared its population has completely vanished."

La Guinguette

Everything about the Chartreuse was original, not only the dancers and the dances but the orchestra, the music, and the manager. Every kind of "percussion" was added to the usual instruments, the noise of money-bags, pistol shots, rows of explosive caps, resounding anvils, and sheets of metal struck to represent the roaring of lions and tigers. All the music was composed by Carnaud himself, who was conductor, first violin, *restaurateur*, composer, and advertisement-writer in one. At every special *fête* he invented a new quadrille and a new exotic word to describe it, such as "la fête des vendanges, quadrille déchirancochicandard," or "l'hôtel des haricots,[33] avec accompaniments de chaînes et de bruits de clefs, grand quadrille exhilarandéliranchocnosophe."

Carnaud was succeeded by the famous Bullier, who altered the name to the Closerie des Lilas and replaced the simple marquee by an Oriental palace with a garden, Moorish pavilions, billiard tables, swings, and a pistol-shooting gallery. A decent orchestra was installed and four admirable waiters. With these improvements the balls, held every Sunday, Monday, and Thursday, began to attract the *beau monde* of the Quartier Latin, and several of the dancers gained the coveted honour of a *sobriquet*. There were Jeanne la Juive, for instance, Maria les Yeux Bleus, Joséphine Pochardinette, and the literary Clémentine Pomponnette, who used to show her admirers a farce she had written "dans les loisirs que lui laissait l'amour." This transformation took place about 1847, and it was then that one of the Moorish pavilions was especially consecrated to Murger's Bohemian set. It is needless to say that the name of Bullier still remains in the Bal Bullier of to-day.

One other popular ball must be mentioned, the Bal Mabille, which for so long was one of the sights of Paris. This public ball was instituted by Mabille, a dancing-master, in the Champs Elysées. The price of entrance at first was fifty centimes, with an extra fee for each quadrille, and in 1843 the whole of the dances were included in an initial sum of two francs. The fame of the Bal Mabille was due first to its polkas, a dance which became the rage at the time, and secondly to the most celebrated of polka-dancers, Elise Sergent, known as La Reine Pomaré. Her dancing was a revelation of fire and passion which won her recognition on the very first evening of her appearance. Crowds came to see her dance, articles were devoted to her by the journalists of the day, and Privat d'Anglemont wrote a sonnet to her. Paris, in fact, went mad about her, and she had many lovers, among whom, it is said, was Alphonse Karr, which brings her into some kind of connexion with Bohemia. But Reine Pomaré and her rival, Céleste Mogador, who also made her *début* at Mabille, were too much on the plane of *grandes cocottes* for any real relation with the Bohemia of their day. They might have danced for love at the Impasse du Doyenné, but Schaunard and Marcel had nothing to offer them to compare with the splendour of the *viveurs* which was laid at their feet. Bohemia found its pleasure at less expense and with less restraint in the company of Mimi and Musette in a Moorish pavilion at the Closerie des Lilas, where Colline's bad puns found appreciative listeners and Schaunard's *pas de fascination* were greeted with rapturous applause.

XII

THE PARIS OF BOHEMIA

Paris sombre et fumeux,
Où déjà, points brillants au front de maison ternes,
Luisent comme des yeux des milliers de lanternes;
Paris avec ses toits déchiquetés, ses tours
Qui ressemblent de loin à des cous de vautours,
Et ses clochers aigus à flèche dentelée,
Comme un peigne mordant la nue échevelée.
THÉOPHILE GAUTIER

The last chapter was devoted to certain accidental adjuncts of *la vie de Bohème* by way of general illustration, though they consisted of simple amusements common not only to the Parisians of the day but to civilized society of most epochs. The present chapter, which I have reserved till the last, might logically have claimed an earlier place, for its subject, as I have already pointed out, is distinctive of the society in which Bohemia played an important part. Bohemia, of course, neither monopolized Paris nor even a portion of it, but the Paris of Bohemia's florescence and decline was a unique background for these events, a necessary condition, though temporary in itself, which it would pass the bounds of human possibility to reconstruct. Interesting as it is to imagine correctly the dress of the Bohemian and his mistress, the places where they dined, or the gardens where they danced, the re-presentation of the city where they lived, so small, so sensitively vibrant, so congested, so hopelessly out of date, except for a few new patches, so dirty, so noisy, and so picturesque, ranks far higher in importance. Yet, though I might have put this chapter first, I choose to put it last because I cannot hope that it will be appreciated by any but those who have already some memory of Paris and on whom the spell of its fascination has, at least, been lightly cast. The general description of Bohemian life may provide some entertainment to those who know not Paris; for their sake I have sought not to break the general interest. My story is now told, and I am free to call those who have breathed, even for a moment, the quick breeze off the Seine or seen the sunshine strike through the trees in the Tuileries Gardens, to stay with me for a last look back upon that city of beauty and adventure which calls, like the East, to those who love it. To have gained even a superficial view of modern Paris, to have caught some of her accents and contrasts—the radiance of the Bois de Boulogne, the vivacity of the boulevards, the *cafés* overflowing on to the pavements, the view from her bridges, the differences between the two banks, the mean alleys lurking mischievously at the back of splendid thoroughfares, the broadest omnibuses comically invading the narrowest streets—is to have formed some general notion with which an earlier Paris can be compared. And with a reader who has penetrated deeper, whose nostrils yearn for her indescribably subtle perfume, who knows the different aspects of her streets from days of diligent tramping, who has seen her river blending with her sky in a hundred harmonies, who has felt her moods and her humours, finding like a true lover her blemishes as adorable as her perfections, who has recognized her past in her present, and who, though a stranger, has divined in ecstasy the wild throb of her romantic heart—with him my task is easier still. Such a one will already have guessed the intoxication of the air which a Roger de Beauvoir delicately breathed, when Paris, her spirit newly quickened with the exhilaration of a potent elixir, was yet unspoiled by modern cosmopolitan vulgarity, and her inner soul shone out, through all her deformities and incongruities, with a gay and unmasked confidence.

She did not shine before an unseeing generation, for the Parisians of the Romantic age adored their city, dandies, Bohemians, and *bourgeois* alike, all passionately conscious of their privileged citizenship, though they could admit with Maxime du Camp that under Louis Philippe she was "one of the dirtiest, the most tortuous, and the most unhealthy" in the world. As they lived in her, so they wrote of her—with pride. Victor Hugo did her great homage in "Notre Dame de Paris" and "Les Misérables," Eugène Sue in "Les Mystères de Paris," and Paul de Kock in all his work, but these achievements appear as slight and partial sketches beside the wonderful and penetrating picture which Balzac drew of Paris—at once the background and the protagonist—in his greatest novels. Balzac, besides giving us a world, gave us a great city. Minute as were the studies he made of the provinces, they are nothing to the picture that he drew of the city which he regarded as the brain of the whole world, the leader of its civilization. He gloated over Paris as a scientist gloats over an interesting organism that he has first observed and then skilfully dissected. He had dissected Paris even on the threshold of his career. In some of his early stories, like a brilliant young surgeon fresh from his researches, he overweights the matter in hand with the results of the laboratory. "Ferragus" begins with a long comparison of the streets of Paris; "La Fille aux Yeux d'Or" with a marvellous tirade on the restless race for money and pleasure that is run by all classes, a tirade which, probing as it does all the strata of society, is an epitome, in some sort, of all his work. Paris, that small *enceinte* which was enclosed within what is now the second line of *boulevards*, still innocent of the reforming hand of Haussmann, becoming rich, but hardly yet industrial, not yet the pleasure-ground of all the world, destitute of railways, squalid, ill-kept, nevertheless was transformed by his wonderful imagination into the type of all great cities, which will ever remain true. To him she was "le plus délicieux des monstres," as he says in "Ferragus." "Mais, ô Paris," he cries, "qui n'a pas admiré tes sombres paysages, tes échappées de lumière, tes culs-de-sac profonds et silencieux; qui n'a pas entendu tes murmures, entre minuit et deux heures du matin, ne connaît encore rien de ta vraie poésie, ni de tes bizarres et larges contrastes. Il est un petit nombre de gens ... qui dégustent leur Paris.... Pour ceux-là Paris est triste ou gai, laid ou beau, vivant ou mort; pour eux Paris est une créature; chaque homme, chaque fraction de maison est un lobe du tissu cellulaire de cette grande courtisane de laquelle ils connaissent parfaitement la tête, le cœur et les mœurs fantasques. Aussi ceux-là sont les amants de Paris...."

There are a happy few to whom it would be enough to say that the Paris of Bohemia was the Paris of Balzac—such devotees, I mean, as have thought it worth while to pay attention to that accurate topography in which Balzac took so great a pride, following it in a contemporary map so that, in their walks about the modern city, streets and houses incessantly recall his characters and his scenes. But life is short for such agreeable exercises, so this chapter must inadequately proceed. I have already touched on the social implications of Louis Philippe's Paris, its smallness and its diminutive population, and my present aim is simply to present more fully its external aspect, which changed so quickly after 1848. The rapidity of the change may well be judged by a passage in Théophile Gautier's article[34] on Paul de Kock, published in 1870. No apology is necessary for transcribing it:

"Those [he says] who were born after the Revolution of February 24, 1848, or a little before, cannot imagine what the Paris was like in which the heroes and heroines of Paul de Kock move; it resembled Paris of to-day so little that I sometimes ask myself, on seeing these broad streets, these great boulevards, these vast squares, these interminable lines of monumental houses, these splendid quarters which have replaced the market-gardens, if it is really the city in which I passed my childhood. Paris, which is on the way to become the metropolis of the world, was then only the capital of France. One met French people, even Parisians, in its streets. No doubt foreigners came there, as always, to find pleasure and instruction; but the means of transport were difficult, the ideal of rapidity did not rise above the classic mail-coach, and the locomotive, even in the form of a chimera, was not yet taking shape in the mists of the future. The physiognomy of the population had not therefore sensibly changed.

"The provinces stayed at home much more than now, only coming to Paris on urgent business. One could hear French spoken on that boulevard which was then called the Boulevard de Gand and which is now called the Boulevard des Italiens. One frequently saw a type which is becoming rare and which, for me, is the pure Parisian type—white skin, pink cheeks, brown hair, light grey eyes, a well-shaped figure of moderate stature, and, in the women, a delicate plumpness hiding small bones. Olive complexions and black hair were rare; the South had not yet invaded us with its passionately pale tints and its furious gesticulations. The general aspect of faces was therefore rosy and smiling, with an air of health and good humour. Complexions now considered *distingués* would at that time have caused suspicions of illness.

"The city was relatively very small, or at least its activity was restricted within certain limits that were seldom passed. The plaster elephant in which Gavroche found shelter raised its enormous silhouette on the Place de la Bastille, and seemed to forbid passers-by to go any further. The Champs Elysées, as soon as night fell, became more dangerous than the plain of Marathon; the most adventurous stopped at the Place de la Concorde. The quarter of Notre Dame de Lorette only included vague plots of ground or wooden fences. The church was not built, and one could see from the boulevard the Butte Montmartre, with its windmills and its semaphore waving its arms on the top of the old tower. The Faubourg Saint-Germain went early to bed, and its solitude was but rarely disturbed by a tumult of students over a play at the Odéon. Journeys from one quarter to another were less frequent; omnibuses did not exist, and there were sensible differences of feature, costume, and accent between a native of the Rue du Temple and an inhabitant of the Rue Montmartre."

Gautier is referring in this passage to the Paris of his childhood, in the second decade of the nineteenth century, but, though by his Bohemian days the Church of Notre Dame de Lorette had been built, omnibuses had been instituted, and railway stations were about to break out on the face of Paris, his picture would have remained substantially true of Paris during the whole of Louis Philippe's reign. There was a certain amount of change during the time: the Palais Royal declined in popularity, ceasing to be "a scene of extravagance, dissipation, and debauchery not to be equalled in the world," as Coghlan's "Guide to Paris" put it; a few old houses were pulled down here and there, and the desert patches on the outskirts began to be filled by a straggling population, but, in general, Louis Philippe's Paris can be considered as a stable whole. Most visitors to Paris do not, of course, realize the boundaries of the large circle which now forms the city, for they enjoy themselves at the centre, though they may, perhaps, remember how far from the terminus a train passes the fortifications. In Louis Philippe's day the outer line of boulevards, on which stood the fortifications and *barrières*, was that second ring of to-day which even visitors reach at times; a *barrière* existed at the Arc de Triomphe, at the Place Pigalle, where the amusements of Montmartre only just begin, at the cemeteries of Père Lachaise and Montparnasse. The actual diameter of the city was then about three miles, but for all practical purposes it was little more than two, for the outskirts were still occupied by large market-gardens, plots of land acquired for future use by speculators, with here and there some mushroom rows of houses, half finished and nearly empty, the work of a bankrupt who had too far anticipated the coming boom, farmyards, chicken-runs, cow-stalls, grass, odd weeds, and all the disfigurements of a landscape over which the impending march of a city has thrown a blight. Only on the northern heights were there still windmills and vineyards. These outskirts had only a scanty population, for there were no thousands of workpeople to spread over the heights of Belleville or Ménilmontant, or southwards over Montrouge, so that it was easy for a starveling company of Bohemians, headed by the Desbrosses and Murger, to find shelter in an old farm by the Barrière d'Enfer—now the busy Place Denfert-Rochereau—or for Balzac's Colonel Chabert to live in a tumble-down cottage well inside the boundaries. The fact was, as the dramatist Victorien Sardou has said in a passage of reminiscence,[35] that under Louis Philippe one-third of the total surface of Paris was not built on. There were gardens everywhere, except in the very centre of the city, and on the left bank, especially, houses were only dotted in the midst of orchards, kitchen-gardens, farmyards, and parks. It was this fact that made Paris, however quick the flame that burnt at her heart, in most respects a provincial city. Only in such a city could Bohemia perfectly have realized itself; an industrial metropolis would have swallowed it or brushed it contemptuously aside.

Paris, then, compared with herself of to-day, would have been almost unrecognizable. There was no sign of the rich and luxurious quarter which has grown up round the Champs Elysées, with its magnificent hotels and fine mansions. The Champs Elysées were used during the daytime for riding or driving, but there was hardly a house to be seen except two or three wretched *cafés*. After sunset it was madness to go past the *rond-point*, for beyond was the home of thieves and cut-throats, the Bois de Boulogne, needless to say, being in a much more wild state than to-day. The Parc Monceau was practically in the country, and even the Quartier du Roule, by the top of the Boulevard Malesherbes, was all market-gardens when Rosa Bonheur lived there as a child. As for the Batignolles, that Kensington of modern Paris, its repute was as unsavoury as that of the London fields now respectably covered by Sloane Square and Sloane Street. The quarter chosen by wealth, as opposed to blue blood, which lived in dreary *hôtels* surrounded by high walls in the Faubourg Saint-Germain, lay in the neighbourhood of the present Saint-Lazare terminus. The favourite street was the Rue de la Pépinière, continued by the Rue Saint-Lazare. Only a small part of the Rue de la Pépinière is now left, most of it being called the Rue La Boëtie, but it retains its old name between the Boulevard Malesherbes and the Rue Saint-Lazare. Another fashionable street was the Rue de Provence, which runs parallel to the south of the Rue Saint-Lazare. In the former was the famous house inhabited successively by seven of Balzac's courtesans,[36] in the latter the charming house of Baron Nucingen. Every Englishman knows the clamour and smell and garish shops of the Rue Saint-Lazare to-day, and the Rue de Provence is just a plain *bourgeois* thoroughfare of shops, *cafés*, flats, and a post-office.

The fashionable boulevards have already appeared in a previous chapter, but a word must be said of the difference between the then and now of that brilliant corner of Paris which most Europeans and Americans see once before they die. To-day, without a doubt, the Boulevard des Capucines, which stretches from the Madeleine to the Opéra, has the most distinguished and luxurious appearance. The Boulevard des Italiens beyond the Opéra is dowdier and more workaday. In the days of Bohemia the Boulevard des Capucines had no social existence. It had as yet not been levelled with the Rue Basse du Rempart, which, some fifteen feet below it, followed the course of the ancient moat; it was flanked by plots of land on which new houses were being erected, and its only traffic was the omnibus which jogged between the Madeleine and the Bastille. The present Opera-house and Place de l'Opéra were not existent, for the Opéra stood just off the Boulevard des Italiens, beyond Tortoni's, while the Rue de la Paix came quietly into the boulevard at a sharp angle, instead of arriving in that busy open space, with Cook's office as its centre, over which traffic plies in all directions with bewildering activity. The Avenue de l'Opéra, also, was not known to Bohemia. At that day a pedestrian who wished to go direct from the top of the Rue de la Paix to the Louvre had to thread a maze of narrow streets—an example of which remains in the Rue des Petits Champs—which became meaner and more sinister as he neared the Louvre. The Louvre quarter, so close to brilliance and luxury, was a squalid plague-spot, that has since been thoroughly cleansed. The brotherhood of the Impasse du Doyenné, I suspect, were careful to have a companion when they ascended the Rue Froidmanteau or the Rue Traversière after dark. If one crosses the Avenue de l'Opéra between the entrance of the Rue de l'Echelle on one side and the Rue Molière on the other, one will have exactly traversed the site of the infamous Rue de Langlade where in "Splendeurs et Misères des Courtisanes" Vautrin found Esther la Torpille on the verge of death, *à propos* of which Balzac has a lurid passage on the thick shadows, the flickering lights, the phantom forms, and disquieting sounds which characterized at nightfall this *lacis de petites rues*.

The Rue St. Denis

On the north-east and the east of the Louvre lay the most unregenerate portion of Paris, a district as tortuous, narrow, and unhealthy as in the Middle Ages, yet the centre of Parisian commerce. Even to-day the visitor may wonder that such a district can exist in a capital city, when he ventures into the Rue Quincampoix, the Rue des Francs Bourgeois, and the other alleys which cut them at right angles. But at least this quarter has been cleared by the thorough reorganization of the Halles and by the construction of some large arteries, the Boulevard de Sébastopol, the Rue Rambuteau, the Rue Etienne Marcel, and the Rue de Turbigo. It is sufficient to glance at a map of Louis Philippe's Paris, such as Dulaure's, to see what a maze it was then. Save for the two narrow thoroughfares, the Rue Saint-Martin and the Rue Saint-

Denis, going from north to south, it had hardly a single continuous street. A stroll in the region of the old church of Saint-Merri will show many of these streets in their original dimensions; there is the Rue des Lombards, for instance, where Balzac's Matifat presided over the wholesale drug market, and the Rue Aubry le Boucher, formerly the Rue des Cinq Diamants, where in the virtuous Anselme Popinot's shop the first measures were taken for the reconstruction of César Birotteau's shattered fortunes. The darkness and insalubrity of this quarter are specially commented on at the beginning of Balzac's "Une Double Famille," where he says that a pedestrian coming from the Marais quarter to the quays near the Hôtel de Ville by the Rue de l'Homme Armé and other streets—practically the route of the present Rue des Archives down to the Place Lobau—would think he was walking in underground cellars. This unsavoury network in the day of Bohemia continued right on to the quays, which have now been cleared by the construction of the Théâtre and Place du Châtelet, the Théâtre Sarah Bernhardt, the Place de l'Hôtel de Ville, and the Place Lobau with its barracks. But in Louis Philippe's reign the Rue de la Vieille Lanterne, where poor Gérard de Nerval was found hanged, occupied the site of the stage of the Théâtre Sarah Bernhardt, and instead of the Place Lobau the Rue de la Tixanderie and the Rue du Tourniquet-Saint-Jean forked at the back of the Hôtel de Ville. The house described in "Une Double Famille" stood in the Rue du Tourniquet-Saint-Jean, which was only five feet wide at its broadest and only cleaned when flooded by a shower. The inhabitants lit their lamps at five in June and never put them out in winter.

Rue de la Tixeranderie

Another typical specimen of the Paris I am describing is to be seen in that curious confluence of three narrow streets, the Rues de la Lune, Beauregard, and de Cléry, just off the Boulevard Bonne Nouvelle. The Rue de la Lune is dominated by the forbidding portals of a gloomy church, and its cobble-stones are quite deserted even when the activity of the neighbouring boulevard is at its height. No flight of imagination is needed to realize its appropriateness as the scene of that tragic close to "Illusions Perdues," where in a garret Lucien writes drinking songs over the corpse of his wretched Coralie to pay the expenses of her burial. This street and the two others,

- 151 -

which meet at an extraordinarily acute angled building, diverge into the squalor of the Rue Montorgueil. It is easier to see the conditions in which *la vie de Bohème* was passed in such spots as these than in the regions towards Montmartre. The Rue de la Tour d'Auvergne still exists, but to search there for the garret of Murger and Champfleury is disappointing. One ascends the cheerful Rue des Martyrs from Notre Dame de Lorette, with its prospect of the Sacré Cœur standing out against the open heavens, and on turning along the Rue de la Tour d'Auvergne one is confronted by a respectable, clean, sleepy street that might grace any neat provincial town in France. All suggestion of Bohemianism is remarkably absent, even on the top floors. In Murger's day this quarter was far less civilized, as may be seen from a water-colour sketch by Victor Hugo which hangs in the Carnavalet Museum. This represents the view southwards from the Rue de la Tour d'Auvergne—a wild foreground of uncultivated land with sombre trees and dilapidated fences, and in the distance all Paris spread out in panorama.

Rue Pirouette

The left bank has changed no less than the right. The luxurious quarter of the Faubourg Saint-Germain has spread immeasurably, and even where old streets remain, as many do in the Quartier Latin, their houses have been rebuilt. Many a Bohemian could probably have told a parallel to Champfleury's touching story of how, long after his mistress had left him, he witnessed by chance the demolition of an old wall of a house in the quarter, and there on the topmost story was laid bare the room, with its very wallpaper unchanged, where they spent so many happy months of youth and love. In particular, this part of Paris was cleared and aired by the construction of those two very important thoroughfares, the Boulevard Saint-Germain, which broke through a host of little streets, including the rampageous Rue Childebert, and the Boulevard Saint-Michel, which replaced and widened the straggling old Rue de la Harpe. Before these were made, the Quartier Latin had not a single main street, though it was not quite so uncivilized as the Halles quarter, nor so large. Southwards by the gardens of the Luxembourg it soon became comparatively *bourgeois* and spacious with pleasant houses and gardens, built originally for rich nobles and prelates, but relinquished at the dictation of fashion to prosperous tradespeople and officials like the Phellions and Thuilliers of Balzac's "Les Petits Bourgeois." Searches for vestiges of Bohemia in general on either side of the Boulevard Saint-Germain are fruitful enough; many an *hôtel garni* recalls that in which Lucien first hid his diminished head, or the early home of Arsène Houssaye, when Nini Yeux Noirs was his divinity and revolution his creed. Specific quests, however, are apt to be disappointing. The Rue des Quatre Vents, the headquarters of d'Arthez' *cénacle*, in Balzac's time "one of the most horrible streets in Paris," remains blamelessly near Saint-Sulpice as dull and decent as the Rue de la Tour d'Auvergne; and the Rue Vaugirard, where the second *cénacle*, headed by Pétrus Borel, held its frantic orgies round the punch-bowl and where Murger wrote his "Scènes de la Vie de Bohème," is devoid of any spark of romance. On the other hand, a visit to the delightful Cour de Rohan, just off the Boulevard Saint-Germain, will land you *en pleine Bohème*, as will certain streets leading up towards the Church of Saint-Etienne du Mont, or the narrow passages by the Church of Saint-Séverin. It is just too late to see another unmistakable relic of Balzac's Paris, for the Maison Vauquer of "Père Goriot" has just been pulled down. Yet to make a pilgrimage to its site gives a very good impression of the gloominess which Bohemian high spirits had usually to combat. The Maison Vauquer stood near the junction of the Rue des Postes and the Rue Neuve Sainte-Geneviève, now the Rue Lhomond, and the Rue Tournefort, south of the Panthéon. I have walked down the Rue Lhomond at three on a sunny autumn afternoon, yet I met no soul in this dingy street, which seemed to catch not a ray of the sun's illumination. It is crossed by two sinister little lanes, the Rue Amyot, at the corner of which Cérizet, in "Les Petits Bourgeois," carried on the business of a small usurer in a loathsome, grimy house, and the Rue du Pot de Fer, before coming to which one passes a high, dark barrack, heavy iron bars shielding its dirty lower windows, the "Institution Lhomond pour l'éducation des jeunes filles"—

poor *jeunes filles*! When the Rue Tournefort meets the Rue Lhomond there is a very steep descent, accurately described by Balzac, into the Rue de l'Arbalète. Almost any of the mournful dwellings with weedy gardens on this slope might have been the hideous *pension* where Goriot died, while at the corner of the Rue de l'Arbalète there is a veritable dungeon, only two tiny windows in cracked frames piercing its high, blank wall. If you proceed into the narrow Rue Mouffetard, one long, smelly vegetable market, you will then realize the general state of all but the best of Louis Philippe's Paris.

It was part of the old world, unconscious of its impending reformation in the light of the new ideals of comfort and sanitation which were to become the accented notes of modernity. It was a provincial city of small compass with no industrial suburbs, no railways—let alone trams or river steamboats—and a population of considerably less than a million concentrated for the most part in its overcrowded quarters by the river banks, where the excitement of its spiritual life made up for the deficiencies of its material well-being. There were few public buildings of recent construction; the Louvre was still disfigured by the *débris* of the Place du Carrousel; the Hôtel de Ville, Notre Dame, and the Palais de Justice were hemmed in by crabbed streets and thickly clustering old houses. Private gardens were many, but public squares were few. Except for the boulevards the streets had medieval paving with central gutters, from which all and sundry were liberally splashed, so that for well-dressed persons to venture in them on foot was an impossibility. An American writing in 1835 says of them: "They are paved with cubical stones of eight or ten inches, convex on the upper surface like the shell of a terrapin; few have room for side-walks, and where not bounded by stores they are as dark as they were under King Pepin. Some seem to be watertight."[37] They were seldom swept, never flushed, and primitively lit. The noise, too, except on the boulevards, was deafening and incessant. Not only did the eternal rumbling of wheels over cobblestones and the sharp clatter of stumbling hoofs assail the ear, but also the ringing of bells, the rattle of water-carriers' buckets, the din of barrel-organs and itinerant singers, and all those street cries of fish-sellers, clothes-merchants, rag and bone men, glaziers, umbrella menders, and fruit-vendors so picturesque in isolated survival, but so unbearable in the *ensemble* of their heyday. It would be a mistake, however, to imagine this Paris as sleepy, stagnant, or unpricked by the progressive spirit; on the contrary, she was exceedingly wide-awake. But, whereas the Englishman at once translates his progressive idea into mechanism, the Frenchman prefers to let the first thorough ferment take place in his mind alone, allowing it, if need be, to inspire in him the primitive actions of attack and defence, but leaving more complicated handiwork to a later date, when the logic of change has been worked out, according to which he then acts rigorously. In this light the Paris of Bohemia must be regarded— picturesquely stagnant externally, seething inwardly—and of this condition

Bohemia was the type. Its extravagant or tattered dress, its Rabelaisian speech and self-indulgence, the antiquated splendours of the Impasse du Doyenné and the equally antiquated hovels and garrets of its poverty, its disregard of public convenience and its real antagonism to democracy, were externals voluntarily or of necessity adopted from an earlier age; they were the old bottles which served for a moment to hold and to flavour with a distinctive tang the new wine of the Romantic vintage. Other vintages of equal potency have quickened men's hearts since then, and every new age, whether its ideals be artistic or social, will have its particular ferment that will find its appropriate vessels, but the past can never return any more than the first delirious headiness can be restored to an old wine that now charms with its matured delicacy. Bohemia is a thing of the past with that irrevocable Paris with its tortuous, noisy streets, its high gables, its wide skirts and embroidered waistcoats, its

Fashionables musqués, gueux à mine incongrue,
Grisettes au pied leste, au sourire agaçant,
Beaux tilburys dorés comme l'éclair passant—

the Paris of Balzac, the Paris of Roger de Beauvoir and Alfred de Musset, the Paris of Théophile Gautier and Gérard de Nerval, the Paris of Rodolphe, Schaunard, and Marcel, the Paris, in fine, which was the only home of *les vrais Bohémiens de la vraie Bohème.*

FOOTNOTES:

[1] "Les Enfants Perdus de Romantisme."

[2] A. Cassagne: "La Théorie de l'art pour l'art en France chez les derniers romantiques et les premiers réalistes."

[3] "Essais de Psychologie contemporaine," the chapter on Flaubert.

[4] Philothée O'Neddy: "Feu et Flamme."

[5] See René Canat: "Du Sentiment de la Solitude morale chez les romantiques et les parnassiens."

[6] See Chapter VII.

[7] Asselineau: "Bibliographie Romantique."

[8] "Causeries sur les artistes de mon temps."

[9] Mrs. Trollope: "Paris and the Parisians in 1835."

[10] "Derniers Jours de Bohème."

[11] "Les Salons de Paris."

[12] Challamel: "Souvenirs d'un Hugolâtre."

[13] "Paris in 1829 and 1830."

[14] Major Fraser's name appears in many memoirs of the time, but I owe the above account to "An Englishman in Paris," by A. D. Vandam.

[15] "Vignettes Romantiques."

[16] Léon Séché tells his story in "La Jeunesse Dorée sous Louis Philippe."

[17] "Histoire du Romantisme."

[18] Jules Claretie: "Pétrus Borel."

[19] Maxime du Camp: "Théophile Gautier."

[20] "Gérard de Nerval."

[21] "Portraits contemporains." The article on the artist Marilhat.

[22] "La Bohème Galante."

[23] Arsène Houssaye: "Les Confessions."

[24] Gérard, to be precise, quotes an earlier and more cruel version:

...La reine du Sabbat
Qui, depuis deux hivers, dans vos bras se débat,
Vous échapperait-elle ainsi qu'une chimère ...

[25] See Chapter xi for a further account of Bohemia's amusements.

[26] In a preface to Gérard de Nerval's "Œuvres."

[27] "Les Confessions."

[28] The following account combines much of the information given in three books: Champfleury's "Souvenirs et Portraits de Jeunesse"; "Henri Murger et la Bohème," by A. Delvau; and the curious little "Histoire de Murger pour servir à l'histoire de la Vraie Bohème," par trois Buveurs d'Eau, the anonymous authors of which are known to be his friends, Lelioux, Nadar, and Noel. It is in the last named that some of Murger's letters are given. There is a certain amount of conflict between the dates given in these different books, but since they are all equally likely to be inaccurate, I have chosen to ignore the discrepancies, which are not very important.

[29] This appears in Charles Monselet's diary printed in the memoir by A. Monselet.

[30] "Histoire anecdotique des Cafés et Cabarets de Paris."

[31] In the summer they took place in the Champs Elysées.

[32] M. Henri d'Alméras in "La Vie Parisienne sous Louis Philippe," from whose book other details of these balls are taken.

[33] The popular term for the prison in which refractory members of the Garde Nationale were confined.

[34] Now printed in his "Portraits Contemporains."

[35] The preface to George Cain's "Coins de Paris."

[36] See "Les Comédiens sans le savoir."

[37] Sanderson: "Paris in 1835."